MALAYS!

Islam
Society
and
Politics

GW01418915

ISEAS Series on Islam

MALAYSIA

Islam, Society and Politics

edited by
Virginia Hooker
Norani Othman

ISEAS

INSTITUTE OF SOUTHEAST ASIAN STUDIES
Singapore

First published in Singapore in 2003 by
Institute of Southeast Asian Studies
30 Heng Mui Keng Terrace, Pasir Panjang
Singapore 119614

E-mail: publish@iseas.edu.sg
Website: http://bookshop.iseas.edu.sg

ISEAS Library Cataloguing-in-Publication Data

Malaysia : Islam, society and politics : essays in honour of Clive S. Kessler / edited by Virginia Hooker and Norani Othman.
1. Islam—Malaysia.
2. Islam and politics—Malaysia.
3. Islam and politics—Malaysia—Kelantan.
4. Islamic law—Malaysia—Kelantan.
5. Malays—Religious life—Malaysia.
6. Malays—Malaysia—Social conditions.
I. Hooker, Virginia Matheson, 1946-
II. Norani Othman.
III. Kessler, Clive S., 1942-
IV. Institute of Southeast Asian Studies.
BP63 M3M232   2003   sls2003002123

ISBN 981-230-156-9 (soft cover)
ISBN 981-230-161-5 (hard cover)

Typeset by International Typesetters Pte. Ltd.
Printed in Singapore by Seng Lee Press Pte. Ltd

CONTENTS

PART II: SOCIETY

PART III: POLITICS

CONCLUSION

PREFACE

This collection of essays has been prepared as a tribute to Clive S. Kessler, Professor of Sociology at the University of New South Wales for over twenty years and former member of staff of the London School of Economics and Political Science, University of London (1969–70), and Barnard College, Columbia University, New York (1970–80). He has been a visiting academic at the Institute for Advanced Study, Princeton; the Institute for Advanced Study, Berlin; the Institute for Malaysian and International Studies, Universiti Kebangsaan Malaysia; and the Faculty of Asian Studies, The Australian National University. In the year 2000, the Australian Academy of the Social Sciences recognized his outstanding contributions to the disciplines of Anthropology and Sociology by electing him a Fellow.

The breadth of Professor Kessler's research interests reflects his immense scholarship, and the depth of his published work is testimony to his intellectual engagement with the major works of Western critical theory. Historical anthropology, peasant societies, Islamic social theory, and the anthropology of Muslim societies, religious symbolism, social and sociological theory, comparative studies of the Abrahamic faiths (Judaism, Christianity, and Islam) and, more recently, globalization are all areas on which he has written. He has also published about Hannah

Arendt's views on organized Zionism, the Asian Values debate, the state and civil society, and Palestinian–Israeli relations in carefully argued pieces which demonstrate his extraordinary and ongoing commitment to a just and civilized world.

The chapters in this volume, written by colleagues and graduate students, focus on Professor Kessler's analyses of Malaysia. Each essay draws on aspects of his published research, taking his insights as points of departure for new studies. Professor Kessler's ideas and observations are thus extended, complemented and updated in ways which emphasize the depth and extent of his influence on contemporary research on Malaysia.

The chapters are divided into three sections: Islam, Society, and Politics. A biographical essay opens the book and describes the formative influences on Clive Kessler as a scholar, public intellectual, and person. This is followed by an introductory chapter which establishes a context for the individual essays. The final chapter outlines Professor Kessler's contribution to the Social Sciences in Malaysia and suggests the themes which might shape future research into Islam, society, and politics in Malaysia during the early decades of the twenty-first century.

In several of the chapters, two sets of dates are given. The first follows the Muslim calendar (AH) and the second the Common Era (CE).

The editors wish to acknowledge the assistance of Vera Joveska and Vernon Kronenberg in co-ordinating the electronic growth of the collection, and Vanessa Kendrick for later additions. Andrea Haese and Barry Hooker masterminded the last vital manoeuvres which brought the work to press. Triena Ong of the Institute of Southeast Asian Studies, Singapore, was extremely helpful and supportive throughout the preparation of the book and we thank her for her patience and advice. Each contributor has responded promptly to editorial queries so that the book could meet a special deadline. It is, however, to Naomi Kronenberg, that the editors owe a particular debt of gratitude. Her wisdom and dedication underpin the book and she played a major role in the editing process. Her spirit shines through the volume.

THE CONTRIBUTORS

Farish A. Noor is a Malaysian political scientist and human rights activist. He has taught at the Centre for Inter-Civilizational Dialogue and the Department of Science and Philosophy at the University of Malaya (UM) and the Institute for Islamic Studies Freie Universität of Berlin. He is presently an affiliated fellow with the Institute for Malaysian and International Studies (IKMAS), National University of Malaysia (UKM). He has just completed his book on the historical development of the Pan-Malaysian Islamic Party (PAS) and is currently studying the socio-cultural and political impact of transnational religious movements in Malaysia.

Kikue Hamayotsu is a Ph.D. candidate in the Department of Political and Social Change, Research School of Pacific and Asian Studies, the Australian National University. She is currently completing her thesis on the institutionalization of state Islamic institutions and state-society relations from a comparative perspective, with special reference to Malaysia. She completed a Master's degree in Southeast Asian politics at the School of Oriental and African Studies, University of London, and has conducted research extensively on state–Islam relations in both Malaysia and Indonesia. Her recent publications include "Islam and Nation building in Southeast Asia in Comparative Perspective" (*Pacific Affairs*, forthcoming).

M.B. Hooker, formerly Professor of Comparative Law, University of Kent at Canterbury, is now Adjunct Professor of Law at the Australian National University, Canberra. He has published numerous books on law, including Islamic law in Southeast Asia. Recently, he completed a study of Indonesian Islam based on contemporary *fatawa* and is currently working on Islamic law in Indonesia with Associate Professor T. Lindsey.

Virginia Matheson Hooker is Professor of Indonesian and Malay in the Faculty of Asian Studies, the Australian National University, Canberra, and Convener of the University's Southeast and South Asia Graduate Programme. She has published widely on pre-colonial and contemporary Malaysia, including *Writing a New Society: Social Change through the Novel in Malay* (2000). Her most recent book is *A Short History of Malaysia: Linking East and West* (in press). Currently, she is researching Islam and social change in Indonesia.

Joel S. Kahn holds a Chair in Anthropology and Sociology at La Trobe University, Melbourne, and is currently Head of La Trobe's School of Social Sciences. He was made a Fellow of the Academy of the Social Sciences in Australia in 1995. He has previously held Chairs at Monash University and the University of Sussex in the United Kingdom, and has published four monographs, three edited collections, and numerous articles and book chapters on development issues in Indonesia and Malaysia and on race, culture, identity, and multiculturalism in Asia, Europe and North America. His most recent book is *Modernity and Exclusion* (2001). He has carried out research in Southeast Asia, the United Kingdom and the United States, and has been awarded grants from the Australian Research Council, the Japan Asia Foundation, and various British funding bodies. He has also undertaken consultancies on community development issues for several Australian companies in Indonesia. He is currently Chief Investigator in a large research project on "Managing Diversity in the Asia Pacific Region".

Naomi Kronenberg graduated from the University of Sydney with a Bachelor of Arts degree and a Diploma in Education. She later pursued studies in sociology and public policy at the Australian National

University, Canberra, where she was awarded a Master of Public Policy degree. She also holds an Associateship of the Library Association of Australia. Naomi has worked as a teacher, researcher, librarian, and public servant and has published articles on the sociology of health, education, and the labour market.

Amrita Malhi was born in Kuala Lumpur and migrated to Australia with her family in 1937, where she completed her schooling in Perth and Canberra. At the Australian National University, she graduated with a Bachelor of Arts in Sociology and History and also completed a Bachelor of Asian Studies in Indonesian and Asian History. She was awarded the Australia-Indonesia Association (ACT) Prize for Excellence in Indonesian in 2000, and is currently enrolled in the Honours programme in Asian Studies at the ANU, researching Islamic thought and politics in Malaysia.

Anthony Milner is Basham Professor of Asian History at the Australian National University. The most recent of his many publications, which cover a range of socio-cultural and historical interests in the countries of Asia, is a book on Malaysia, *The Invention of Politics in Colonial Malaya*, published in 2002 in a revised paperback edition.

Norani Othman is Deputy Director of the Institute of Malaysian and International Studies (IKMAS) at Universiti Kebangsaan Malaysia and, concurrently, a Research Affiliate (AGORA Fellow) at the Institute for Advanced Study, Berlin. She was educated in Malaysia and the United Kingdom and has held a Fulbright fellowship in Islamic Studies at the Law School of Emory, Atlanta, and at the Carnegie Foundation, New York. Her publications cover social and sociological theory; law and society; gender studies; human rights and Islam; and intellectuals in Third World society. Recent publications include an edited collection of essays (with Sumit Mandal) on Malaysia's experience of globalization, and a book entitled *Capturing Globalization* (2001).

William R. Roff is Emeritus Professor of History at Columbia University, New York, and Honorary Fellow in Islamic & Middle Eastern Studies, University of Edinburgh. He is the author or editor of *The Origins of Malay Nationalism* (1967); *Kelantan: Religion, Society* *and Politics in a Malay State* (1973); *Islam and the Political Economy of Meaning: Comparative Studies of Muslim Discourse* (1987); and numerous other books and articles.

Shamsul A. B. is Professor of Social Anthropology and, currently, Director of the Institute of the Malay World and Civilization, Universiti Kebangsaan Malaysia, Bangi. He researches, lectures and writes extensively on politics, culture, and economic development with an empirical focus on Southeast Asia. He has published numerous essays on identity formation and contestation in Malaysia and the role of colonial knowledge in the construction of knowledge on Malaysia. His best known book is *From British to Bumiputera Rule* (1986), a phenomenology of class relations in a Malay rural community.

Maila Stivens did postgraduate work in Anthropology at the University of Sydney and at the London School of Economics. She has carried out research on middle-class kinship in Sydney and in Malaysia on "matrilineal" Negeri Sembilan, on modernity, work and family among the new Malay middle classes, "public and private" in Southeast Asia, and, most recently, on the "Asian Family" and "Asian Values". She was lecturer in Anthropology at University College London (1977–87) and is now Director of Gender Studies at the University of Melbourne. She was also a visiting fellow in Gender and Development at the Institute of Development Studies, Sussex, in 2000. Her main publications include: *Why Gender Matters in Southeast Asian Politics* (editor, 1991); *Malay Peasant Women and the Land* (with Jomo Sundaram and Cecilia Ng, 1994); *Matriliny and Modernity: Sexual Politics and Social Change in Rural Malaysia* (1996); *Gender and Power in Affluent Asia* (jointly edited with Krishna Sen, 1998); and *Human Rights and Gender Politics: Asia-Pacific Perspectives* (edited with Anne-Marie Hilsdon, Martha MacIntyre and Vera Mackie, 2000).

1

CLIVE KESSLER
Some Biographical Reflections

NAOMI KRONENBERG

Clive Samuel Kessler, my brother, was born to Hannah and Albert Kessler in Sydney on 15 September 1942. Our father, Albert, had been born in Sydney in 1905 to Jewish immigrants from Poland. Hannah, also a Jew, was born in Germany in 1909. She met Albert in Antwerp during a business trip he made to Europe and they married, after a short courtship, in London in 1937. At the time of Clive's birth, World War II was raging. That dark backdrop to Clive's arrival, along with situations and events related to the conflict, was to have a profound influence on his formation as a scholar and a member of society.

It is an honour for me to have been asked by the editors of this volume to write a biographical piece about Clive. It has also been a considerable responsibility, as my wish to do him justice is greater than my capacity to do so. There are also more general issues facing the would-be biographer — issues such as scope and purpose, for example. The latter became a focal point for me in this project and provided me with an organizing principle to use. The purpose of the chapter, I concluded, is to provide biographical material and observations on Clive, in order to shed light on his work and scholarly interests, as depicted in this Festschrift. My contribution, therefore, will describe and discuss a number of major themes in his life, rather than provide a strictly chronological and exhaustive list of his achievements and experiences. By selecting what I see as formative and indelible influences and vicissitudes, I hope to give the reader some flavour of what has shaped this exceptional and inspiring person. My purpose is to provide material which will add resonance to the reader's perusal of the other chapters in this commemorative volume.

Clive was named in honour of his maternal lineage (the family name, van Cleef, echoing in "Clive") and his paternal grandfather, Samuel Kessler, who had died some two years earlier. The Dutch, rather than the German, form of the prefix "van" points to the location of our mother's forebears in Ostfriesland, close to the Dutch border. The milieu into which Clive was born was, in many respects, typical of middle-class Sydney. We lived in a rented flat in Darling Point — a rather different suburb from the gentrified retreat it has since become but, nonetheless, with a beauty and graciousness then, which has been lost in its modern, gloating opulence. Our father worked in a small gem trading business, where he earned an adequate but not lavish income, which brought us a comfortable but unadorned standard of living. The business had been established by Albert's father. Unusually for that time, our mother worked in the business alongside our father and her remarkable energy and determination to participate in what was then a "man's world" had a profound influence on her children. Her efforts not only ensured that the family maintained its simple but independent place in the world, during the times when Albert was away serving in the Australian army, but her outlook and daily routines also registered a fundamentally important message in our minds about the equality of men and women (and, by extension, of all people). Married women working outside the home was not a commonplace occurrence in urban Australia in the 1940s. I recall that most of our female teachers in school were spinsters, perhaps because their sweethearts were away, serving in the Armed Forces, some never to return. Whatever the reason for that situation, our young minds were imprinted with the rarity of married women in the workforce.

Our household was perhaps a little unusual in another way. It included our maternal grandparents, Else and Edmund van Cleef, who, by what now seems like a miracle, were rescued at the eleventh hour from transportation to a concentration camp. Edmund had already been held in a transit facility, ready for departure to an extermination camp. After our parents' brief introductory meeting at an afternoon tea party in Antwerp, where Hannah was enjoying a brief holiday with friends, our father had courted her, mainly by letter, and by visiting her in Germany. Albert was determined not to marry in Germany under the Nazi regime, so London was chosen as the venue in a stopover on their return to Australia. Once the newlyweds had resettled in Sydney, our paternal grandfather, Samuel Kessler, was able to act as sponsor and guarantor for our maternal grandparents to immigrate. They were not the only ones he sponsored — a number of relatives and acquaintances living in Europe at the time were also recipients of Samuel's support. These people went on to make unassuming but palpable contributions to their new country.

Clive and I therefore had, woven into our daily existence, a growing awareness — even if we could not articulate what we observed — of war and its disruptive social effects, of dislocation, loss and upheaval, and of social, religious and cultural distinctions and enmities, all of which, I venture, made their mark on Clive's later formation as a social theorist and anthropologist. There is a story in Clive's history, which provides a graphic symbol of the formative influence of the war upon him. On the evening of 31 May 1942, Hannah, pregnant with Clive, was sitting in the lounge room at the flat in Darling Point. Three midget Japanese submarines entered Sydney Harbour, aimed at destroying United States warships berthed there, particularly the *USS Chicago*. In the Japanese attack, the Australian ship, *Kuttabul*, was sunk by torpedo, with the loss of nineteen lives. The reverberations of the firing dislodged a piece of the lounge room wall, from where Hannah had moved just in time to avoid injury. A week later, one of the mother submarines, in which the midget submarines had nested on their voyage to Sydney Harbour, surfaced off Bondi Beach and shelled the suburbs of Rose Bay, Bondi, and Bellevue Hill, resulting in damage to several dwellings. The vibrations were felt over a wide area and

Hannah was reminded of her fortunate escape from injury the week before. This figurative reach of the war into Clive's very being was borne out in his later life.

After the war, Clive began his primary schooling at Double Bay Public School, the closest government school to our home. As was the case with Darling Point, the suburb of Double Bay was then populated largely by a mixture of working-class and middle-class residents. The suburb was charming, with a spacious park and short beachfront near the school. Double Bay, in those days, despite a few grand domestic buildings dating from the colonial period, had none of the meretricious connotations it has today. It was a gentle, neighbourly suburb, displaying some of the best aspects of Australia's growing social diversity and tolerance. While lodged in the traditionally blue-ribbon, conservative federal electorate of Wentworth, Double Bay, through its shops, houses and streets, seemed to be home to more middle and working-class residents and trades-people than were the adjoining sister suburbs of Point Piper and Rose Bay.

Double Bay Public School reflected the character of the surrounding suburb and the growing pluralism of Australian society. The school drew some students from wealthier backgrounds, who went on to private schools for their secondary education. Far outnumbering these children, however, were the sons and daughters of working- and middle-class Australians and wartime immigrants from all over Europe. The school was smaller and its practices more informal than those of the government primary schools in the nearby suburbs of Bellevue Hill, Bondi, and Rose Bay. Double Bay School also featured a fair proportion of interesting and inspiring teachers, who taught the mainstream subjects in the standardized way required by the central Department of Education but who also gave expression to their own broad interests and intellectual passions. These teachers made their mark on Clive, an impressionable and highly intelligent child, who often presented the teachers with challenges in return. Clive was unwilling, even in those early years, to abandon his fledgling sense of justice and there were several occasions when the staff had to take Clive's concerns into account. One example was an attempt to require the Jewish pupils to participate in sessions on Christianity and Christian cultural events. Clive successfully led the move to have this practice rescinded. The example of a child of very young years acting to preserve minority rights and sensitivities is quite remarkable and very typical of him!

Another important event occurred during Clive's time at Double Bay Public School. Students at all schools underwent periodic health checks and, during one such check, Clive's eyesight was found to be considerably limited, the impairment probably genetically-based, passed through our mother from her father, Edmund. The problem (basically, one of short-sightedness) could be surmounted by prescribing spectacles and suitable exercises, such as covering one lens of the spectacles for a time to make the "lazy", exposed eye work harder (such was the thinking at the time). In one way, what the sight test revealed could be seen as a great burden for Clive and I remember a sense of great protectiveness which I felt towards him. On the other hand, correcting the deficiency became the basis for an enormous expansion of his powers and capabilities. I remember, at the time, standing with him on the verandah of our paternal grandmother's (Samuel's widow's) flat, opposite the seaplane base at Rose Bay. It was a common pastime to watch the seaplanes land and take off and one we used to engage in with great enthusiasm, every time we visited our grandmother. With his new glasses, Clive saw the planes, literally, for the first time. He was astonished and captivated by the details of machinery and water views, the colour and the movement. My parents and I were taken aback and deeply moved by Clive's experience and by what the school health check had brought about.

We were so fascinated that we asked Clive, "Why didn't you say before that you couldn't see clearly?" His answer was simple and heart-breaking. He said: "I didn't know that anybody else saw different things from what I was seeing." Years later, I was reminded of this incident when I heard Daniel Barenboim speaking about his early life. Because everyone in his household played a musical instrument, he had no idea that other people did not necessarily have this skill and pastime — he thought everyone grew up in a music-filled environment, as a matter of course. One is struck by the impressive logic which children display in drawing out, from their own perceptions and experiences, a sense of their immediate surroundings and the world beyond.

The weakness in Clive's eyesight in his early years also had a profound, formative effect on his intellectual development. It made the basis of his reception of stimuli and his communication preferences more auditory than visual. It was an important factor in making him a superb communicator and a consummate observer of people and social phenomena, through the expression of their spoken and written history and culture. These skills, which Clive has developed to such a high level, became major building-blocks in his contributions as an anthropologist, social and political historian, and social theorist. His sensitivity to the nuances of human speech and written records and his ability to detect the hidden meanings behind overt statements and arguments owe much, I believe, to this early focus. Clive's achievements in this area are exceptional and did not arrive easily — they derive from his assiduous and rigorous efforts. Nonetheless, a major motivator for those efforts was the nature of his early experiences in perceiving and constructing his world.

Alongside his love of music, which aligns so obviously with his auditory sensitivity, Clive displays, perhaps more unexpectedly, a thoughtful and individual appreciation of art and visual images. He has been drawn, particularly, to artists whose work displays proportions and perspectives different from the mainstream — Modigliani, and El Greco, for example. Clive is also a keen observer of the changes in the techniques and brushstrokes of artists whose eyesight changes and fades with the passage of years — Monet and Renoir are two examples. Clive's greatest love in the realm of images and representations is, however, for old maps. In the maps' blend of words and images, their figurative rather than direct representation of topography, as well as in what they tell us about people's attempts to know the world and their place in it, Clive has found a distillation of many of his own passions.

In 1947, our parents purchased a cottage in Bellevue Hill and the family, including our beloved grandparents, moved from our rented accommodation to our new home. Clive and I stayed on at Double Bay School, as our parents did not want to disrupt our schooling by moving us. The house was on the side of Bellevue Hill abutting Bondi Junction, a centre of shops and offices of a lower-middle to middle-class character. Our home seemed worlds away from the other side of Bellevue Hill, which reached into Rose Bay and Point Piper and contained two exclusive private boys' schools — Cranbrook and Scots College. Our new home was very much a continuation of our previous milieu, but with a backyard (symbolizing the "great Australian dream") and respite from one or two cantankerous and prejudiced neighbours in our erstwhile apartment building, who grumbled about the noise of the children's rather tame games and whispered about "reffos" (immigrant refugees) as undesirables. Like Darling Point and Double Bay in those days, our part of Bellevue Hill gave no hint then of the ostentation and sumptuous way of life which characterize it today.

In 1953, Clive moved to Woollahra Opportunity School for his final two years of primary schooling, a school dedicated to educating the brightest of all students from Sydney's eastern suburbs catchment area. The school provided enriching programmes for exceptionally intelligent children and aimed to extend their skills and horizons, to enlarge their interests and to motivate them to take up additional pursuits. Clive excelled in his studies at Woollahra and was well prepared by the school to move on to his secondary school education.

After Woollahra, Clive followed the usual path of graduates from that school to Sydney High School, one of the foremost public selective secondary schools in Sydney, then and now. In one respect, Clive's enrolment at Sydney Boys' High could be seen as unexpected. Our father, Albert, had attended Sydney Grammar School, a first-class private school, and Albert's sisters had been to privileged private girls' schools. Most parents who had undertaken their schooling at private schools were committed to that form of education and ensured that their children followed in their footsteps. Albert Kessler, and our mother Hannah, espoused a different educational and social philosophy. They had strong social democratic allegiances in all aspects of their lives and, for them, public education — ensuring the highest quality in learning for all members of society — was the key to improving society locally, nationally, and at the global level. For our father, educated in a different milieu, the intensity of his commitment to the broader public good was a testament to his decency and the independence of his thought. The educational aspirations of our parents for their children were strictly for excellence within a system that provides for all, not just for a moneyed few.

Our parents' passion for public education and their view that well-supported, high-quality schooling for all is the basis for building a civilized society was passed on to Clive and received renewed support and commitment from him. One of the great motivators of Clive's professional life has been his teaching and his assistance to students from all walks of life and educational backgrounds. He has gone out of his way on many occasions to provide help and encouragement to students caught up in difficult circumstances, students without the range of resources and advocates enjoyed by the wealthy and influential. Clive's insistence on high standards of intellectual content in the courses which he teaches and oversees and his promotion of assiduousness, acuity, and scholarship reflect his devotion to the ideal and practice of excellence for all in their pursuit of education and work. With the increasing attention being given by political, social, and educational institutions to commercial considerations, often at the expense of intellectual and professional quality, Clive has made huge efforts to defend his ideals and to keep on implementing them. He has determinedly protected his courses and his students from a dilution of educational standards. His position is not one of conservative nostalgia, rather it is his own conscious adaptation to the present day of the principles he first absorbed at an early age from the words and example of his parents.

Clive's education at Sydney High opened new areas to his inquiring mind. His love of history, seeded during his primary school years, blossomed in a realization of the significance of this subject in understanding today's world. This view has continued to play a large role in Clive's erudition and intellectual achievements to this day, and is not a mere restating of a conventional cliché. To cite just one example, Clive has undertaken a thorough and mindful study of the history of the Crusades. He undertook this work not only for the sake of the subject itself but also as an illumination of geopolitical and religious tensions at work over time in the interrelations of the three Abrahamic religions — Christianity, Islam and Judaism — which themselves form another branch in Clive's professional activities and interests.

Sydney Boys' High School also exposed Clive to the art and practice of debating. He, together with two other boys, Graham Delaney and Phillip Dryden, made up the three-person debating team which was fielded in competitions against the top debaters from other schools, including teams from the most exclusive private schools in the Sydney region. The rules were quite demanding — the topic for the debate and the position of affirmative or negative argument were not selected by the teams but assigned to them, in a room where they were isolated, about an hour before the debate began. Clear thinking, an ability to develop logical yet persuasive arguments, a breadth of general knowledge (apart from a dictionary, no books were allowed in the preparation room) and prodigious public-speaking skills were the basis of the string of successes achieved by Sydney High's debating team. All three boys possessed these abilities in impressive proportions.

Debating tied in closely with Clive's penchant for the spoken and written over the visual, the word over the picture. Debating refined his skills and, when hearing him speak today, I often have flashbacks to those evenings when our parents and I would join the audience at the debating competitions in which the Sydney High team participated. Another very important aspect of Clive's involvement in this activity was, I believe, the approbation which it brought. For a bookish child, whose main strengths lay outside the areas of physical prowess, visual acumen, and manual dexterity, the debating crown affirmed the value of his cerebral and verbal achievements.

The debating team mirrored the fruitful mix of cultures and backgrounds which characterized public education at the time. Phillip Dryden was a recent immigrant from England, an "English rose" in appearance, with gentlemanly ways. Graham Delaney's background was Irish-Catholic, a significant subculture throughout Australia's history. Clive's European-Jewish background complemented that of the other two boys beautifully. At first sight, there was nothing disparate about them — they appeared to be average Australian schoolboys — but a deeper realization brought home the richness of their differences. It is sad for me to write a footnote to this episode — Pip (Phillip) Dryden died of leukaemia in 1962, aged only 20, and Graham Delaney died a few years ago of a heart attack, having made a notable contribution as a lawyer and teacher.

Clive's exceptional skills as a writer and orator owe something of their origins to capabilities in this same area which our parents possessed. Our mother had been studying journalism at the University of Berlin, when the Nazi ban on Jewish students and teachers came into force and terminated her studies. She nevertheless pursued, as a lifelong interest, her love of, and talent in, languages, writing and speaking. Her command of English, after a few years in her beloved country of refuge, was widely acknowledged as far superior to that of many native English speakers. Over the years, with the extension of her skills and confidence, she was much in demand as a public speaker at functions in support of causes which she cherished, in a wide area covering, *inter alia,* the Jewish community, the general community, social justice, education, children's rights, minority rights, and feminism. She chaired meetings efficiently and creatively and also wrote essays, articles, and letters. Her legacy as a speaker and writer to Clive is obvious to all who know both mother and son.

Our father's influence on Clive has been as profound, if somewhat more diffuse. A quiet man, particularly outside the perimeters of his home and family, Albert made talking around the dining table and sitting room a subtle yet uproarious art. Albert was a diffident master of word-plays, puns, double entendres, conundrums, and curiosities. His gift as a humorist fired large bursts of joking, persiflage, and laughter in all of us sitting around the room. The distancing from annoyances and misfortunes which humour provides was, in our household along with many other homes of the dislocated and dispossessed, a way of dealing with life's difficulties without surrendering one's humanity. Clive has clearly inherited not only our father's great gift with words and their underlying subtleties but also Albert's remarkable and unusual sense of humour. Clive also possesses a rare appreciation of, and insight into, the use of humour as a social implement, a capacity derived from the way that humour was used and promoted in our family circle. Clive, for instance, in a lecture recently, made the observation that so-called "ethnic" jokes largely draw on those national groups that had either never possessed a homeland; had enjoyed a homeland but had lost it; or had endured unusual setbacks in gaining a homeland — among them, the Kurds, the Poles, the Irish, and the Jews. The brilliance of Clive's insights, his understanding of history and social forces, and the origins of these talents in his family setting are so evident in this example.

After completing his secondary education with first-class honours in English and History, Clive postponed his university course for a year in 1960, in order to pursue study and work experience in Israel, under the auspices of a Jewish youth group. That year set the foundation for Clive's enduring interest in the Abrahamic faiths and their interrelationships and became a rich resource for him to draw on, in his ongoing commitment to justice for all parties in the Middle East.

Clive saw what the young country of Israel had achieved in areas such as building, immigration, agriculture, technology, and education. Even at that young age, he nurtured the beginnings of his enduring penchant as a traveller — to look more closely; to see behind the scenes and beyond the surface; and to assess a country or culture, in large measure, not so much on the merits of its material achievements but rather on the weight it gives to clear vision, an understanding of its full history in relation to the histories of other groups, a realistic appraisal of the claims of all its constituents; and the pursuit of social justice. This view was explored and developed by Clive, during his year away, in conversations he had with Dr Daniel Cohen, one of our mother's cousins, who had immigrated as a child to British-mandated Palestine during the 1920s. Daniel was a historian and held, for many years, the position of Director of the Central Archives of the History of the Jewish People in Jerusalem. In him, Clive found an admirable debating companion and a guide endowed with wisdom and experience, in their discussions of world history and politics and of Middle Eastern affairs. Daniel was a spur to the commitment, which Clive developed during his year away from home, to a broad sense of justice, security, and peace for all people in the region and elsewhere in the world. Clive's travels at that time became a foundation for his ongoing endeavours in the area of social justice, at home and abroad. He was one of the early supporters of a two-state solution for Israel and Palestine and his reasoned approach, for which he has nobly endured, over an extended period of time, the recriminations of hardliners from all quarters, is rooted in those days.

Another fundamental part of Clive's view of the world and his role in it was clearly developing over the years of his growth into adulthood. Clive has always asserted the primacy of intellectual, philosophical, and spiritual goals and activities over material ones. This belief, like so many others in his repertoire, is grounded in attitudes and practices passed on by our parents. Clive carries strong memories of our parents' constant assertion that material and financial achievements and status are all well and good but that they are a means to an end, a way of dealing with basic needs to free people to pursue higher aims. Material security, moreover, despite its outward appearance of solidity and permanence, is paradoxically the very opposite — ephemeral and unreliable. This opinion, probably acquired by our parents as they themselves grew up, resonated with new meanings for them through their experiences of World War II, becoming an unforgettable maxim. I remember our mother, in urging us to acquire a solid education, saying that she had learned that a person can lose everything in life — material possessions, loved ones, even life itself — but that the one thing that could not be stripped away was one's education, "...what a person can do with their minds and their hands." I still see her, Clive standing next to me, as she gestured in her eloquent way, first touching her forehead to indicate the mind, then holding her hands out, palms upward, to drive the message home. Throughout his life, Clive has embodied this principle, shaping it in his own way according to his own experiences. The material world is important and has a place in creating a decent standard of living for all. Excessive material cravings and pastimes are vacuous and sterile, however, once one's physical and material needs are met, and striving for justice, truth, and goodness are the true purpose of human endeavour.

On his return home in 1961 from his post-school sojourn overseas, Clive enrolled at the University of Sydney. In that environment, his prodigious intellectual abilities flourished. In his first year, he studied English, history, philosophy and anthropology, the last a new subject for him and one which, at the outset, had not yet had the chance to evoke in him the level of interest and commitment he felt for the other three subjects. Yet, in time, anthropology captivated him and became the chosen path for his intellectual and professional pursuits during his lifetime. The growth of Clive's interest in anthropology from his undergraduate days drew on his conclusion that this body of knowledge, as carved out and developed by its theorists and practitioners, has served as a cornerstone in the assemblage of disciplines humans have used to discover and explain their world. Clive came to see, in anthropology, a bridge between the sciences and the humanities, a point of confluence for history, philosophy, psychology, and social theory, in the task of exposing and making sense of our place in the universe. This desire — to explore and understand human endeavour, in all its manifold forms and varieties and, by doing so, to highlight ways in which people may understand their own and their neighbours' yearnings — has been one of the guiding principles throughout Clive's work and in his life beyond work.

Clive graduated with first-class honours and the university medal in anthropology after four years of study. Before his honours year in anthropology, Clive studied higher-level courses in both anthropology and history in his second and third years, as part of the preparation for his honours year. His capacities as a scholar flourished remarkably, under the guidance and example of some outstanding teachers. There was Ernst Kohn Bramsted in history, for whom Clive felt not only respect in terms of Bramsted's status and activities as a historian but also a strangely familiar affection, evoked by Bramsted's background as an immigrant from Germany and his similarity in appearance and manner to our maternal grandfather. In anthropology, there were many respected scholars to inspire young students; indeed, the Department of Anthropology at the time was recognized world-wide as one of the foremost centres of theory and field work. A. P. Elkins' work on the Australian Aborigines is the foundation for much of the understanding and rigour, which now informs the best work on Australian indigenous peoples and cultures. Elkins' activities and findings also illuminated research on indigenous cultures in other countries. Ian Hogbin, Les Hiatt, Michael Swift, and particularly Chandra Jayawardena, also widely recognized, inspired and guided their students in exploring and analysing subjects and methods of great substance and complexity. All this was food and drink to Clive, the nourishment of his intellect and humanity. The late Chandra Jayawardena was a particularly strong and nurturing influence — he and Clive developed a very warm and lasting relationship and Clive regards Chandra to this day, in a filial way, as a formative and supportive spirit.

After graduation, Clive travelled to London, enrolling in further studies at the London School of Economics, where he encountered as teachers renowned anthropologists, such as Raymond Firth and Maurice Freedman. During his studies in England, Clive made a few trips, some involving extended stays, to Malaysia, to undertake fieldwork in Kota Bahru, Kelantan, and surrounding areas. The result of his work was a thesis, leading to the award of a Doctor of Philosophy degree, jointly by the University of London and Cornell University. The thesis was soon afterwards published as a book entitled, *Islam and Politics in a Malay State: Kelantan 1838–1969* (Ithaca, N.Y.: Cornell University Press, 1978), which, as noted elsewhere in this Festschrift, has become a classic in studies of

Malaysian politics and society and in the application of social theory to specific field situations.

In the late 1960s, after completion of his Doctorate of Philosophy and his work as a lecturer at the London School of Economics, Clive was appointed as a lecturer at Barnard College in New York, an institution under the aegis of Columbia University. He worked there for many years and, in the course of his teaching, research, and professional activities, earned the respect and affection of his colleagues and his students. During those years, Clive also undertook spells of work outside Barnard — for example, a residential fellowship at Princeton University.

At the beginning of 1980, Clive returned to Australia to take up a Chair of Sociology at the University of New South Wales, where he has worked up to the present. During these years Clive has taught, undertaken research, organized and participated in conferences, and been called on by radio and television journalists as an expert commentator on topics dealing with religion, politics, and developments in the Asian region. He has undertaken administrative duties and provided support in the day-to-day running of his School. Clive has worked unstintingly and always placed the good of the discipline and of his colleagues and students above his own well-being.

Not long after Clive's return to Australia, our father became seriously ill, with the strains on his heart over a long period building up. Some months after Clive arrived back, our father underwent heart by-pass surgery, as one of Dr Victor Chang's first patients in the fairly new field of cardio-vascular surgery. Despite the intervention, our father died some months later in July 1981. Our mother died in her sleep in November 1982. She had also endured cardiac problems for many years but, in our minds, her death was overwhelmingly related to the unending grief she experienced at her husband's death. Clive's care and devotion to both our parents during this difficult and sorrowful time were absolute and creditable. Our parents' deaths were a grievous blow to Clive, so recently returned to Australia after years of living away from his family.

Clive's arrival in Australia, after a considerable time in the Northern Hemisphere, was a homecoming for him. Australia had always held a special significance for him and he was aware, in his highly insightful way, of the problems facing Australia and of Australia's unusual and marginalized position in the world — located outside Europe and the Americas, not part of Asia either culturally or geographically, and too small to possess the weight and influence of the more powerful brokers in international deals.

Clive has always considered himself to be something of an outsider, a person of hybrid origins, standing at the margins, enjoying the life around him but able to distance himself, when necessary, to observe the hurly-burly and discern the underlying tensions. For Clive, the outsider can fulfil a valuable function, as observer and commentator, and he has found parallels for himself, at the national level, with Australia's place in the world. In Clive's view, this seemingly odd and uncomfortable position brings with it great blessings and great possibilities, if they can be realized through careful and honest thinking and action. Where others might see little that Australia can do on the world scene, by reason of its isolation and smallness, Clive sees an exemplary position for Australia to take, by dint of the very attributes which others may see as limiting. It is one of my cherished hopes that Clive, on his sixtieth birthday and beyond, enjoys the fruits of his great efforts over the years and finds that the country, which gave his family such benign refuge, continues to grow in the compassion and ingenuity, for which he himself has so long striven.

2

MALAYSIA

Still "Islam and Politics" But Now Enmeshed in the Global Web

VIRGINIA HOOKER

One of Professor Clive Kessler's lesser known accomplishments is a mastery of Kelantan Malay. This colourful dialect of standard Malay is laconic but rich in earthy metaphors, direct and subtle at the same time, and for non-Kelantanese Malays and foreigners alike, a challenge to their forbearance and tolerance. The people of Kelantan, in general, make few concessions to outsiders and take pride in their independence of spirit and behaviour. Undaunted by this reputation, the young Kessler chose as his "case study" the township of Jelawat in rural Kelantan and lived among the people of Jelawat for almost two years. He observed not only their history, politics, religion, economy, and culture but also learned their language, without which a true insight into Kelantanese life would not have been possible. From this intense experience was distilled one of the classic works of Southeast Asian anthropology, Kessler's *Islam and Politics in a Malay State: Kelantan 1838–1968*, a work which has become a benchmark for studies of Malay society.

In part motivated by the failure of the "old paradigms" of social science to engage with social reality, Clive Kessler argued for an integrated and holistic approach which "seeks to draw together, as complementary aspects of the same reality, class and culture, 'material' and 'ideal' factors, 'existence' and 'consciousness' " (Kessler 1978, p. 19). In his first book, Kessler develops the methodology which he has maintained and refined in later writing. As he himself describes it:

> Ultimately, through a detailed analysis of one concrete case, ... to address what is both a basic question of social theory and an urgent matter of human concern, the complex interdependence between the material and the ideological dimensions of political life (Kessler 1978, p. 7).

Kessler's study was remarkably percipient about the role of Islam in local Malay politics and its potential for attracting rural Malays away from secular, nationalist parties. Throughout his book, Kessler emphasized that, for Kelantanese peasants, religion was not a "mysteriously disembodied presence" but "an idiom whereby people may shape and express their own experience of themselves both as the products and the producers of their society's history" (Kessler 1978, p. 244). It is this ability to identify the basic elements and underlying trends in Malaysian society which raises his analyses above the ephemeral and not only lends them longevity but also imbues them with a certain prescience.

As early as in 1969, for example, based on his understanding of the long-term strategies of the leaders of the Islamic party Parti Islam SeMalaysia (PAS), Kessler had argued that the party would use its ability to take votes from the United Malays National Organization (UMNO) to "make their own party irresistible to it as a prospective coalition partner" and even, perhaps, to use this leverage to force the UMNO to adopt some of the objectives of PAS (Kessler 1978, p. 242, fn. 5). In 1972, this was indeed what eventuated and PAS, previously an opposition party, joined a new coalition (the National Front) in the name of national unity following serious racial violence in 1969. In the mid-1970s, he suggested that if the PAS failed to continue to serve the interests which had brought it to power, its supporters would change their allegiance (Kessler 1978, p. 243). A generation of younger PAS leaders, critical of their elders' co-operation with the

UMNO, moved for the party to withdraw from the governing coalition. Although the short-term effect was disastrous for PAS, in the longer term it led to a generational change of leadership so that, by the mid-1980s, the party was reinventing itself, as will be described later in this chapter.

As we look back from the early twenty-first century, it is clear that the period of Kessler's dedication to analysing Malaysian society has spanned the phase of its most rapid economic transformation, resulting in equally rapid socio-cultural change.[1] Malaysian independence was achieved on the basis of an understanding between a number of leaders of the Indian, Chinese, and Malay communities about power-sharing in government. Essentially, this was enacted through a coalition of political parties into an Alliance which, although representing each of these communities, would be dominated by the UMNO, the Malay-based party. The UMNO was led by English-educated Malays, many of whom also had close connections with the traditional Malay aristocracy. The Chinese and Indian parties were also headed by wealthy and well-connected leaders. During this period, PAS was one of the few non-Alliance parties which was able to attract sizeable support. It campaigned for the implementation of Islamic principles in society and government and was critical of the secular and élitist flavour of the UMNO.

In the general election of 1959, PAS won nine of the ten federal seats and sent a message to the Alliance in Kuala Lumpur that it was neglecting local interests in Kelantan.[2] During the 1960s, dissatisfaction with the ability of the Alliance to represent the interests of the poor and marginalized inhabitants (especially in the urban areas) of Malaya was expressed through the formation of two new political parties (the Democratic Action Party and the Gerakan, or Malaysian People's Movement) which worked together to attract votes from the Alliance. As a result, in the general election of May 1969, urban voters, particularly the Chinese, supported the new parties, which gained more than two-thirds of the urban vote. Their enthusiastic celebrations at the prospect of victory in several states were countered by plans for a mass UMNO rally on 13 May. In Kuala Lumpur, this resulted in two days of extreme violence as Malays and non-Malays clashed furiously, causing loss of life and property. A State of Emergency was declared, Parliament was suspended, and authority for restoring order was entrusted to the Deputy Prime Minister, Tun Razak, and the National Operations Council. Repressive measures were invoked in the name of national security, many of which have remained on the books and have been used by Dr Mahathir Mohamad's government, several decades after the 1969 riots.

Under Tun Razak, a new Department of National Unity was established to focus on race relations, and a national ideology was drafted as a basis for new programmes in civics and citizenship. Working with a National Consultative Committee composed of representatives of all Malaysians, Tun Razak (who became Prime Minister in 1970) reviewed the factors which had led to the racial violence of May 1969. It concluded that, as PAS had already recognized in Kelantan, rural development programmes had not reached the people and areas where they were most needed and the ethnic group overwhelmingly disadvantaged by this misdirection was Malay. Malays (closely followed by Indians) had the highest unemployment rates and Malays held only one per cent of investment in registered businesses. Although the most senior positions in the civil service were held by Malays, they were poorly represented in more junior positions. Tun Razak and his advisers concluded that a radical transformation of the Malaysian economy was the only way of improving economic performance and that Malays must have a greater share of the investment sector.

The programme to restructure the economy was implemented in 1971 under the title, the New Economic Policy (NEP). It emphasized those elements of the Constitution which claimed a special position for Malays and other "native peoples" within the nation (Funston 2000, p. 171). On this basis, affirmative action policies for Malays and the native peoples of Sabah and Sarawak (referred to collectively as *bumiputera*, or sons of the soil) were extended and increased, and much greater attention was given to improving access to higher education. The NEP's primary aim, however, was to achieve national unity through a more equitable distribution of wealth across all Malaysia's social and economic groups but, even at the time, there was some concern that national unity would not necessarily flow from improved economic circumstances.

Closely linked with the NEP was a National Cultural Policy (NCP), which was intended to develop a "national soul" for Malaysia based on the formation of a National Culture, in which Islam was an important component and in which "suitable" elements from non-Malay cultures could be included. It has been convincingly argued, however, that rather than achieving cultural unity, the NCP "has politicised culture and made Malaysians more aware of cultural differences among themselves."[3]

The NEP also had some unforseen outcomes. One was the growth of a campus culture of political involvement in social issues in the 1970s, as students protested against the government on behalf of the rural poor. This was countered by a Bill passed in 1975 prohibiting student involvement in politics, a law which still remains. However, tertiary graduates were not the only educated Malays produced by the NEP policies. There were also thousands of young men and women from the rural areas who moved to the newly created Free Trade Zone areas and became employees in foreign-owned industrial enterprises, which had been attracted to invest in Malaysia by the NEP. Both these groups of blue collar workers and their white-collar counterparts were entering the work-force during the period when the international profile of Islam was rising as a result of the Arab–Israeli conflict, the increase in oil prices, and the revolution in Iran. At home and abroad, these young Malays became aware that Islam could play a much greater role in their personal and national lives. Many of them began to intensify their personal devotion to Islam and also to join *dakwah*, or proselytizing groups, to persuade Muslims to be more "Islamic", and non-Muslims to become converts.[4]

Few observers, let alone the National Front itself, had foreseen this intensification of devotion to Islam among the Malay beneficiaries of the NEP. Various organizations were founded to express in diverse ways this focus on Islam. One was the Malaysian Muslim Youth Movement (ABIM), whose dedicated leaders included the young Anwar Ibrahim. From the mid-1970s until he was persuaded to join the UMNO in 1982, he was a loud and articulate critic of government policies of élitism. The individual who is credited with persuading Anwar to join the UMNO was Dr Mahathir, who became Prime Minister in 1981. Aware of the appeal of Islam to the growing class of urban Malays as well as to their rural brothers and sisters, he had been incorporating some elements of "modern" Islamic practice into government-sponsored projects. Following this principle, the government had contributed to the establishment of an Islamic Bank, an International Islamic University in Kuala Lumpur, and an Islamic insurance company, and had encouraged the creation of Islamic think-tanks. Anwar's apparent defection to the UMNO was criticized by many, but his supporters claimed that, on the contrary, he was increasing the government's Islamization activities (more of which are described in Kikue Hamayotsu's chapter in this volume). The response of PAS to this increasing attention by the government to the incorporation of Islamic elements into official life is discussed in several parts of this book (see in particular chapters by M. B. Hooker, Farish Noor, and Amrita Malhi).

As mentioned above, in the mid-1980s the new generation of PAS leaders began a campaign to present PAS as the party which protected the poor and oppressed, and criticized the NEP as being racially oriented and against the Islamic principle that all are equal. This position was challenged by Dr Mahathir in 1991 when he launched a new programme for Malaysia's continued development and modernization, known as Vision 2020. In a thirty-year plan designed to replace the NEP, he outlined his aims to create a united Malaysia in which all its citizens lived in prosperity and harmony in a technologically advanced society which valued knowledge, economic success, and dynamism, and was inspired by the values of tolerance and compassion.

Some of the material aspects of this Vision were implemented through the 1990s when the infrastructure for a Multimedia Super Corridor linking Kuala Lumpur with the new "smart city" of Putrajaya was constructed and foreign investors were urged to join in developing a Malaysian version of Silicon Valley. These developments were severely curtailed with the economic crisis of 1997. The fall of prominent Malaysian tycoons, corporate collapses, and rumours of corruption and mismanagement caused deep divisions within the UMNO about how the crisis should be handled. That these divisions had reached the very highest levels of the UMNO became apparent when some of Anwar's supporters openly criticized the government for mishandling the crisis, a position interpreted as a direct attack on Dr Mahathir. Between late June and August 1998, a campaign of innuendos about Anwar's private life was waged and in early September he was dismissed as Deputy Prime Minister and shortly afterwards expelled from the UMNO. The sacking of the man expected to be Prime Minister and his subsequent detention under the Internal Security Act (including his assault while in custody) deeply shocked Malaysians. Thousands took to the streets in protest and, in general elections held in November 1999, showed their displeasure by voting strongly for an opposition coalition which included PAS. Despite the major swing against the UMNO by Malay voters, the National Front government was convincingly returned to power.[5]

Following the 1999 elections, it appeared that the government was on the back foot but the opposition coalition failed to push home its advantage and became fractured by internal wrangles. The tragedy of the terrorist attacks in the United States on 11 September 2001, which have been linked with the acts of extremist Muslim groups, has provided Dr Mahathir with the unexpected opportunity to increase his criticism of PAS, as analysed in Amrita Malhi's chapter. The Islamization of politics and the politicization of Islam continue in contemporary Malaysia in ways which Kessler first noted during his fieldwork in Kelantan in 1968.

Although from time to time he has published analyses of politics, more specifically political culture in Malaysia,[6] Kessler has been steadfast in his focus on "the underlying sociocultural currents running through Malaysian society, rather than the flow of surface political manoeuvres and events" (Kessler 2000, p. 106). Undoubtedly for Kessler, one of the strongest of those underlying currents is Islam. His interest in Islamic history goes back to his schooldays, but a stay in Jerusalem in 1960, the holy city of the Abrahamic faiths, inspired him to deeper study. Later, his direct experience of observing the popularization of the Islamic vision of society through the rhetoric of the Pan Malaysian Islamic Party (PMIP) in Kelantan also made him acutely aware of the tensions between morality and reality which beset individuals as they endeavour to practise their faith.[7] He saw the rituals of Islam as essential to sustaining the Islamic vision of a "good society".

> So long as the good society remains unactualized, that ideal, instead of being projected into the world to come, is made to bear upon the life of this world through recurrent rituals, during which the normal social order, with all its inequities and imperfections prompted by self-interest, is suspended.[8]

One of the most dramatic of these public rituals is the demanding pilgrimage to Mecca, one of the five "pillars" of Islam, which is enjoined on all able Muslims, if they have the means to accomplish it. Kessler takes up the phenomenon of "ritual reversal" (a suspension of the normal social order through participation in ritual) in his analysis of the meaning of the pilgrimage for Kelantan peasants and refers to "the moral, social and political significance of Islam's rituals of transient equality."[9] William Roff takes this as his starting point for the first chapter in this volume in the section entitled "Islam."

Inspired by Kessler's understanding of the significance of the *hajj* for Malays, Roff raises the issue of "how best may those of us who are not Muslims go about understanding the 'cryptic phenomena' of the ritual practice known as the *hajj*?" In his chapter, Roff tests several Western theories of ritual as a symbol of transformation to understand the significance of the pilgrimage. For, as Kessler himself wrote, "The drama of movement, travel, and transformation, even sacralizing metamorphosis, is at the very core of Islam itself" (Kessler 1992, p. 148). Beginning with Van Gennep's theory of *rites de passage* and describing its elaboration half a century later by Victor Turner, Roff identifies two insights which are relevant to studies of the pilgrimage. He draws on them to analyse the assemblage of rituals through which the pilgrimage is accomplished and supplements his analysis with quotations from the reflections of individual pilgrims.

At several points in his chapter, Roff addresses the question of the potential conflict between Western analyses of Islam and those of the Muslims themselves. One way to avoid this problem, Roff suggests, is to pay close attention to the texts "according to which Muslims claim to act". Among the most crucial of these texts are the classical works of legal thought, based ultimately on the two sources of Islamic law, the Qur'an and *Hadith* (the sacred records of the actions and sayings of the Prophet and his Companions). In his chapter, M. B. Hooker analyses a late twentieth century Islamic legal code, drafted in Kelantan. Although formulated by Muslim scholars, Hooker demonstrates that, from the perspective of the sources of classical Islamic jurisprudence, the code is flawed and, moreover, that it resorts to the English system of legal reasoning which is alien to Islamic law (Syariah).

Hooker predicates his chapter on Kessler's observation about the Islamic vision of "the good society." According to that vision, the individual is inspired to do good by his submission to Allah, to whom he is bound "by meticulously defined rights and duties" (Kessler 1978, p. 212). Hooker argues that the aim of the Kelantan Code, drafted in 1993, is to "make manifest Revelation in the temporal world of the twentieth century" and to "translate an individual's obligation to God into a social duty enforced by the state". As the chapter shows, through the Code the state government of Kelantan is trying to expand the jurisdiction of the religious (Syariah) courts beyond the limits allowed by the federal Constitution. The concluding argument emphasizes that, in essence, the Code raises the issue of authority in regard to the power to define and implement the Islamic vision of society.

The issue of authority is continued in Kikue Hamayotsu's chapter, "Politics of Syariah Reform: The Making of the State Religio-Legal Apparatus". Kessler's insights into the relationship between Islam and politics in Kelantan are extended in Kikue Hamayotsu's study to argue that, in a Muslim society, the influential factors in contestations for power are not doctrinal forms but, rather, patterns of political agency. Islamization of the state, the chapter argues, is overwhelmingly associated with the implementation of Syariah law and, as a case study, the chapter examines the government-led programme to reform the system of religious courts in Malaysia.

Through her carefully argued examples, Hamayotsu indicates the complexity of the issues surrounding the government's involvement in what is essentially an increase in the Islamization of the state. The most obvious of these is the government's claim that its attention to Syariah demonstrates its commitment to the principles of Islam. Because the government is setting the agenda, however, and because the reforms are overseen by a religious agency within the Office of the Prime Minister, it is clear that changes to the state religio-legal system will not be in conflict with any of the government's non-religious policies. The chapter also describes how, through the reforms to the religious judicial system, some of the leading Islamic scholars in Malaysia have been drawn into the state bureaucracy and have become dependent on the state, not only for their authority but also for their promotion and careers. In his chapter, M. B. Hooker raises the question of the effect on the Syariah of state intervention, arguing that this resulted in a form of Islamic law which was no longer purely Islamic in its sources of authority. Hamayotsu argues also for the diminution of the credibility of some Muslim scholars as arbiters of Islamic law because of their co-option into the bureaucracy of the secular state.

In the second section of the book, "Society", the chapters tease out the meaning of "Malayness" from a very diverse range of perspectives. Shamsul A. B. takes up Kessler's concept of the "idiom" chosen by a community to shape and express "their own experience of themselves both as the products and the producers of their society's history" (Kessler 1978, p. 244). The focus of Shamsul's study is an élite group, which, over time, has constructed the way Malaysians present knowledge and truth and sustain mythologies.

This group of "knowledge constructors" includes non-Malays from the period before and during the colonial era, as well as Malaysian intellectuals. In particular, Shamsul explores their influence on the concept of "Malay Studies." He demonstrates the link between the development of a concept of "the social" as a theoretical category and field of study from which the subject, "social science", emerged. The objectivity of social science is critical, he argues, to counterbalance the functional goals of modern society. The co-optive power of the nation-state, at work in the religious bureaucracy as outlined in Hamayotsu's chapter, is emphasized also in Shamsul's chapter. He argues that the nation-state incorporates the social sciences into institutions of national purpose and, when this happens, there is a risk that the views of social scientists who disagree with national policy may be silenced.

Shamsul reminds readers that the usually uncontested "facts" about Malaysia, on which scholarship and administrative policies were based, were assembled largely during the pre-independence period by colonial officials. As a result, the early and often defining and shaping of what constituted "knowledge" of the Malay world was accomplished by foreigners. While political independence consolidated Malaysia in the physical and geographical sense, it was more difficult for Malaysians to redraw the map of their own understanding of "knowledge". The founding and development of the Institute of the Malay World and Civilization in the early 1970s, in the context of renewed nation-building activities and the National Cultural Policy, is used as a prime example of Malaysian attempts to redefine and reshape knowledge of the Malay world.

Maila Stivens' chapter on recent claims to rights by groups of Malaysian women examines the complex challenges these groups face, as well as some of the strategies they have devised to further their causes. Even the terminology which the women choose to express their position can be subject to criticism and here a link may be drawn with Shamsul's chapter, where he argues that Western-derived terminology may have inhibiting consequences for the momentum of national initiatives.

A further link between Stivens' and Shamsul's chapters is the acknowledgment of the socio-economic as well as political context within which groups and individuals have to negotiate "space" for their projects and activities. In her chapter, Stivens identifies some of the challenges: a nation-state which has established official development programmes (currently Vision 2020) within which the roles of women and the family are already defined; an official view of what constitutes "modernity" and its attainment in the case of state-sponsored projects; complex relationships between ethnic groups and the politics of identity; and, perhaps most obviously, "a politicised Islam, within an ongoing Islamization of Malaysian society".

Through the example of the women's group, Sisters in Islam (Puteri Islam), Stivens identifies at least two strategies used to pursue a greater recognition of women's rights. A small, but well-organized group, its members have won recognition as public intellectuals and they use this role to work for women's rights through what they term "cultural dialogue". The Sisters study local (Malaysian) Muslim culture and hold discussion groups and conferences, to make Malaysians aware of the cultural norms within which they operate and then to explore possibilities for gender rights within those norms. Secondly, and linked with the issue of cultural norms, the Sisters have worked to increase communication between different women's organizations and to encourage discussion of gender rights in local idioms as well as universalist terms.

Stivens' chapter concludes that, in their negotiations for more diverse opportunities for women in Malaysian society, the groups take account of domestic (national) as well as global (international) issues. This chapter pays considerable attention to the critical positions associated with the relationship Malaysians are establishing with their immediate context and with the wider world. This is expressed by the author in terms of universalism, particularism, and cultural relativism.

Joel Kahn also addresses these issues in his chapter, "Islam, Modernity and the Popular in Malaysia." His focus is not women's rights but the influence of the concept of modernity, as well as its actualization, in Malaysian society. Malaysia's national programmes of modernization and, in particular, the projects associated with the Multimedia Super Corridor have linked Malaysia directly with the global network of international information technology. While acknowledging their status as global players, many Malaysians also claim that their culture is unique and they have developed what Kahn terms "a self-exoticising discourse".

Kahn sees this paradox as an essential aspect of modern Malaysian culture and warns that to ignore it runs the risk of distorting our understanding of contemporary Malaysia. Clive Kessler, according to Kahn, has "been more successful than any other anthropologist of the Malays in keeping this paradox constantly in the frame...".[10] Kahn turns not to Malay villages, the usual sites for anthropological studies, but to the modern popular entertainment industry. He argues that this industry, even more than print culture, has shaped Malays' understanding of "the modern" and he takes as his examples the great actor and musician P. Ramlee and contemporary *nasyid* vocal groups.

Through an analysis of the *nasyid* groups, whose songs are in Malay but who perform in costumes inspired by Middle-Eastern fashions and against the backdrop of desert locations, Kahn shows that increased globalization has not (in this case) brought increased Westernization. By placing the *nasyid* phenomenon within its local context of urban Malaysian youth culture, Kahn reveals the paradox that, whereas *nasyid* may appear exclusively Malay, as a part of "youth culture", it also acknowledges the diversity within the youth culture. Furthermore, in its Islamic aspect, it acknowledges the existence of non-Muslims, for whom in Islam there is a model for co-existence.

Kahn's chapter concludes with the suggestion that transformations within Malay popular culture provide evidence that a new phenomenon is emerging: "a vision of Malayness that is both exclusive and inclusive at the same time". This vision, however, may threaten the communally based voting patterns on which Malaysian politics rests. The results of the 1999 general election indicated that large numbers of Malays did *not* vote for the UMNO, a radical departure from previous behaviour. Undoubtedly linked with this loss of Malay votes has been an increased emphasis on Malay nationalism by the UMNO leaders, especially Dr Mahathir.

The final section of this volume is devoted to politics and begins with a study of the Malay monarchy, the traditional focus for Malay loyalty. In the pre-colonial history of Malaysia, government was conducted through a delegated system of authority originating from the royal and supernatural power of the sultan. Each traditional Malay polity was centred on such a ruler and, although British colonial rule re-organized many aspects of traditional government, the position of the Malay ruler was maintained and, some claim, was even enhanced by British support. In his chapter "How 'Traditional' is the Malaysian Monarchy?" Anthony Milner examines the relationship between the pre-colonial culture of the Malay world and political behaviour and experience in Malaysia today.

Milner's starting point is one of Clive Kessler's studies of Malay political culture in which he gives examples of how the present can be the prism through which the past is refracted (Kessler 1992a). In his study, Kessler describes some continuities between characteristics of the Malay system of kingship and modern political culture. Milner takes up this issue to present a detailed examination of the concept of monarchy after colonial influence made itself felt in the Malay states. Milner makes it clear that the royal courts were responding not only to Western interventions but also to challenges from among their own élites.

Through his analyses of several publications and documents emanating from the royal courts in the late nineteenth and early twentieth centuries, Milner gives examples of the new ways in which the rulers were being presented to their people (and to British colonial officials). In several of the Malay States, increased emphasis was given to the rulers' achievements as administrators and as protectors of the interests of their people, who increasingly were viewed as citizens rather than merely "subjects". In the post-independence period, emphasis was placed on the sultans' dedication and service to their states, highlighting the state itself as an object of loyalty.

The central argument of Milner's chapter is that the Malay monarchy in modern times has transformed the way it presents itself to Malays. Its survival has been accomplished through a process of transformation so that its present form, although integrated into modern Malaysian political life as a "traditional" monarchy, is essentially a manifestation of accommodation to the modern nation-state.

The last two chapters are devoted to the politics of Islam in Malaysia, a subject of crucial concern to Clive Kessler. His doctoral thesis had as its main title "Islam and Politics in Malay Society" (amended to "Islam and Politics in a Malay State" when revised for publication), and this focus has remained a primary research interest. In his chapter, Farish Noor, like Milner, draws on some of Kessler's thoughts published in an article entitled "Archaism and Modernity in Contemporary Malay Political Culture" (Kessler 1992). Like Milner, Farish Noor focuses on power, but rather than analysing the monarchy, he takes as his subject Nik Aziz, the spiritual leader of PAS. Farish Noor's approach, inspired by Kessler, is the cultural mediation of politics through religion, in this chapter exemplified by the religious teachings and interpretations of the Qur'an by Nik Aziz.

Farish Noor argues that, although the Muslim religious scholars (*ulama*) of Malaysia see themselves as responsible for upholding and protecting their religion, they are not immune to change. The Malay rulers, according to Milner, responded to challenges to their authority by becoming more responsive to change, and the *ulama*, Farish believes, also recognize that they must be aware of social and political changes in their constituencies. "Constituencies" is an appropriate term, because many *ulama* have joined political parties and even become politicians. The political rivalry between the UMNO and the Islamic party PAS provides the background to this chapter.

Nik Aziz is one of Malaysia's most effective politicians and also a charismatic religious teacher. His Islamic credentials are impressive and he has used his authority as a leading *ulama* to enhance his political career. To analyse how he has achieved this synergy, Farish carefully analyses passages from Nik Aziz's commentaries on the Qur'an. Farish Noor is able to move beyond their surface messages to disclose their pointed political critiques. Their rhetorical strength derives from Nik Aziz's skill in expressing Quranic exegesis in vernacular idioms, using also the richness of Kelantan Malay (the dialect mastered by Clive Kessler).

Farish's analysis highlights the ability of Nik Aziz to "localize the universal and universalize the local" so that Islam becomes a living reality in the daily lives of ordinary Kelantanese. One of his most potent political messages, couched in religious terms, is that all people are equal in the sight of God but the poor are closer to God than the rich. Unlike the leaders of the UMNO, who have displayed conspicuous materialism, Nik Aziz has insisted on simplicity and modesty among his fellow PAS politicians, and has himself succeeded in defining his personal image according to these values.

Amrita Malhi continues the theme of political rivalry in her chapter, "The PAS-BN Conflict in the 1990s: Islamism and Modernity." Instead of Qur'anic exegesis, she uses speeches, documents, and a video clip circulated by members of the UMNO, or groups closely associated with it, analysing their strategies for discrediting the policies of PAS. Particularly since 11 September 2001, the Malaysian Government and Dr Mahathir have presented PAS as backward, extremist and, by associating it with the Taliban and terrorism, have suggested that it is also dangerous. The association of PAS's policies with those of the Taliban, Malhi suggests, is part of the government's strategy to portray PAS as not only extreme in its interpretation of Islam but uneducated, backward, and unable to operate effectively in a modern, technological world. One of the key terms in such government-sponsored rhetoric is *jahil*, an Arabic word which is associated with ignorance of Islam, barbarity, and backwardness.[11] Mahli notes that when presenting his own policies and programmes for Malaysia's future development, Dr Mahathir uses terminology which, although acknowledging the importance of Islamic values, places great stress on material advancement, progress, and the importance of efficiency and good management. The audience for this message of continuing modernization, Malhi argues, is the growing number of upwardly mobile, middle-class Malaysians who want a share of the global capital they can witness on satellite television in their technologically rich, high-rise apartments.

The gulf between the affluent, urban élites and the peasants of Kelantan (described by Farish and, earlier, by Kessler) is indeed wide. While Dr Mahathir and his colleagues may very often (but not exclusively) say that they direct their messages to middle-class urban Malaysians, the leaders of PAS are less exclusive in targetting their audiences. Malhi refers to statements by the late Dr Fadzil Noor, parliamentary leader of PAS, which show that PAS (or at least some of its leaders) are concerned to implement development projects which will benefit the poor in village and city alike, and be implemented without damage to society and the environment.

To raise again the concept of paradox as described in Joel Kahn's chapter, Malhi provides some evidence that the National Front's provocative criticisms of PAS may have stimulated it to respond with more progressive policies. Certainly, PAS has employed the rhetoric of social justice and equality (as described also in Farish's chapter) to win supporters and to criticize the National Front. It was on the basis of social justice and the need to reform the government that common grounds were found between PAS and a group of other non-government organizations to form the opposition coalition keADILan in 1999. After the general election of that year, and particularly after the events of 11 September 2001, internal disagreements led to a breakdown in the coalition and a consequent serious weakening of its position.

Malhi's chapter devotes considerable attention to the representation of modernity by both the National Front and PAS. It is an issue Clive Kessler himself addressed after the 1999 general election. In his view, the National Front had failed to develop and then communicate a " 'modernist Muslim' alternative" to the policies of PAS (Kessler 2000, p. 119). In Kessler's view, such an alternative could be presented as:

> A persuasively elaborated and effectively institutionalised understanding of Islam that was consonant both with the rational, democratic and emancipatory values of the Muslim faith at its formative historical moment and of subsequent Islamic civilisation and with the analogous values and spirit of advancing and increasingly inclusive modernity (Kessler 2000, p. 119).

Kessler reminds us that in the early twentieth century, a group of Malays (known now as the Kaum Muda, or the Young Generation) did articulate and widely circulate their vision for a modern-minded and Islamically inspired society which would bring progress to the Malay world. They had considerable impact on Malay thinking but never attained political power. There are lessons here, Kessler seems to be saying, which contemporary Malaysians might study.

The chapters in this volume, prepared as a tribute to the scholarship of Professor Clive Kessler, have each in a variety of ways acknowledged that, although contemporary Malaysia is fully part of the globalized world, its citizens continue to express their membership of that world in characteristically Malaysian idioms. This position was described over sixty years ago by one of Malaysia's best-loved writers. In the late 1930s, Ishak Haji Muhammad, also known as "Pak Sako", published two satirical novelettes which were banned by British colonial officials for their criticism of the colonial domination of Malaya. In them Pak Sako created characters who drew on indigenous knowledge and invented their own devices to lead lives which were independent of Western-derived technology.[12] Pak Sako's vision for Malay(si)an society, like that of the Kaum Muda, has been superseded. The independence of spirit, however, which inspired both visions lives on in many parts of contemporary society, as the chapters in this book testify.

Notes

1. This period is outlined more fully in Matheson Hooker (2003). The author wishes to thank Dr John Funston for critical input to this chapter.
2. The reasons for this electoral victory are analysed in Kessler (1978), pp. 120–26.
3. An excellent description of this policy and reactions to it is Gomes (1999), pp. 87–94.
4. Kessler has written on this phenomenon. See especially Kessler (1980).
5. One of Kessler's most perceptive commentaries on contemporary Malaysia is his essay, "Malaysia in Crisis, 1997–2000". See Kessler (2000).
6. Particularly his pieces for the website *Asian Analysis* [www.aseanfocus.com/asiananalysis]
7. Explored in more depth in Kessler (1972).
8. Kessler (1978), p. 216.
9. Ibid., pp. 216–17.
10. Kessler's perception of paradox ranges widely throughout Malay society. For another example, see Kessler (1985), p. 164, where he describes how by acting upon "their own implicit and Islamically-informed theory of political behaviour", which they had been told by political rivals was inappropriate, the Kelantanese paradoxically achieved a political victory and simultaneously validated their belief in Islamic principles.

11. Kessler explains the term, as understood in Kelantan during the period of his fieldwork in the 1960s. He also gives an example of PAS accusing the UMNO of following *politik jahil* (see Kessler 1978, p. 221 and p. 227). The UMNO did not always have a monopoly of the term.

12. The novelettes are *Putera Gunung Tahan* and *Anak Mat Lela Gila* first published in 1938 and 1941 respectively. Details of their author's descriptions of indigenous knowledge are given in Hooker (2000), pp. 137–42.

References

Funston, John. "Malaysia: Developmental State Challenged". In *Government and Politics in Southeast Asia*, edited by John Funston, pp. 160–202. Singapore: Institute of Southeast Asian Studies, 2000.

Gomes, Alberto G. "People and Cultures". In *The Shaping of Malaysia*, edited by Amarjit Kaur and Ian Metcalfe, pp.78–98. London and New York: Macmillan Press and St Martin's Press, 1999.

Hooker, Virginia Matheson. *Writing a New Society: Social Change through the Novel in Malay*. St Leonards: Allen & Unwin, 2000.

———— . *A Short History of Malaysia*. St Leonards: Allen & Unwin, 2003.

Kessler, Clive S. "Islam, Society and Political Behaviour: Some Comparative Implications of the Malay Case". *British Journal of Sociology* 23, no. 1 (1972): 33–50.

———— . *Islam and Politics in a Malay State: Kelantan 1838–1969*. Ithaca and London: Cornell University Press, 1978.

———— . "Malaysia: Islamic Revivalism and Political Disaffection in a Divided Society". *Southeast Asia Chronicle*, no. 75 (October 1980): 3–11.

———— . "The Politics of Islamic Egalitarianism". In *Readings on Islam in Southeast Asia*, compiled by Ahmad Ibrahim, Sharon Siddique, and Yasmin Hussain, pp. 159–64. Singapore: Institute of Southeast Asian Studies, 1985.

———— . "Archaism and Modernity: Contemporary Malay Political Culture". In *Fragmented Vision: Culture and Politics in Contemporary Malaysia*, edited by Joel S. Kahn and Francis Loh Kok Wah, pp. 133–57. North Sydney: Allen & Unwin Pty Ltd, 1992a.

———— . "Pilgrims' Progress: The Travelers of Islam". *Annals of Tourism Research* 19, no.1 (1992 b): 147–53.

———— . "Malaysia in Crisis, 1997–2000". *Review of Indonesian and Malaysian Affairs* 34, no. 2 (2000): 99–128.

PART I

Islam

3

SOCIAL SCIENCE APPROACHES TO UNDERSTANDING RELIGIOUS PRACTICE

The Special Case of the *Hajj*[1]

WILLIAM R. ROFF

For much of the 1980s, I was a member of an international Committee for the Comparative Study of Muslim Societies, established under the joint auspices of the American Social Science Research Council and the American Council of Learned Societies. The focus of our interest was not "Islam" in some disembodied, essential and timeless sense, but Muslims, the social actors who, as believers, interpret, understand, enunciate, and enact all that "Islam" means to them in whatever time and place. Interpretatively, we were interested in trying to understand and employ indigenous conceptual systems rather than imposing on Muslim social behaviour Western analytical categories. Wilfred Cantwell Smith declared many years ago that "Anything that I say about Islam as a living faith is valid only in so far as Muslims can say 'amen' to it. ... Where the encounter is between the academic tradition of the West and [Islam] the statement that is evolved must satisfy each of two traditions independently and transcend them both by satisfying both simultaneously".[2] The anthropologist Victor Turner (whose work is

central to this essay) quoted at one point an earlier anthropologist, E.
E. Evans Pritchard, who is said to have remarked that "it is all too easy,
when translating the conceptions of other people into our own, to
transplant our thought into theirs", and Turner himself goes on to
speak of the problems of, as well as the need for, making intelligible
many of the "cryptic phenomena" of religion in societies other than
our own.[3] Counsels such as these are salutary, but not always easy to
follow. What is important however, I assume, is to listen carefully to
what people say, while attending with equally close attention to the
texts according to which they claim to act.

I first became interested in the *hajj* and its implications — in my
case for Malay society, whose history I was studying at the time —
when at the outset of my research in Malaysia forty years ago I went
to live with a Malay family in a village near a small town — to learn
the language properly and as much as I could about Malay life and
thought. The head of the family was a carpenter with the Public
Works Department but he was also a *haji* who had made the *hajj* or
"pilgrimage" — I shall come back to that term — to Mecca in the
mid-1920s, and I understood that this title was important both to him
and to his neighbours. I slept in the *anjung*, or front part of the house,
on the floor but more particularly on a silk *selimut* (quilt) which my
host had brought back from Mecca in 1927. On the wall nearby was
a framed lithograph of the Kaaba, and across the room a current,
slightly tatty Common Era calendar (this was October) promoting the
services of a local *shaykh haji* (pilgrimage agent), which similarly
depicted some Meccan scene. My host himself — when dressed for
salat (ritual prayer), for giving lessons in *mengaji Qur'an* (reciting the
Qur'an) to the young pupils whose houses he visited for that purpose,
or for any other occasion that required him to assume his religious
persona — was accustomed to wearing the white skull cap which
denoted his *haji* status. In other words, it rapidly became clear to me
that the accomplishment of the fifth pillar of Islam had immense
personal and social significance, symbolized in a host of separate ways.
I was aware, of course, that this was true not only for the many
thousands of Malays who over the years had made the *hajj*, but also
probably in similar form for countless others from end to end of the
Muslim world. How do we go about understanding this "cryptic
phenomenon"?

One answer, methodologically, may be to look for help to studies in the sociology of ritual. This is not the place to embark on a lengthy disquisition on the evolution of ritual studies in sociology, even were it in my power to do so. The anthropologist Talal Asad, however, in his essay, "Towards a genealogy of the concept of ritual", has usefully documented the important shift in Western social thought from the eighteenth century (and earlier) idea of ritual as a text or script regulating (principally Christian) religious practice to the early twentieth century idea of ritual as a type of practice, not necessarily religious (let alone Christian), that is interpretable as symbolizing or expressing some further set of meanings, and which, as practice rather than script, relates differentially to individual consciousness and social organization.[4] The importation into understandings of ritual of the need to recognize both text and the individual and social context of ritual performance was to be of great consequence.

It is this especially that is reflected in Arnold Van Gennep's seminal work, *Les Rites de Passage*, published in 1908. In pursuit of an exercise in the classification of what he termed "magico-religious acts or rites",[5] he noted the universal and frequent occurrence in human societies of the movement of individuals from one status to another — generational, occupational, marital, sacerdotal, etc. — each transition or passage marked by ceremonies whose aim is to ensure that the transition is made successfully. In elaborating this insight and developing his theoretical argument, he made two initial observations of importance. The first concerns the prevalence in rites of transition of territorial or spatial passage across real or symbolic frontiers, which led him to develop his ideas about the threshold between profane and sacred space. The second was his insistence that rituals be analysed in their totality and in cultural and temporal context, as "ceremonial wholes", without extrapolating elements from them for conjunct analysis as the folklorists tended to do.

Van Gennep saw in physical, territorial passage, then, the archetypal framework for analysis of the ritual assemblages he called *rites de passage*. Departure from the profane, movement towards the sacred, arrival at a boundary or threshold, entry — he sets out, map-like, the classic stages of what he called the "ceremonial sequence", each accompanied by its rites, reducible to three — those accompanying separation, transition, and incorporation. Van Gennep styled rites of separation "pre-liminal", rites of transition "liminal", and rites of incorporation "post-liminal" — terminologies that make clear the centrality and importance for him of the "liminal" stage.[6] Though it may now seem obvious that an analytical framework of this kind is perhaps especially relevant for understanding religious pilgrimage, Van Gennep says very little about this, confining what remarks he makes to a couple of pages in a chapter entitled "Other types of rites of passage". He does, however, refer to the Muslim pilgrim "who has pledged to go to Mecca … in a special state called *ihram* from the moment he enters the limits of the sacred territory", and having assumed this condition is "outside ordinary life and in a transitional state". He suggests also that the "special rites" while in Mecca include "rites of incorporation into the divine (touching the Black Stone, and perhaps originally the rite of stone throwing)".[7]

Despite the suggestiveness of Van Gennep's theory of *rites de passage* for pilgrimage studies, they have seldom been taken up by Islamists. The French scholar, Maurice Gaudefroy-Demombynes, whose *La Pélerinage à la Mekke*, published in 1923, is the first monographic and analytical (as distinct from descriptive) study of the *hajj* to be published in a European language, subtitled "A study in religious history", clearly knew of Van Gennep but cited, as far as I can ascertain, only one largely unrelated folklorist article of 1919. Nonetheless, Demombynes uses terminologies that recall Van Gennep, noting, for example, that while the departure of a Muslim for an ordinary journey is likely to be surrounded by precautions and propitiatory ceremonies, these, when they concern the *hajj*, "take on more clearly still the character of *rites de passage*". The "ensemble of rites" that attend departure form "a first stage between lay life and an existence that comes to be more and more neighbour to the sanctuary". He writes, "Before leaving the faithful erases all his past and prepares himself to become another person", and quoting from Al-Qalyubi (d. 1004/1596) says that the pilgrim sets out "as if he were leaving this world", concluding "it is without doubt 'a death of the past', a *rite de passage*".[8]

This was to be the last we were to hear for many years about *rites de passage* and the *hajj*. G.-H. Bousquet, a French orientalist-administrator who wrote extensively on the Maghrib, has two chapters on the *hajj* in his 1949 work *Les Grands Pratiques Rituelles de l'Islam*,[9] but is not remotely interested in the analysis of ritual or in ritual theory. Gustave Von Grunebaum, in a lengthy and more scholarly section on the *hajj* in his *Muhammadan Festivals* (published in 1951),[10] seeks only to provide description, with some quotation from textual authorities. Such comments as he has on ritual structure are quoted from the eleventh century philosopher, al-Ghazali. A more recent monographic work, published in 1982 with the perhaps promising title, *La Doctrine Initiatique du Pèlerinage à la Maison d'Allah*, turns out on inspection to be an admirably detailed but analytically sparse work of devotion by (I assume) a convert, Charles-André Gilis, who was strongly influenced by French Sufism.[11] The sole monographic work of which I am aware that makes a serious attempt to analyse the *hajj* in terms of ritual theory (in this case from within the discipline known, especially in America, as History of Religions) is the unpublished doctoral dissertation completed by Harry B. Partin for the Divinity School at the University of Chicago in 1967, entitled "The Muslim pilgrimage: Journey to the center".

In a chapter entitled, "The religious structure of the pilgrimage", Partin says that, "While there is need to distinguish pilgrimage [in general] from other religious phenomena, it is also necessary to see that pilgrimage belongs to a more general class of religious phenomena, namely, rites of passage".[12] Taking up Van Gennep's three-fold schema — rites of separation, transition, and incorporation — he expresses surprise that Van Gennep says little or nothing about pilgrimage, "for in pilgrimage one finds the three-fold pattern of rites on not one but two scales" — at the place of pilgrimage itself and on the larger scale of the journey.[13] (This is a useful comment, given the wide extent of the Muslim world within a couple of centuries of its establishment, but I shall come back to it.) Following discussion of pilgrim travellers in a variety of cultural traditions, Partin does look briefly at the ensemble of *hajj* rites in Van Gennepian terms — instancing the assumption of *ihram* (ritual clothing) as a rite of separation, and *tawaf* (circumambulation of the Kaaba) as a rite of incorporation. However, he is more interested, prompted by the work of his teacher, Mircea Eliade, in returning to an examination of pilgrimage as a symbolic journey, and in developing Wensinck's notions about "the ideas of the Western Semites concerning the navel of the earth", and relating these to Muslim beliefs in the cosmic centrality of Mecca.[14]

It was the anthropologist Victor Turner who in the 1960s took up afresh Van Gennep's ideas concerning what he would shortly call "ritual process", and in due course applied them to religious pilgrimage. In a lecture to the American Ethnological Society in 1964, entitled "Betwixt and between: The liminal period in *rites de passage*", later published in *The Forest of Symbols*,[15] Turner set out to explore "some of the sociocultural properties of the 'liminal period' in that class of rituals which Arnold van Gennep has definitively characterized as '*rites de passage*'".[16] Such rites, Turner suggested, indicate and constitute transitions between "states", by which term he meant any "relatively fixed or stable condition", including both such social constancies as legal status, office, profession, or rank, and the degrees of social maturation signified by adulthood, marriage, and the like. Turner summarized this by saying, "State, in short, is a more inclusive concept than status or office and refers to any type of stable or recurrent condition that is culturally recognized."[17] Recalling Van Gennep's tripartite division of transition rites, Turner saw the separation phase as marked by symbolic behaviour signifying the detachment of the individual from the social structure in which he is otherwise embedded, and his entry into a "liminal" phase — which he, like Van Gennep, saw as possessing a centrality and importance that demands from the observer special attention — characterized by becoming rather than being, by "interstructure" (he later termed this "anti-structure"), of "betwixt and between". It is the characteristics of this liminal phase that were his main subject of inquiry, based primarily on his fieldwork among the Ndembu people of Zambia, and he ended his lecture with an invitation to investigators of ritual to "focus their attention on the phenomenon and processes of mid-transition".[18]

Turner up to this point had said nothing about religious pilgrimage — his Henry Morgan lectures in 1966, published three years later as *The Ritual Process: Structure and Anti-Structure*, were similarly based on analysis of Ndembu data. He was well aware, however, of the paradigmatic nature of Van Gennep's schema for religious pilgrimage, which interested him personally as a practising Roman Catholic, and in the 1970s he embarked on a comparative study of pilgrimage systems.[19] This found shape initially in an essay entitled, "The center out there: pilgrims' goal", subsequently reprinted in his collection of essays, *Dramas, Fields and Metaphors*, with the title "Pilgrimages as social processes".[20]

Already, in *The Ritual Process*, Turner had introduced a term of his own with which to describe the function as well as the essential characteristic of the liminal period of transition rituals. Liminal phenomena, he wrote, present a "blend ... of lowliness and sacredness, of homogeneity and comradeship ... in a 'moment in and out of time' ... which reveals, however fleetingly, some recognition of a generalized social bond ... an unstructured ... and relatively undifferentiated *communitas*, community, or even communion of equal individuals...".[21] *Communitas*, he continued, "is almost everywhere held to be sacred or 'holy', possibly because it transgresses and dissolves the norms that govern structured and institutionalized relationships and is accompanied by experiences of unprecedented potency."[22] He went on to provide a taxonomy of *communitas* phenomena, distinguishing between what he called "existential or spontaneous" *communitas*, which he likened to a "happening"; "normative" *communitas*, in which over time spontaneous *communitas* is organized "into a perduring social system", and finally "ideological" *communitas*, in which a model is prescribed for its generation.[23] When, later, in "Pilgrimages as social processes", he turned to pilgrimage to exemplify his understanding of the social processes that accompany *rites de passage*, he referred explicitly to the *hajj* on a number of occasions to illustrate his argument. In particular, he quoted Malcolm X's well-known account of how the experience of the *hajj* transformed his view of human societies through "the love, humility, and true brotherhood that was almost a physical feeling wherever I turned", although Turner went on to suggest that behind the spontaneous *communitas* evoked here lay the normative *communitas* of rule-governed (and perhaps textually supplied) behaviour that underpinned it.[24]

Turner, then, I suggest, accomplished two things of consequence in his reworking of Van Gennep which are important: the problematization of the concept of the "state" or condition — and how we are to understand this — which is transformed by ritual process, and the development of the concept of *communitas* as the central feature of the liminal or transformative stage of *rites de passage*. Both may be seen as relevant to any study of the ensemble of Islamic rituals known as the *hajj*.

Though the *hajj* consists essentially, and only, of the sequence of rituals performed in Mecca and its vicinity at a fixed time each (lunar) year, it is most frequently referred to (in English and French, and analogously in many other languages) as the "pilgrimage" to Mecca. This is understandable. The root meaning of "pilgrimage" is, of course, journey, and from early in the history of Islam increasingly large numbers of Muslims, for whom the *hajj* is, subject to certain limited conditions, obligatory, have lived far from Arabia. It is not surprising, therefore, that the undertaking of the journey to Mecca, in order to perform the *hajj* while there, has become surrounded in most Muslim societies, not least the furthest flung, with rites relating to preparation, departure, voyaging, and return. Harry Partin, as I noted earlier, saw in religious pilgrimage Van Gennep's threefold schema reproduced on two scales — at the place of pilgrimage itself, and on the larger scale of the journey. I once tried, in an article entitled "Leavetakings: The 'separation' stage of the Meccan pilgrimage",[25] to discuss some of the issues arising, beginning with a quotation concerning the Sufi Abu'l Qasim al-Junayd (d. 298/910) which well conveys this process: "A man who had just returned from the pilgrimage came to Junayd. Junayd said: From the hour when you first journeyed away from here have you also been journeying away from all sins? He said: No. Then, said Junayd, you have made no journey. At every stage where you halted for the night did you traverse a station on the way to God? No, he replied. Then, said Junayd, you have not trodden the road, stage by stage. When you put on the pilgrim's garb at the proper place, did you discard the qualities of human nature as you cast off your clothes? No. Then you have not put on the pilgrim's garb."[26]

The anthropologist Dale Eickelman, in his contribution to the article on rites of passage in *The Encyclopeadia of Religion*, noted that, given the diversity of cultural and historical contexts within which Islam has been and is practised, "some transitions, including ... the pilgrimage (*hajj*) to Mecca, are specifically Islamic, yet how these occasions are ritually marked varies considerably with location."[27] This is especially true of local rites accompanying the departure and return of pilgrims, but also of those involved in local celebration of the *hajj* on the appropriate days. Regarding departure, Eickelman noted the way in which many North African pilgrims "first ritually circumambulate their town or village, visiting its principal shrines in the company of friends and relatives", and carrying flags or banners.[28] In Southeast Asia, a *selamatan* or *kenduri*, a communal meal, is held in an intending pilgrim's house, attended by relatives and neighbours, restating the social matrix from which the pilgrim is about to separate himself, and when the time for setting forth arrives he must in some areas descend by the house-ladder that lies nearest the rising of the sun and, having set his foot to the ground, not go back until he comes home. Regarding return, the remarkable series of housefront and wall paintings, reproduced in the volume *Hajj Paintings: Folk Art of the Great Pilgrimage*, depict the emblematic as well as the celebratory aspects of *hajj* completion and homecoming, in this instance in Egypt.[29] The marking in the diaspora of the *hajj*, most frequently centred on the *'Id al-Adha* (the Day of Sacrifice or *'Id al-Kurban*) on 10 Zulhijjah, is accompanied in most Muslim societies by special rituals, described vividly for Aceh in Sumatra, for example, by James Siegel, as evoking "the hope that men will 'bind themselves together with the rope of God, the rope that neither rots in the rain nor cracks in the sun'"[30]

Any full discussion of the ritual process as it applies to the *hajj* would certainly need to take into account the meaning and experience of the journey to and from the Holy Places, and the celebration of the festival at home. I am primarily concerned here, however, to look — if necessarily rather briefly — at the ritual ensemble of the *hajj* proper in the light of the sociological materials I have been discussing. I shall not attempt to distinguish between *ʿumra* (the "lesser" pilgrimage, made outside the *hajj* season, or curtailed during the latter) and *hajj*, but speak of the *hajj* entirely; nor will I detail any of the numerous differences between schools about the minutiae of ritual performance.

There may be said to be six main ritual elements: *ihram, tawaf, saʿy, wuquf* at Arafat, lapidation, and *kurban*.

Assumption of *ihram* (clothing consisting solely of two pieces of unsewn white cloth) in the past took place mainly at the *miqat* or places of entry to the sacred territory; nowadays, with the prevalence of air travel, pilgrims often change before boarding their aircraft.[31] Donning *ihram* is prefaced by a statement of intention (*niyat*) of the kind of pilgrimage one is making — *ʿumra; hajj* and *ʿumra;* or *hajj* alone (between which I shall make no distinction here) and by a major ablution and depilation. The prescriptions for this rite emphasize that *ihram* symbolizes the pilgrim's separation from the profane world and the resulting commonality of the human condition before Allah, shorn of rank, status, gender (though, in fact, women, though unveiled, remain somewhat distinguishable in dress from men) and worldly possessions and adornments. Reinforcing this, the *ihram* garments themselves are often perceived (and eventually employed, after being soaked in water from the *zem-zem* well in the Masjid al-Haram, the Great Mosque) as the wearer's burial shroud. As a modern Muslim commentator puts it: "The scene [at the *miqat*] is like the day of judgement. From one horizon to another a flood of 'whites' appears. All the people are wearing Kafan [burial shrouds]. No one can be recognized. The bodies were left in Miqat and the souls are motivated here. Names, races, nor social status make a difference . An atmosphere of genuine unity prevails. It is a human show of Allah's unity. Everyone 'melts' himself and assumes a new form as 'mankind'. The egos and individual traits are buried. The group becomes a 'people' or an '*Umma*'. All the 'I's' have died in Miqat; what has evolved is 'We' ".[32]

Such descriptions obviously recall the discussion by Van Gennep, elaborated by Turner, of pre-liminal rites of separation and the nature of the resulting phase of liminality. For Turner, it will be recollected, liminality presents a blend of lowliness and sacredness, of homogeneity and comradeship, in a time "in and out of time", revealing the emergence of a *communitas* that transgresses and dissolves the norms that govern structured and institutionalized relationships, accompanied by experiences of unprecedented potency.[33]

Crying aloud the *talbiyah*, a prayer announcing the pilgrim's presence, the throng then moves upon Mecca, the Masjid al-Haram, and the Kaaba, around which is performed, individually but as part of a vast collectivity, the second important rite, the *tawaf* of arrival, preceded again by a statement of intention. This sevenfold anti-clockwise circumambulation of the Kaaba is started, if possible, by kissing the Black Stone set in its eastern corner or, if that is not possible, by touching it or, if that is not possible, by saluting it by raising both hands level with the ears, facing the palms towards the stone, saying *takbir* and *tahlil* prayer formulae and kissing one's hands. There is much more that one might say about subsidiary practices associated with the performance of *tawaf*,[34] but though these may intensify or heighten the experience, they do not affect its essential character. This is well described, again, by Ali Shariati: "During Tawaf ... you cannot enter the Kaaba nor stop anywhere around it. You must enter into and disappear from the crowd. You must be drawn into the roaring river of people who are circumambulating. This is how you will become a Hajj. … [I]t is 'people' representing 'mankind' who are making Tawaf. … Those who are detached from themselves are alive and moving collectively. Those who are not separated from themselves are stagnant and dead. … When you give up your life in the way of Allah, in your warm blood you will approach Shahadat and be called a Shaheed."[35] These repeated references to transitional states of the self and the potency of shared experience seem certainly to reinforce the idea of *tawaf* as, in Van Gennep's and Turner's terms, a rite of incorporation.

The *tawaf* of arrival is followed by performance of the *sᶜay*, the traversing seven times, back and forth, of the route between the raised hillocks of Safa and Marwa, in imitation and memory of Hajar's running between these places in search of water for her son Ismail. Completion of this ritual marks the completion also of the ᶜumra, for those who are either leaving temporarily the state of *ihram*, or not continuing to the *hajj* proper. I shall proceed without a break — as many pilgrims do — direct to the next stage, the *wuquf*, or "standing", at Arafat.

Doctrinally, this is the central and essential moment of the *hajj*, without which there is no *hajj*. Following a special *khutbah* (sermon) in the Masjid al-Haram on 7th Zulhijjah, the participants make their way from Mecca on the 8th, by way of Mina, and congregate on the 9th in the measureless concourse that fills the plain of Arafat. Here, from mid-day, following exactly the model of the Prophet Muhammad's "farewell pilgrimage" three months before his death, on which the entire ritual ensemble of the *hajj* proper is based, those assembled listen to two *khutbahs* associated with combined *zuhr* and *ᶜasr* (mid-day and afternoon) prayers, and spend the hours between then and sunset in contemplation of the Almighty and seeking forgiveness of their sins and acceptance of their *hajj*. Al-Ghazali, quoted by Von Grunebaum, says of the *wuquf*: "In ᶜArafa, the crowds, the shouting, the many tongues, the grouping of the nations by their leaders should remind you of the plains of the Last Day when the nations will assemble round their prophets, desirous of their intercession, fearful and perplexed."[36] Innumerable participants have spoken of the awesome experience that the *wuquf* at Arafat affords.

The fifth and penultimate principal ritual element in the *hajj* follows, the lapidation or stoning of the pillars, accomplished at Mina on the 10th Zulhijjah, the day after the *wuquf* at Arafat. As with the *s^cay* I shall not treat this at any length here. Like the *s^cay*, it is structured by a secondary narrative — within the master narrative based on the Prophet Muhammad's farewell *hajj* — which looks back to the time of Ibrahim, and recalls the instruction given to Ibrahim by the angel Gabriel to reject Satan's temptations to disobey Allah, by pronouncing the *takbir* (the formula *Allahu Akbar*, God is Great) and stoning him. As with the *s^cay*, it embodies moral lessons that, expressed in the solemn intention required before it is performed, contribute to the common sense of ethical purpose engendered by *hajj* participation.[37]

Let me proceed, finally, to the *kurban* (sacrifice), which occurs on the same day, and also in Mina. Obligatory for all pilgrims (broadly speaking), it too has an internal narrative, commemorating what I personally have always regarded as the most terrifying moment in the entire Islamic and Christian traditions, the readiness of Ibrahim in obedience to the Almighty to sacrifice with his own hands Ismail, his dearly beloved son by Hajar, and when the Almighty is satisfied with Ibrahim's submission to his will, permitted the last-minute substitution of a sheep.[38] Is it the inherent and terrible drama of this story and its message that has led to 10th Zulhijjah, 'Id al-Kurban, being marked in the Muslim diaspora as the central day of the *hajj* celebrations rather than the 9th, the *wuquf* at Arafat? Siegel puts it rather differently for Aceh. Reproducing verbatim the local *khutbah* on this occasion, which evokes the participants at Mina commemorating the Ibrahim and Ismail story, he notes that the image presented of the pilgrims dressed uniformly in *ihram* thinking of the sacrifice is an image "not merely one of men without society. It is also an image of *akal* ... the faculty by which man knows, and its function is to know God's commands, and so to obey them." He goes on: "The final image [of the *khutbah*] is that of Ibrahim with his knife raised, about to kill Ismail. Yet, this is not the entire image for it also includes, as we have seen, the pilgrims thinking of Ibrahim about to kill Ismail as well as the audience thinking of the pilgrims thinking of Ibrahim. ... Only after the audience itself is added to the picture of the pilgrims is the story of Ibrahim actually told."[39]

Following desacralization, celebration, and a final *tawaf* of the Kaaba, the pilgrim, now "*haji*" (or, if a woman, "*hajah*"), is free to return home. In doing so, do the pilgrims return changed — as both Islamic teaching and social science theorizing, in their different but perhaps convergent ways, would predicate of them? Plainly, many do in a variety of obvious and outer, symbolic ways — wearing, maybe, Arab dress in distinction to that in which they arrived; often, at least in the past, having taken new and more "Islamic" names in token of their rebirth; and with a new status denoted by the title "*haji*". It may reasonably be assumed that pilgrims return also changed in their perceptions of Islam and the Muslim 'Umma, its imperatives and strengths. They are graduate members in consequence both of this larger community and of their own national, local, rural, or urban one and, by virtue of having re-enacted the origins of the faith at its font, they are uniquely capable of linking the two and revitalizing in their persons that to which they return.

The power of Turner's *communitas* to reorganize perceptions of social relations and dissolve or restructure prior conceptions of the relationship between Man and the Infinite, seems evident in many personal accounts of the *hajj*, from which I shall cite only two passages here, one of which is particularly well known. Malcolm X, in his account of the *hajj* sent to the then newly formed Harlem Mosque, wrote that "there were tens of thousands of pilgrims, from all over the world. They were of all colors, from blue-eyed blonds to black-skinned Africans. But we were all participating in the same ritual, displaying a spirit of unity and brotherhood that my experience in America had led me to believe never could exist between the white and the non-white ... [O]n this pilgrimage what I have seen and experienced has forced me to *re-arrange* much of my thought-patterns previously held, and to *toss aside* some of my previously held conclusions."[40]

A different figure altogether, the Iranian left-wing social critic and writer Jalal Al-e Ahmad, made the *hajj* in 1964, not long after Malcolm X. He kept an impressionistic, day by day journal. His account of the *hajj* is full of wry observations about many of the more regimented and unattractive aspects of "*hajj* tourism", about the commercialism of the organizers, the quarrelling and greed displayed by several of his companions, and his own tendency to a rather cynical worldliness.

However, he ends his account as follows: "The way I see it I've come on this trip mainly out of curiosity, the same way I poke my nose into everything, to look without expectations. Now I've seen it, and this notebook is the result. This was an experience too, in my case, or perhaps a very simple event. Every one of these experiences was simple and 'uneventful'. Although it was quite ordinary it was the basis of a kind of awakening, and if not an awakening, at least a skepticism. In this way, I am *smashing the steps of the world of certainty one by one* with the pressure of experience, beneath my feet."[41]

Let me end by referring again to the questions I asked at the outset: how best may those of us who are not Muslims go about understanding the "cryptic phenomena" of the ritual practice known as the *hajj*? Does the sociology of ritual help? I think it does, though we should recall that questions such as these are likely, by definition, to be framed primarily by non-Muslims, and that if the answers to them do not satisfy Muslims, we may be talking only to ourselves. Does that matter? I'm not sure. However, the thought remains, to quote Fredric Jameson: "To what extent is the object of study the thought pattern of the theorist rather than the supposed object, ritual".[42]

Notes

1. In a chapter dealing with "religious ideas and social reality", in his *Islam and Politics in a Malay State: Kelantan 1838–1969*, drawing on the work of earlier anthropologists and alluding in particular to James Siegel's *Rope of God*, Clive Kessler refers to "the moral, social and political signficance of Islam's rituals of transient equality" (p. 217). The present essay is an exploration of one aspect of this significance. It was originally presented at Professor Muhammad Khalid Masud's MA seminar on "Text and practice in Islamic ritual" at the Institute for the Study of Islam in the Modern World in Leiden in 2000, and subsequently at the Kulliyah of Islamic Revealed Knowledge and Human Sciences, International Islamic University of Malaysia, the Anthropology Department of St Andrews University, and the Middle East history seminar at the School of Oriental and African Studies, London, to all of which I am grateful for discussion and comment.
2. Smith (1959), pp. 43; 53.
3. Turner (1969), p. 4.
4. In Asad (1993), pp. 56–57.

5. Van Gennep (1960) [originally published in 1908], p. 15.
6. Ibid., p. 21.
7. Ibid., p. 185.Van Gennep cites in support of these remarks W. Robertson Smith's *Lectures on the Religion of the Semites*; and Ciszewski, *Kunstliche Verwandschaft bei den Sudslaven*. The second of these references is obscure to me.
8. Gaudefroy-Demombynes (1977), pp. 155–56.
9. The chapters on the *hajj* are at pp. 69–107.
10. The section on "pilgrimage" is at pp. 15–49.
11. Gilis (1982).
12. Partin (1967), pp. 155–56.
13. Ibid., p. 157.
14. Ibid., p. 169.
15. Turner (1967), Chapter IV, pp. 93–111.
16. Ibid., p.93.
17. Ibid., p.94.
18. Ibid., p110.
19. Turner (1974), p. 65.
20. Ibid., Chapter 5, pp. 166–230.
21. Turner (1969), p. 96 (emphasis in original).
22. Ibid., p. 128.
23. Ibid., pp. 132. See also Turner (1974), p. 169.
24. Ibid., p. 170.
25. Roff (1993).
26. Cited in Nicholson (1963).
27. Eickelman (1987), p. 398.
28. Ibid.
29. Parker and Neal (1995). See especially "The Homecoming", pp. 96–113.
30. Siegel (1969), pp. 275. The section on "The pilgrimage" is at pp. 260–75; cf. also the appendix, "A note on *communitas* and the rope of God", pp. 279–83.
31. For two *fatwas* on this, in 1980 and 1981, in Indonesia, see Mohammad Atho Mudzhar (1993), pp. 160–63 & 140–43 (text in Indonesian and English.)
32. Ali Shariati (1978), pp. 10–11. For a qualification of this ideal view, see Siddiqui (1982), p. 15, republished in Khan and Zaki (1986).
33. See Turner (1969), p. 96.
34. Most descriptive accounts and *manasik* guides detail these. See, for example, Gaudefroy-Demombynes (1977), chp. 4, pp. 205–24, "Les tournees rituelles a la Kaaba (*tawaf*)"; and Matthews (1977), "Tawaf", chp. 8, pp. 63–88.

35. Shariati (1978), p. 28–29. The *shahadat* is the Islamic confession of faith; to be a *shahid* is to be a witness to the faith, and in some (especially Shiʿi) contexts, to manifest extreme witness to the faith through martyrdom.
36. Quoted from al-Ghazali, "Ihya ʿUlum ad-Din", in Von Grunebaum (1976), pp. 46–47.
37. Further stonings take place after the 10th Zulhijjah.
38. The most moving evocation of this episode with which I am familiar is Benjamin Britten's setting of the text of the Chester Miracle Play version in Canticle 2, "Abraham and Isaac", Opus 51. On the substitution of Ismail for Isaac in later Islamic tradition, see Reuven Firestone, "The evolution of the Abraham-Ishmael legends in Islamic exegesis", pp. 135–51. I am grateful to Peter Riddell for drawing this work to my attention. It should also be noted that, in Judaism, the parallel event and its associated rituals are similarly surrounded with awe.
39. Siegel (1969), pp. 272–73.
40. Malcolm X (1966), p.140 (emphasis in the original).
41. Jalal Al-e Ahmad (1985), p. 123 (emphasis added).
42. Cited by Bell (1992), p. 31, apparently from Jameson (1981).

References

Ali Shariati. *Hajj*. Translated by Somayyah and Yaser. 2nd edition. Bedford, Ohio: Free Islamic Literatures Inc., 1978.

Asad, Talal. *Genealogies of Religion: Discipline and Reasons of Power in Christianity and Islam*. Baltimore: Johns Hopkins University Press, 1993.

Bell, Catherine. *Ritual Theory, Ritual Practice*. New York: Oxford University Press, 1992.

Bousquet, G. G. *Les Grands Practiques Rituelles de l'Islam*. Paris: Presses Universitaires de France, 1949.

Britten, Benjamin. *The Canticles (Canticle 2). "Abraham and Isaac"*, Opus 51. London: Decca Recordings, 1963, CD 425-716-2.

Eickelman, Dale F. "Muslim Rites". In *The Encyclopedia of Religion*, edited by Mircea Eliade, vol. 12, p. 398. New York: Collier Macmillan, 1987.

Firestone, Reuven. *Journeys in Holy Lands*. Binghampton, NY: State University of New York, 1990.

Gaudefroy-Demombynes, Maurice. *La Pélerinage à la Mekke: Étude d'Histoire Religieuse*. Philadelphia: Porcupine Press, 1977. (Photomechanical reprint of the original 1923 edition, Paris: Presses Universitaires de France, 1949).

Gilis, Charles-André. *La Doctrine Initiatique du Pélerinage à la Maison d'Allah*. Paris: Les Editions de l'Oeuvre, 1982.

International Hajj Seminar, London, 1982. *Hajj: A Ritual at the Heart of the Islamic Movement. Summary and Recommendations of the Seminar, London 1982 (1402).* London: The Open Press, for the Muslim Institute, 1983.

Jalal Al-e Ahmad. *Lost in the Crowd*, translated by John Green et al. Washington, DC: Three Continents Press, 1985.

Jameson, Fredric. *The Political Unconscious.* Ithaca, NY: Cornell University Press, 1981.

Khan, Zafarul-Islam, and Yaqub Zaki, eds. *Hajj in Focus.* London: The Open Press, 1986.

Kessler, Clive S. *Islam and Politics in a Malay State: Kelantan 1838–1969.* Ithaca, NY: Cornell University Press, 1978.

Malcolm X. *The Autobiography of Malcolm X.* New York: New Grove Press, 1966.

Matthews, Anis Daud. *A Guide for Hajj and 'Umra.* Lahore: Kazi Publications, 1977.

Mohammad Atho Mudzhar. *Fatwa-Fatwa Majelis Ulama Indonesia: Sebuah Study tentang Pemikiran Hukum di Indonesia, 1975–1988/Fatwas of the Council of Indonesian Ulama: A Study of Islamic Legal Thought in Indonesia, 1975–1988.* Jakarta: Indonesian-Netherlands Cooperation in Islamic Studies, 1993.

Nicholson, R. A. *The Mystics of Islam.* London: Routledge & Kegan Paul, 1963 [originally published 1914].

Parker, Ann, and Avon Neal. *Hajj Paintings: Folk Art of the Great Pilgrimage.* Washington, DC: Smithsonian Institute Press, 1995.

Partin, Harry B. "The Muslim pilgrimage: Journey to the center". Unpublished doctoral dissertation. Chicago: University of Chicago, School of Divinity, September 1967. Available from the Department of Photoduplication, University of Chicago Library, Thesis No. 22915.

Roff, William R. "Leavetakings: The 'Separation' Stage of the Meccan Pilgrimage". In *Muslim and Arab Perspectives* (New Delhi) 1, no. 1 (October 1993): 220–28.

Siddiqui, Kalim. "The hajj in the context of contemporary history". In *Hajj: A Ritual at the Heart of the Islamic Movement. Summary and Recommendations of the International Hajj Seminar, London, 1982 (1402)*, pp. 9–26. London: The Open Press for the Muslim Institute, 1983. (Republished as *Hajj in Focus*, edited by Zafarul-Islam Khan and Yaqub Zaki, pp. 1–18. London: The Open Press, 1986.)

Siegel, James. *Rope of God.* Berkeley, Ca: University of California Press, 1969.

Smith, Wilfred Cantwell. "History of religions: Whither and why?" In *The History of Religion: Essays in Methodology*, edited by Mircea Eliade and J. M. Kitagawa. Chicago, Ill: University of Chicago Press, 1959.

Smith, W. Robertson. *Lectures on the Religion of the Semites*. London: A. and C. Blick, 1907.

Turner, Victor. *The Forest of Symbols: Aspects of Ndembu Ritual*. Ithaca, NY: Cornell University Press, 1967.

————. *The Ritual Process: Structure and Anti-Structure*. Chicago, Ill: University of Chicago Press, 1969.

————. *Dramas, Fields and Metaphors: Symbolic Action in Human Society*. Ithaca, NY: Cornell University Press, 1974.

Van Gennep, Arnold. *The Rites of Passage*. Translated by Monica B. Vizedom and Gabrielle L. Caffee. Chicago, Ill: University of Chicago Press, 1960 [1908].

Von Grunebaum, Gustave. *Muhammadan Festivals*. London: Curzon Press, c. 1951, 1976.

Wensinck, A. J. *The Ideas of the Western Semites Concerning the Centre of the Earth*. Amsterdam: Johannes Muller, 1916.

4

POLITICS OF SYARIAH REFORM
The Making of the State Religio-Legal Apparatus

KIKUE HAMAYOTSU

Introduction

Exercises in authority building are intrinsically related to the quest for state-making. Moreover, the expansion of modern state institutions in itself is a highly political process and the effects of this process are similarly political. In a Muslim society, Muslim leaders readily utilize the idiom of religion to engage with such a process of state-making. Various Islamic actors[1] — over a wide ideological spectrum — strive for the attainment of a vision of state and nation on both ideological and institutional fronts. Some aspire to the creation of an "Islamic state" — based on the Islamic canons and tradition. Others adopt a less dogmatic approach to establish authority based on religious-inspired moral principles.

In a more modern context, this contestation over the nature of the state, as Clive Kessler elegantly showed in his classic study on Muslim-Malay politics in Kelantan, is transferred into the arena of party politics (Kessler 1978). What the outcomes of these contestations are, as Kessler emphasizes elsewhere, depends not on the irrevocable influence of doctrinal forms, but on historically, sociologically, and ideologically determined patterns of political agency (Kessler 1979).

The jurisdictional expansion and institutionalization of the Islamic (Syariah) judicial mechanism in Malaysia offer an intriguing case for examining the process of state-making. A reform drive in the Syariah judicial apparatus since the 1980s, spearheaded by the UMNO (United Malays National Organization) (which has dominated government) has brought about an unprecedented institutional development on the constitutional, legislative, and administrative fronts. The apparatus of the Syariah courts was upgraded, with their jurisdiction expanded within the country's still essentially "secular" judicial system. This apparent "Islamization" trend has corresponded with the organizational expansion of the state machinery administering Syariah matters, including the increased employment of better-qualified Syariah personnel. One important overall effect of this process is the rise of highly institutionalized state mechanisms regulating Islamic agencies and actors. The Syariah reform, thus, has the potential to reinforce state authority in society at large. Given the fact that some actors benefit — while others do not — from this reform initiative, the process is inherently contentious and thus highly political.

The relatively high degree and the particular type of institutionalization of the Syariah regime, which have been taking place, raise an intriguing puzzle for observers of religion and politics in Malaysia and beyond: Why and how has institutionalization of the Islamic judicial apparatus proceeded to the level and in the particular way it has? A well-institutionalized state apparatus here matches a rationalized set of bureaucratic authority structures in a Weberian sense.[2] This chapter attempts to go some way towards solving the puzzle.

Legal reform in general is not a simple business; it is a matter of "fashioning working relationships between judges, prosecutors, police, advocates, notaries, bureaucratic personnel, law faculties, political leadership, and more, all under the influence of ideological principles and myths constantly reinforced by near daily repetition and experience" (Lev n.d., p. 28). In brief, the short- and long-term interests of various actors get in the way, making a reform process complex, time- and resource-consuming and, most of all, highly political.

The complexity of this universally acknowledged problem of legal reform is multiplied by at least two other factors in the case of Malaysia's Syariah judicial reform. First, what is at stake is not simply a matter of law and courts, but one of religion. In Malaysia, Islam is the official religion of the Federation. Despite the country's otherwise highly centralized politico-administrative system, Islamic matters — including the administration of Syariah courts and laws — were nonetheless placed under the control of the Sultan, assisted by State[3] religious agencies, the Majilis Agama Islam (Council of Islamic Religion or Religious Council) and the Department of Religions Affairs (or Religious Department).[4] These religious authorities at the State level are highly resistant to federal interference, jealously guarding their administrative turf. This federal-state tension over religious authority has a high potential to hold back the reform process.

Secondly, Malaysia's multi-ethnic/religious circumstances add a further complication to the Syariah reform. Questions abound: does the jurisdictional expansion of the Syariah court ever affect non-Muslims and, if so, in what way? Do non-Muslims care about Syariah issues at all? A recent "Islamic state" controversy, provoked by the electoral success of the opposition Islamic party, PAS (Parti Islam Se-Malaysia) following the dismissal of Anwar Ibrahim as Deputy Prime Minister in 1998, seems to suggest that they do (Lim 2001). If, as therefore seems likely, they do care, can they influence, by supporting these interests or by other means, an institutional adjustment of Muslim affairs? These questions raise the issue of nation-building, one of the biggest challenges to the post-colonial national leadership. Ultimately, these issues also have links to the problem of political legitimacy for ruling élites.

Seen against the backdrop of such difficulties foreseen for the reform process, the degree of institutionalization of the Syariah legal apparatus appears comparatively high, from both a cross-national and cross-sectional perspective. Interestingly, apparent "Islamization" of the judicial apparatus has come with "modernization" of the Syariah mechanism, reminiscent of the process seen under the British colonial regime (Yegar 1979). At that time, a selective approach was taken and any move to introduce a "Draconian" type of Islamic law was carefully rejected as a result.

Conventional wisdom suggests that institutionalization of the state religious apparatus in Malaysia is a result of societal pressures, often represented by the opposition Islamic party, PAS. Societal pressures, often cited as an explanation of policy change, are not the sole determinants, however. Societal pressures alone are not sufficient for explaining the level and type of institutionalization of the state religious apparatus. Horowitz's study on Islamic law reform (1994) looks beyond these social influences to find complementary causes. He attempts to combine "a much broader current of approbation for Islamisation" with a more actor-oriented intentionalist approach, emphasizing the interplay of the agents of state authority with the legal profession (Horowitz 1994, especially pp. 250–54).

In recognition of the value of Horowitz's actor-oriented approach, this chapter aims to shed light on the role played by the political incentives impinging on state actors. It advances a claim that the incentive structures of the Muslim ruling élite within the UMNO to manage a system of patronage-based legitimization have had a decisive effect on the way in which — and the degree to which — the religio-legal mechanism has been institutionalized. The UMNO's incentive structure is broken into three components: (1) the level of threats from "extremist" and/or "deviant" Islamic agencies; (2) the salience of non-Muslim (especially Chinese) interests and the level of "organized" pressures posed by them; and (3) the pressures of corporate business interests. These elements combine to capture the substantial range of the political stakes facing the ruling party in the area under discussion. The chapter's emphasis on the role played by the incentive mechanisms of the ruling élites is an attempt to fill a gap that is evident in Horowitz's study on the legal reform: the political dimensions of the reform process.[5]

The chapter proceeds as follows. The first section introduces an overview of institutional changes at the constitutional, legislative, and administrative levels. The following section demonstrates the role played by state–society and intra–state co-ordination in the process of Syariah reform. The limitation of this explanation is noted by offering an alternative argument, emphasizing the political incentives at work within the ruling UMNO party. Next, an analysis of two cases demonstrates how the UMNO's incentive structure operated to bring about the particular outcome observed. The chapter concludes with an analysis of the political effects of the institutionalization of the religio-legal apparatus.

The Jurisdictional Expansion of the Syariah Legal Apparatus

A most important dimension of the Syariah reform launched by the UMNO government was the jurisdictional expansion and increased autonomy of the Syariah courts and Islamic laws *vis-à-vis* their civil counterparts within the entire judicial/legal structure. This does not mean to suggest, however, that the civil legal apparatus has been replaced by the one based on the Syariah. Nor does it intend to hint that the country's judicial system has grown more "Islamic" in essence. In theory and in practice, Malaysia's judicial system, inherited from the British colonial regime, remains very much civil dominant. The authority of the civil courts has hardly been threatened by the rise of a more authoritative Syariah court mechanism. The tradition of English common-law practices still remains intact. What counts, however, is that the Syariah reform has had the effect of upgrading the status of the Syariah courts and officials through the use of constitutional, legislative, and administrative instruments. Physical conditions, the qualification of officials and the bureaucratic machinery overseeing the Syariah legal service were improved dramatically. Such institutional restructuring in the Syariah area had a profound effect overall, promoting the empowerment of the state administrative apparatus governing Islamic legal affairs.

In view of the universally acknowledged difficulty entailed in legal reform, the move towards a relatively high level of institutionalization of the Syariah judicial apparatus is striking. Prolific co-ordination problems, stemming from the transfer of authority from one place to another, were resolved quite effectively. The federal government, under the leadership of JAKIM (Jabatan Kemajuan Islam Malaysia, or Islamic Development Department), the central religious authority, managed to minimize a "separatist" tendency apparent in individual State religious authorities. This prevented them from building a completely separate religious-legal regime based on their own localized interpretation in each State. The containment of this tendency in turn facilitated the establishment of a relatively coherent and

authoritative religious-legal apparatus nationwide, despite some
unresolved procedural problems.

The Post-colonial Judicial System: "Inferior" Status of the Syariah Courts

A brief overview of the overall judicial system surrounding the
Syariah courts provides a background for appreciating the effect of
the institutional reform under discussion. At independence,
Malaysia inherited a highly institutionalized judicial system from
the British colonial regime. Under the system strongly influenced
by British rules and traditions, the civil courts enjoyed a wide range
of jurisdiction. On the other hand, the powers of the Syariah
courts — running in parallel with the civil courts — were restricted,
defined as separate from, and made "inferior" to, those of the civil
courts in the wake of colonial rule. Islamic law was strictly applied
to Muslims in matters relating to family and inheritance and
in some aspects of Islamic offences. In the field of criminal law,
in particular, the jurisdiction of the Syariah courts was very
limited. With Islamic affairs placed under the influence of the
sultans in their respective states, the Syariah courts were excluded
from the federal system dominated by the civil courts. Moreover,
this system of Syariah courts comprised only two levels: the
Court of the Chief Kadis (Kadi Besar) and the subordinate Court
of the Kadis (Wu 1999, pp. 63–64). The leading figure of the
Syariah reform, the late Professor Ahmad Ibrahim, characterizes the
common perception among Syariah personnel about their inferior
position in this way:

> In contrast [to the civil courts] the Syariah courts were for a
> long time neglected and forgotten. There was no independent
> judicial and legal service for them and the judges and officers
> belonged to the general administrative service and were subject
> to the control of the Religious Councils and the religious
> departments. The judges of the Syariah High Courts did not
> have the independent status, remuneration and terms of service
> of the civil judges. The facilities provided for the Syariah courts
> were far below those provided for the civil courts (Ahmad 2000,
> p. 194).

Such jurisdictional disparity between the civil and Syariah courts, in favour of the former, continued to fuel a sense of discontent, envy, and inferiority among Syariah officials and experts. It is against this backdrop that the UMNO government has undertaken the Syariah reform since the 1980s.

Overview of the Institutionalization of the Syariah Judicial Apparatus

The government implemented historic and influential statutory initiatives to enhance the overall authority of the Syariah courts and officials. In the constitutional sphere, the Federal Constitution was amended in 1988 to give more jurisdictional leverage to the Syariah courts. Article 121 (1A) was added to ensure that decisions made within the jurisdiction of the Syariah courts could not be reversed by the civil courts.[6] Although the jurisdiction of the Syariah courts still remains restricted to matters concerning family, inheritance, and religious-related offences and regulations, this constitutional amendment has had an immense effect in upholding the legitimacy of the Syariah courts and officials, and protecting their administrative turf.

Legislation pertaining to the administration of the Syariah laws and courts was also passed in each State under the auspices of the federal religious authorities. Unlike the former administration of Muslim Law enactments, which concentrated power in the Majlis Agama Islam, the new laws made a clear distinction among three principal authorities, namely, the Majlis Agama Islam, the *Mufti*,[7] and the Syariah courts (Ahmad 2000, p. 140). A most important effect was the separation of the Syariah judicial apparatus from the State Religious Departments and Religious Councils. This division guaranteed greater independence to the former — in a physical, administrative, and financial sense — as well as the authority to execute its functions in the Syariah courts. Furthermore, the Syariah courts were reorganized into a three-tier hierarchy: the Syariah Subordinate Court, the Syariah High Court, and the Syariah Court of Appeal (Ahmad 2000, p. 140; and Wu 1999, p. 164).

For the purpose of introducing these statutory adjustments, the federal religious authorities exercised a high level of leadership in inducing the otherwise fragmented religious legal apparatus to comply

with the federal line. Together, the newly formed Islamic legislatures
were intended to upgrade and standardize the operation of the Syariah
judiciary system nationwide.

In the administrative sphere, a most significant development was
the establishment in 1998 of the Department of Syariah Judiciary
(Jabatan Kahakiman Syariah Malaysia or JKSM) under the Prime
Minister's Office. This was an alternative administrative instrument
which the federal authorities were *testing* — given the latter's
jurisdictional constraint on the Syariah courts in constitutional terms
— in an effort to "nationalize" the Syariah judicial apparatus. On
agreeing to join this federal system, Syariah judges and officials
previously employed by an individual State government were to be
placed under the Syariah official common-use scheme (*Skim Guna
Sama Perkhidmatan Pegawai Syariah*) (*Berita Minggu*, 28 May 2000; *Utusan
Malaysia*, 23 December 1998). Under this system, Syariah judges could
be transferred between the participating States, allowing them better
chances of promotion. This career-focused incentive did, in fact, appeal
to many Syariah officials. Despite the State religious authorities'
continuing resistance to any steps which hinted at federal intervention,
Syariah judges in all the States, including even Kelantan which was
ruled by the opposition PAS, agreed to join this federal scheme initially.
Although, for a variety of reasons, some States have yet to join the
scheme, this pseudo-federal mechanism is expected to help close intra-
State gaps in the procedures and execution of the Syariah judicial
machinery.[8]

State–Society and Intra-State Co-ordination Mechanisms

The relative success of the institutionalization of the Syariah
judicial apparatus, in part, stemmed from a remarkable co-ordination
between governmental and private actors — on both the Syariah
and civil sides. The pivotal force in this pact was the strong
leadership of the late Professor Ahmad Ibrahim, a famous figure
in Malaysian judiciary and legal circles. He was the most vocal
proponent of the establishment of a comprehensive judicial system
based on Syariah principles. The pre-colonial indigenous system of
laws, in his view based on the Syariah, should be the law of the
land because the present Malaysian legal structure was inherited

from the British colonial regime involuntarily (Ahmad 2000, pp. 131–33).

Against the backdrop of the rising tide of Islamic consciousness, public objection was hardly heard. On the contrary, strong support for Professor Ahmad's stand was expressed openly — especially by a group of Syariah-educated academics and officials. It is, in fact, unsurprising that the group of Syariah-educated scholars and officials was extremely positive about — and highly mobilized by — Professor Ahmad's proposal to expand the Syariah judicial system and laws. To understand the judiciary's aspiration for "Islamization", one has to take note of the subordinate status unwillingly assumed by the Syariah courts and officials in the post-colonial era. The Syariah experts had been ranked as second-class in the civil-dominant judicial system, and were looked down upon by their civil counterparts. Public confidence in the Syariah system was very low. In addition, these Syariah instrumentalities came to be overtly criticized by increasingly vocal — and widely publicized — women's groups, to the extent that they were depicted almost as the prime source of the problems faced by the Muslim community. (For instance, see *Far Eastern Economic Review*, 18 December 1997). The Syariah reform was meant to remedy this long established damage and indignity, by elevating the system of Syariah not only physically but also administratively and constitutionally. Furthermore, such unprecedented attention to the Syariah branch of court and law — hinting at "Islamization" of the judicial apparatus — meant that more official resources would be allocated to the teaching of classical religious studies at the tertiary level. For Islamic scholars and teachers, the Syariah reform project thus offered an opportunity not only to extend their career prospects but also to apply in practice their learning and their interpretation of the classic texts of Islam.[9]

What is striking about the Syariah reform was that support came not only from the Syariah experts but also from the officials and experts on the civil side. This phenomenon is especially intriguing, if one considers the fact that the jurisdictional expansion of the Syariah side meant the transfer of some authority away from its civil counterpart. The better co-ordination between the Syariah and civil courts is primarily explained by two factors: first, the large majority of the Bench is comprised of Muslim judges. Being Muslim, the judges themselves were not immune to the growing Islamic consciousness in the Muslim community. For them, assisting the upgrading of Syariah meant offering service and doing justice to the *ummah* (Muslim community) at large. As an example of this type of service, some higher court judges sit on the Syariah Appeal Court panels in some States, despite little material incentive to do so.[10]

Secondly, Professor Ahmad was a key driving force and a valuable asset for mobilizing a wide range of actors with particular vested interests to work for the common goal of establishing a better Islamic legal system. He wielded extraordinary authority, not only in Syariah but also in civil legal circles. It is widely acknowledged that there was none comparable to him in terms of expertise and experience both in civil and Syariah laws. He founded the Law Faculty, first at the Universiti Malaya (UM or University of Malaya), and later at the Universiti Islam Antarabangsa Malaysia (UIAM or International Islamic University) and taught and trained large numbers of high-profile judges, lawyers, and legal officers. To honour his contribution, UIAM's Law Faculty incorporated his name into the Faculty's title. Many of his students came to hold senior posts in the Bar, Bench, Attorney-General's Chambers, and government, and in other positions which influenced decision-making and the drafting of laws on both civil and Islamic matters. His students' high regard for his authority — and confidence in his substantial expertise — helped a wide spectrum of groups and individuals to reconcile their conflicting interests and views and to work for their common goal of establishing a better system of Syariah. Large numbers of experts — civil and Syariah judges, common law and Syariah law academicians, lawyers as well as both religious and legal officials — sat together in the committees chaired by Professor Ahmad in an effort to co-ordinate Syariah and common laws and to upgrade the standard of the Syariah service.

These actors, whose work strongly suggests the significance of societal input, no doubt played a very important role in pushing for the demanding task of Syariah reform. "Islamization" of the state is almost universally equated with the implementation of Syariah. The significance attached to Syariah among the Muslims in general, and religious élites in particular, was translated into a pressure for, and acceptance of, Islamization of the legal system. Nevertheless, such societal pressures do not adequately account for the particular type of legal administrative arrangements that emerged from the 1980s onwards, as outlined above. The task of drafting Islamic laws, for example, was not left entirely to Syariah and legal experts. The committees for Syariah and civil law co-ordination in charge of the practical drafting of the Islamic laws were placed under the JAKIM, a central Islamic agency directly under the Prime Minister's Office. The drafts submitted by the committees were almost always scrutinized closely and altered, if necessary, before being passed in the Parliament, where the ruling party's dominance was unquestioned. The best example in this respect concerned the handling of apostasy. The provisions pertaining to specific rehabilitative and regulatory measures on apostasy — although included in an original draft presented by the co-ordination committees — were excluded from a final model draft, which was scheduled to be presented to the State governments.[11]

What was crucial, it has to be noted, were the *political incentives* of state actors — specifically, ruling élites within the UMNO. Lavish government sponsorship — political, institutional, and financial — was lent to the advocates of Syariah reform, as long as they remained within the boundaries and rules set by the interests of the UMNO. It is known, for example, that Professor Ahmad Ibrahim was pressured by the UMNO leaders not to talk on behalf of, let alone lend expertise to, the opposition Islamic party, PAS. At the same time, former Deputy Prime Minister Anwar Ibrahim, known personally to Professor Ahmad, continually promised him full government backing. Most importantly, the leadership of UIAM's Law Faculty — an experimental arrangement in that institution, combining the two branches of law (civil and Syariah) under one roof — was given to Professor Ahmad in 1983, the year in which UIAM was established.

UIAM's role in the development of the Syariah system was extremely important. Two factors have to be emphasized. First, equipped with a large number of both national and international legal experts on a wide range of legal matters, both Syariah and civil, the Faculty offered a central forum and bank of expertise for the reform of the Syariah judiciary and laws, with a regular series of seminars and workshops. Secondly, the Faculty offered comprehensive legal training programmes, combining both Syariah and civil elements. These measures, among others, were implemented with the intention of training a new breed of Syariah officials, familiar with both

Islamic and common laws and procedures (Ahmad 1993; and Mahmod Saedon 1993).

These UIAM-trained Syariah experts were expected to be more sensitive to, and compatible with, Malaysia's local cultures and circumstances, unlike the traditional Syariah experts educated in — and hugely influenced by — the Middle-Eastern system, who customarily dominated the Malaysian Syariah courts.

The UMNO and Syariah Reform: Political Incentives of the Ruling Élite

The extensive governmental support for Syariah reform — and the particular nature of the institutionalization of the religious legal order — was primarily determined by the political incentives of the UMNO politicians — incentives to manage a system of patronage-based political legitimization. The political incentives at the top echelon of political leadership — converted into powerful pressures — helped to forge better co-ordination between the federal government on the one hand and the State religious authorities and societal actors on the other. The ruling party's incentive structure, broken into three components, combined to make Syariah reform politically attractive.

The first component of the party's strong incentives was aimed at dealing with a threat of "extremist" and "fanatical" Islam to the UMNO's political-economic interests. For the UMNO leaders, this "extremist" threat — in a most organized and powerful form — came from the oppositional Islamic party, PAS. The ensuing electoral implication made the level of the threat in this religious-legal sphere considerably high.[12]

PAS's involvement in the Syariah issues remained a source of serious concern to the UMNO leaders. Differing from the UMNO's more secular outlook, PAS had long aspired to establish an "Islamic state" based on Islamic law and principles in Malaysia. Its single-minded commitment to this goal meant that the Islamic party kept placing oppositional pressure, in terms of its interpretation of Islam, on the UMNO in the electoral sphere. Furthermore, from the UMNO's "liberal" perspective, the vision of an "Islamic state" espoused by PAS represented *nothing less than* a "threat" to the UMNO's plan to create a "modern" Muslim urban-middle class.

Within the context of rising Islamic consciousness among the UMNO's traditional support base (the Muslim-Malay community), the party was alarmed that PAS's commitment to the full and stringent implementation of Syariah law might divert Muslim support away from the ruling coalition, the Barisan Nasional (BN). The UMNO's defensiveness against PAS was all the more understandable when its preoccupation with economic development is taken into account, a factor which PAS claimed was a cause of "secularization" and moral decay. The UMNO's frequent use of "threat" rhetoric — rhetoric to embellish the "threat" of PAS in the "extremist" light — was intended to contain this electoral threat from PAS. Furthermore, the UMNO leaders even proclaimed that Malaysia was already an "Islamic state", an attempt largely seen as a measure to counter the unprecedented electoral "threat" from the Islamic opposition since the Anwar crisis in 1998. (See, for example, *Star*, 6 October, 2001; and *Utusan Malaysia*, 1 October 2001).

The UMNO's concern about the threat emanating from PAS's Islamic assertion was rooted in a problem of political legitimacy within the Muslim-Malay community. As Islam grew important as a factor defining legitimacy to rule the Muslim *umma* (community), the UMNO needed to be seen as doing good for the Islamic cause but without hampering the party's modernist credentials. Standardizing and upgrading the Syariah judicial system nationwide became an instrument to achieve this end. Importantly, the effort also served to pre-empt PAS in its attempt to fulfil its aspiration of building an "Islamic state" on its own terms. A *hudud* (Islamic criminal codes) Bill, proposed by the PAS-led Kelantan state government, and ensuing tension between the UMNO and PAS in the early 1990s, illuminate this point. (For further discussion, see Chapter 5 by M. B. Hooker.)

Despite the electoral threat posed by the "extremist" PAS, a strategy simply to emulate PAS was not a viable choice for the UMNO. The ruling party's political legitimacy no longer derived only from the mandate of its old party base — Muslim-Malays in the rural areas. The relevance of various issues changed dramatically, as the Muslim community experienced unprecedented social transformation, both horizontally and vertically. At the same time, the UMNO's relationship with non-Muslim communities went through some significant readjustments. To fully understand the choices taken by the UMNO leadership in the process of Syariah reform, two other factors have to be taken into account.

The second factor shaping the UMNO's incentive structure was the low level of non-Muslim (Chinese in particular) pressures in this religious-legal arena. It is generally assumed that the Chinese in Malaysia were not particularly concerned about Syariah-related issues, unless their interests were directly affected. The increasingly intense electoral competition between the UMNO and PAS, however, aroused anxiety and suspicion among the non-Muslims. Their fear was that the UMNO government would take more drastic Islamization measures to stem the tide of PAS's influence.

Balancing the weight of the "Islamic threat" on the one hand, and the pressures from the non-Muslim communities on the other, posed serious legitimacy questions for the UMNO leadership on three grounds. Firstly, the UMNO government set the goal of attaining a "developed country" status before the year 2020. This goal — symbolized in the national slogan "Vision 2020" — was to create "modern" national citizens, not only in material terms but also in social and cultural terms. To this end, establishing a cordial partnership between Muslims and non-Muslims was essential in minimizing the political and socio-economic costs and risks inherent in unstable ethnic relationships. It was especially so, since Malaysia was heavily dependent upon risk-averse foreign capital for its economic growth. The UMNO government could not afford to have the Chinese community in general, and Chinese capital in particular, lose confidence in its leadership.

Secondly, the recession in the later 1980s (and again the region-wide financial crisis in the late 1990s) exposed the fundamental weakness of *bumiputera* (sons of the soil, or Muslim-Malay) entrepreneurs, many of whom depended on the UMNO's patronage for their selection, performance, and survival. On the other hand, Chinese businessmen showed their entrepreneurial strength and viability by not only surviving the crises but also by bouncing back with little assistance from the government. In the context of an increasingly competitive international market, the UMNO leadership, especially Prime Minister Mahathir, found that vibrant Chinese capital, together with the energetic Chinese workforce, was a vital asset to the Malaysian economy. Under such circumstances, the UMNO leaders opted to entertain Chinese interests and demands (Gomez 1999, p. 189).

Finally, the UMNO politicians began building a personally based patronage, linked to prominent Chinese corporate figures, as intra-party competition for the party's top posts grew strong. Winning these high-reward posts became extraordinarily expensive as a result. This patronage relationship in turn made the UMNO politicians even more vulnerable to pressures from the Chinese community (Crouch 1992, pp. 32–25; and Gomez 1999, chp. 4). Given the UMNO leaders' increasing dependence on Chinese capital, and the Chinese workforce more generally, the absence of more co-ordinated and organized community-wide opposition from the Chinese constituency was crucial. This factor reduced the net political costs for the UMNO in pushing for "Islamization" of the legal system.

The third and final element constituting the UMNO's incentive structure centred on corporate business interests, a most important support-base for the ruling party. Since the Syariah jurisdiction was tightly restricted to areas concerning family, inheritance, and more general religious-related matters, the "Islamization" campaign in this legal sphere did not pose a serious threat to the interests of the corporate business sector. One important effect was a lack of reaction from the corporate business actors on this issue.

There was no reason for the corporate actors to be seriously bothered about whether the UMNO politicians wanted to make the judicial system slightly more Islamic for their own political ends, as long as Malaysia's liberal-capitalistic business practices were kept untouched. On the other hand, the "Islamization" of laws was quite welcomed when it was found to advance economic outputs. A few yet unprecedented legal changes took place in the business sector to promote economic transactions based on Islamic principles. The Islamic Banking Act was passed in 1983 as an effort to regulate the increasingly popular Islamic banking service (Zakariya 1988). A law pertaining to *Takaful* (Islamic insurance) was a similar mechanism introduced to oversee Islamic insurance activities (Mohammad Hashim Kamali 2000a, chp. 12). Moreover, the Syariah and Civil Law Co-ordination Committee under the federal government is proposing to introduce additional "Islamic" laws in this area — for instance, one dealing with the administration of property.[13]

Two important facts have to be noted here. First, these business-related Islamic laws were introduced without replacing paralleling laws on the civil side. Secondly, the administration of these laws remained under the jurisdiction of civil courts. These facts suggest that the "Islamization" of law in the business-related area was primarily intended to facilitate business activities, for both Muslims and non-Muslims, without altering the basic judicial framework. In other words, there was almost no real effect on the jurisdiction of the Syariah courts and officials in this area.

A greater threat to corporate business interests, in fact, was posed by the inauguration of a more conservative PAS regime. There was concern that PAS's "extremist" application of Syariah laws might scare off foreign investors and hamper domestic business activities. Such fear compelled the corporate business sector, both Muslims and non-Muslims, to keep favouring the more liberal legal regime under the UMNO. The minimal level of pressure from large-scale corporate business meant significant flexibility for the UMNO's decision-making, which in turn had a strong positive effect on the way in which the Syariah reform proceeded.

Two high-profile cases illustrate how the political dynamics outlined above shaped the outcomes of the Syariah reform. The first case is the Selangor Islamic administration laws enactment controversy in 1989; and the second is the Hudud Bill controversy in 1993. Our final section examines these cases.

Selangor Islamic Administration Laws Enactment Controversy (1989)

This first high-profile case is based on the enactment of the State Islamic administration laws passed in the State of Selangor in 1989. The controversy which arose related to two sections of the enactment. The first involved Section 67, which provided that a person could convert to Islam if he or she had attained the "age of maturity according to Islam." The second involved Section 70, which provided that under-aged children of non-Muslim parents who convert to Islam automatically become Muslims. The age of maturity under Islamic law is younger than eighteen years, as defined by civil laws.[14] Chinese-based political parties, therefore, expressed strong opposition to this provision. Their concerns centred on two issues. The first related to the question of whether the Islamic definition should be applied to non-Muslims. Such an Islamic definition was seen as impinging on the "freedom of religion", the rights that the non-Muslims were constantly afraid of losing, and wanted to defend, in Malaysia's Muslim-dominant context. The second issue of contention was that this provision was seen as facilitating the conversion of non-Muslims to Islam. This fear involved the question of inter-ethnic power balance. Non-Muslim leaders suspected that this provision was meant to reinforce the influence of Muslims, while further weakening the position of non-Muslims.

After the enactment was passed at the State Assembly, eight MCA (Malaysian Chinese Association) assemblymen expressed objections against the passage — despite voting for the Bill — and threatened to resign unless the provisions were amended (*Star*, 29 November 1989). The issue was consequently transferred to an extra-parliamentary arena, resulting in a divide between the two largest partners of the ruling coalition, the MCA and the UMNO (*Utusan Malaysia*, 30 November 1989). Although there was strong objection from the MCA, the issue was settled in favour of the UMNO, forcing the MCA leaders to withdraw their demands and to admit their "mistake" (*Utusan Malaysia*, 5 December 1989).

Despite the significance of Chinese interests then acknowledged by the UMNO leadership, the Chinese parties were not very successful in mobilizing communal-wide opposition against the ratification of the enactment. This was partly due to the low level of awareness among the non-Muslims about how much this particular law would affect their interests. By and large, non-Muslims tend to think that Syariah laws will have little effect on their personal lives. This general indifference among the non-Muslims — and the absence of organized pressure and of a forum to mobilize resistance in the extra-parliamentary sphere — weakened the position of the MCA and other non-Muslim-based parties in negotiating and striking a better deal with the UMNO.

From the UMNO's perspective, the price of being seen in the Muslim constituency as "not pushing enough for the Syariah cause" was much higher than a possible loss of support — probably a very limited one — from the Chinese community. An additional drawback was related to the keen efforts of the UMNO leadership under Dr Mahathir to put its house in order after the 1987 intra-party power struggle, which had left the party split into two blocks: the

Mahathir-led new UMNO (UMNO *Baru*) and the rival Razaleigh-
led Semangat 46 (Crouch 1992). With the next general election on
the horizon and the strengthened oppositional Muslim force centred
on PAS, the UMNO could not afford to lose Muslim support further
by showing any deficiency in handling a crucial Syariah issue.
Furthermore, this case suggested that constitutional codes could be
ignored when considered necessary by the UMNO, indicating the
UMNO's high stake in the Syariah area.

Hudud Bill Controversy (1993)

The second case, the *Hudud* (Islamic criminal codes) Bill controversy
occurred in the wake of the introduction of the *Hudud* Bill by
the PAS government in Kelantan in 1993 (*Asiaweek*, 5 June 1992,
pp. 27–31; Ismail 1995; Kamarul Zaman 2000; and Mohammad Hashim
2000b). The key problem was that the implementation of the law
required the amendment of the Constitution. Even if the UMNO
had agreed to introduce such an amendment, it would have needed
to persuade the non-Malay parties in the Barisan Nasional coalition
to support the amendment with the necessary two-thirds majority.

Unlike the case of the Selangor Islamic administration laws, the
constitutional rules were not only maintained but also emphasized to
defend the interests of non-Muslims. The UMNO leaders at the
federal level upheld the argument that the treatment of non-Muslims
under this "cruel" law was their utmost concern, despite the PAS's
decision to exclude non-Muslims. It is worth noting that the Kelantan
Muslims themselves were not particularly averse to the introduction
of the *hudud* laws. The proposal was, in fact, very popular.[15] Based on
this popularity, even the UMNO assemblymen in the State felt obliged
to support and pass the Bill.

The UMNO leaders' steadfast objection and their ultimate decision
to scrap the Bill are explained, again, by the ruling party's incentive
structure. As mentioned above, the UMNO leaders perceived Islamic
extremism, or whatever appeared "fanatical" and/or "extreme," as a
major threat to their capital accumulation and nation-building activities.
Such instances of "extremism" were not at all welcome because bias
against Islamic extremism was widespread among non-Muslims, both
within and outside the country. The UMNO leaders feared that such

antipathy might discourage investment from Chinese and foreign capital. To promote foreign direct investment, on which the Malaysian economy heavily relied, a politically conducive (namely, an "extremism-free") environment was a prerequisite. For the modernist leaders within the UMNO, the *hudud* laws symbolized no more than a fanatical element of Islam, which they did not want to see becoming too visible. Among the urban business and middle-class constituencies, the UMNO managed to mobilize such sentiments, contributing to tacit support for the UMNO's stand on the controversy. The source of trouble needed to be nipped in the bud, although this meant that the UMNO might sacrifice some votes in the rural Muslim constituencies.

The *hudud* controversy exemplified the UMNO's unease with, and intolerance of, "extremist" and "fanatic" varieties of Islam — domestically "represented" by the UMNO's arch rival, PAS. To tame these unfavourable elements, seen as the greatest threat to the party's interests, the UMNO leaders readily exploited whatever resources — be they state or societal — available to them. The costly efforts to upgrade and standardize the Syariah judicial machinery were one such device, contributing to a relatively strong institutionalization of the religio-legal apparatus. The weaker organized communal-wide opposition from the Chinese — evidenced in the Selangor Islamic laws controversy — and the very low level of pressure from corporate businesses were also factors of great consequence. These factors contributed further to the institutionalization of the Syariah legal mechanism dictated by the UMNO's liberal initiative.

State and Religious Élite: The Making of the Religio-legal Apparatus

The Syariah reform is still far from complete and various procedural problems remain unresolved. Moreover, problems of jurisdictional conflict between the Syariah and the civil court will continue to surface as long as the aspiration to introduce more Syariah laws in the legal system stays alive. Nonetheless, the reform process has brought about an extremely important consequence: expansion of the state apparatus overseeing Syariah judicial affairs.

The administrative apparatus was institutionalized to a relatively high degree and in a way that made it more professional and efficient. At the same time, this made the Syariah system less vulnerable to private interests — both within the state and the societal spheres — and to corrupt practices. Despite a potential vulnerability to intervention from the ruling politicians, whether UMNO or PAS, the jurisdictional expansion of the Syariah legal apparatus has provided Syariah officials with much sought-after authority and jurisdictional independence — from interference by the civil court and the Religious Council, as well as by the Department of Religious Affairs.

Given the significance attached to the Syariah-based religious legal order among the more self-consciously Islamic Muslims in general and the religious élites in particular, the visible empowerment of the Syariah establishment, beyond doubt, had the effect of conferring extra Islamic credentials on the UMNO and the government it dominates. More importantly, raising the status of the Islamic judiciary helped to incorporate a top echelon of the religious-educated *ulama* (Islamic scholars) into the public service. This incorporation process has had some important effects on the political front. First, a relatively few, highly-qualified, Islamic élites came to be heavily dependent upon the state for their authority as well as for material reward. Secondly, with their authority as well as their socio-economic standing upgraded, these religious-legal officials were given what they saw as their rightful place in the process of national development. Third and finally, religious-legal authority was firmly placed under the state administrative machinery.

The still-incomplete Syariah reform has been put on hold since the onset of the Anwar crisis in 1998, which coincided with the death of Professor Ahmad Ibrahim, a crucial motivator for Syariah reform. His leaving the scene supports the proposition that the efficient and effective institutionalization of the state apparatus requires a good deal of resource inputs from societal actors. Furthermore, a greater degree of participation by societal actors offered a "check-and-balance" mechanism to the institutionalization process, which was otherwise highly vulnerable to the influence of the ruling politicians.

Conclusion

The emphasis on the role played by the ruling élites' incentive structures does not mean to suggest that societal actors themselves did not have any significant effect in determining the outcome of the Syariah reform. Societal pressures did offer a basic prerequisite for such reform but it is nonetheless important to note that these pressures for the Islamic cause were not a unitary force aimed at achieving a common end, based on a common ground. In the case of Syariah reform, Syariah experts were interested not only in upgrading their socio-economic status but also in maximizing their jurisdictional boundaries. They also saw this reform project as an unprecedented opportunity for them to apply in practice their specialized knowledge of classical religious texts and to develop further the institutions of religious learning and training for the generations that follow.

Women's groups, on the other hand, wanted to see Syariah judges become better-qualified and, above all, show a fair and more sensitive approach to women's needs and predicaments. These groups were not at all interested in seeing the Syariah courts being given more power and influence. It was the political incentives of the ruling party, the UMNO, which mediated various societal inputs to bring about a final result. The three elements underlying the UMNO's incentive structure — that is, an "extremist" threat (particularly from PAS), the salience of organized Chinese pressures, and the presence of corporate business interests — combined to maintain a system of patronage-based political legitimization for the ruling party. This view concurs with a position advanced by Lev in his study on law and the state in Indonesia: "creating an effective legal system takes a great deal of time, as a glance at legal history anywhere will demonstrate, and how it evolves is largely determined by *local political authority* with an eye on economic, and social imperatives" (Lev, n.d., p. 28). In short, the particular type and the comparatively high level of the institutionalization of the state religio-legal apparatus were primarily explained by a set of incentive structures established by the Muslim ruling élite, represented by the UMNO. By establishing a case that focuses specifically on the political dimensions, this chapter has sought to build up on the actor-oriented, intentionalist approach proposed by Horowitz (1994).

The powerful political element implicated in the institutional change — against the backdrop of widespread patronage practices in Malaysian politics — had an important political consequence. The institutional expansion has brought with it opportunities for political patronage — in the form of offices, funds, perks, and various other benefits that could be distributed to existing as well as potential UMNO supporters. Such patronage politics has, in turn, helped to enhance the power base of the ruling party by making an important segment of the religious-legal authorities dependent on the state, in terms of their career and authority aspirations. The institutionalization of religious authority alone may not be sufficient to explain entirely the most intriguing aspect of political Islam in Malaysia — specifically, the UMNO-PAS competition — for which Kessler has offered the most convincing explanation to date (1978; 1979). Nonetheless, the effect of splitting the religious leadership to have it later reconstituted under the opposition Islamic party will have a long-term and crucial effect on the outcome of the political contest between the two self-confidently "Islamic" parties in Malaysia in years to come.

Notes

1. The use of the term "actor" in this context derives from the work of Horowitz (1994), which is discussed on p. 3 ff.
2. Max Weber's work (Gerth and Mills 1948) includes a discussion of his theory of the social order in different societies and the movement from the ritualistic to the rational in this area.
3. In this chapter, State (with a capital letter) is used to refer to a state government unit in the federal system (for example, Kelantan), while state (without a capital letter) indicates an administrative authority structure in a conceptual sense.
4. The Council and the Department share religious authority at the State level, with separate jurisdictions supervised by the one or the other. The balance of influence between these two agencies varies from one State to another. For the case of Johor, for instance, see Abdullah Alwi (2000); for Kelantan, Roff (1974).
5. Horowitz seems to pay more analytical attention to the outcomes of the legal reform — in terms of the contents of law — rather than the political dimensions of the reform process.
6. In a number of cases in the past, there was a conflict between the decisions of the Syariah courts and the civil courts, and the civil rule usually prevailed. After the constitutional amendment, this trend has been reversed. For a general background of the amendment, see, for instance, Ahmad (1989).

7. The *Mufti* is the supreme authority in respect of all matters concerning Syariah law in the respective States. He is authorized to issue, modify, or revoke a *fatwa* (Islamic ruling) on any unsettled or controversial question of Syariah law (see, for instance, Ahmad and Ahilemlah 1995, pp. 52–53). In recent years, whether a *fatwa* should be subjected to the normal legislative processes has become a focus of controversy (for instance, *New Straits Times*, 22 July 1997). For this issue and related debates, see Mohammad Hashim (2000a, chp. 13).

8. Interviews with Syariah judges, Public Service Department (JPA) officials, and legal experts at the International Islamic University.

9. The author acknowledges an observation of Virginia Hooker on this point.

10. Interview with a high-ranking civil judge.

11. The sensitivity of the apostasy regulation was evident in recent controversies prompted by the apostasy Bill proposed by the Perlis State government (*New Straits Times*, 6 October 2000; *Star*, 30 September 2000; and *Utusan Malaysia*, 8 April 2000).

12. It has to be noted that the threat of "extremist" Islam to the UMNO leadership does not always come from outside the government; it comes from *within* the government, too. The tension between Islamic religious government officials and the UMNO's modernist leadership became more evident in the late 1990s over various contentious issues. The UMNO leaders had perceived the former as a "threat" to their more liberal regime and attempted to crack down upon them. The confrontation between these two cliques culminated in the beauty contest controversy in 1997.

13. Interview with a legal official.

14. Under Syariah law, the age of maturity for boys is fifteen, while girls are considered to have come of age when they have their first menstrual period.

15. The author appreciates an observation of Harold Crouch on this point.

References

"A Woman's Place". *Far Eastern Economic Review*, 18 December 1997, pp. 44–46.

Abdullah Alwi Hassan. "Sejarah Perkembangan Jabatan Dan Majlis Agama Islam Johor" [History of Development of the Department and Council of Islamic Religion, Johor]. Paper presented at the Seminar Sejarah Dan Budaya Johor Tahun 2000 [Seminar on Johor History and Culture, Year 2000], Johor Bahru, 3–6 May 2000.

Ahmad Ibrahim. "The Amendment to Article 121 of the Federal Constitution: Its Effect on Administration of Islamic Law". *Malayan Law Journal* 2 (1989): xvii–xxii.

————. "Law Studies in the International Islamic University". *Malaysian Law News*, January 1993, pp. 27–29.

Ahmad Mohamed Ibrahim. *The Administration of Islamic Law in Malaysia*. Kuala Lumpur: Institute of Islamic Understanding (IKIM), 2000.

Ahmad Ibrahim and Ahilemlah Joned. *The Malaysian Legal System*, edited by Ahmad Ibrahim. Second edition. Kuala Lumpur: Dewan Bahasa dan Pustaka, Kementrian Pendidikan Malaysia, 1995.

Crouch, Harold. "Authoritarian Trends, the UMNO Split and the Limits to State Power". In *Fragmented Vision: Culture and Politics in Contemporary Malaysia*, edited by Joel S. Kahn and Francis Loh Kok Wah, pp. 21–43. Sydney: Asian Studies Association of Australia in association with Allen & Unwin, 1992.

Gerth, H. H., and C. Wright Mills, ed. and trans. *From Max Weber: Essays in Sociology*. London: Routlege and Kegan Paul, 1948.

Gomez, Edmund Terence. *Chinese Business in Malaysia: Accumulation, Ascendance, Accommodation*. London: Curzon, 1999.

Horowitz, Donald L. "The Qur'an and the Common Law: Islamic Law Reform and the Theory of Legal Change". *American Journal of Comparative Law* 42 (1994), Part I: 233–93; Part II: 543–80.

"Islam and the Law". *Asiaweek*, 5 June 1992, pp. 27–31.

Kamarul Zaman Haji Yusoff. *Debat Hudud dalam Politik Malaysia* [Hudud Debates in Malaysian Politics]. Kuala Lumpur: IKDAS Sdn Bhd, 2000.

Kessler, Clive S. *Islam and Politics in a Malay State: Kelantan 1838–1969*. Ithaca: Cornell University Press, 1978.

Kessler, Clive S. "Islam, Society and Political Behaviour: Some Comparative Implications of the Malay Case". *British Journal of Sociology* 23 (1979): 33–50.

Lev, Daniel. "Law and State in Indonesia". Unpublished paper, n.d.

Lim Kit Siang. *BA & Islamic State*. Selangor: Democratic Action Party, 2001.

Mahmod Saedon Awang Othman. "Pengajian Syariah dan Undang-undang di Universiti Islam Antarabangsa Petaling Jaya [Syariah and Law Studies at International Islamic University, Petaling Jaya]". Paper presented at the Seminar Pengajian Syariah dan Undang-undang di Institusi-institusi Pengajian Tinggi di Malaysia Peringkat Kebangsaan [Seminar on Syariah and Law Studies at Institutions of Higher Learning at the National Level in Malaysia], Bangi, 25–26 August 1993.

Mohammad Hashim Kamali. *Islamic Law in Malaysia: Issues and Developments*. Kuala Lumpur: Ilmiah Publishers, 2000a.

————— . *Punishment in Islamic Law: An Enquiry into the Hudud Bill of Kelantan.* Selangor: Ilmiah Publisher, 2000b.

Roff, William R. "The Origin and Early Years of the Majlis Ugama." In *Kelantan: Religion, Society and Politics in Malay State,* edited by William R. Roff, pp. 101–52. Kuala Lumpur: Oxford University Press, 1974.

Rose Ismail, ed. *Hudud in Malaysia: The Issues at Stake.* Kuala Lumpur: SIS Forum (Malaysia) Berhad, 1995.

Wu Min Aun. *The Malaysian Legal System,* second edition. Selangor: Longman, 1999.

Yegar, Moshe. *Islam and Islamic Institutions in British Malaya: Politics and Implementation.* Jerusalem: The Magnes Press, Hebrew University, 1979.

Zakariya Man. "Islamic Banking: The Malaysian Experience". In *Islam and the Economic Development of Southeast Asia: Islamic Banking in Southeast Asia,* edited by Mohamed Ariff, pp. 67–102. Singapore: Institute of South East Asian Studies, 1988.

Newspapers and Periodicals

Asiaweek
Berita Harian/Berita Minggu
Far Eastern Economic Review
New Straits Times
Star
Utusan Malaysia

5

SUBMISSION TO ALLAH?

The Kelantan Syariah Criminal Code (II), 1993

M. B. HOOKER

argues that K Syariah law, taking in early Arabian rules and punishments out of context 'minimalist'

Introduction

Almost thirty years ago Clive Kessler, in commenting on Islam in Kelantan, said:

> It is, for example, a standard contention of quasisociological Muslim apologetics that alcohol and gambling are prohibited, not as worldly pleasures that must be renounced for salvation, but on pragmatic grounds: to minimise dissension and foster social harmony. But while the presumed consequence of observing these injunctions may be social, their justification is not. These prohibitions are enjoined by Allah because they are deemed socially beneficial, yet they are observed (and their observation is rewarded) because they are enjoined by Allah. A duty imposed upon the individual by his divine origins, conformity to such obligations is owed not within society to others, but to an extramundane creator. The fundamental relationship of the good society as envisaged by Islam is that of the individual inspired to good by his submission to Allah, to whom, more than

80

to any other individuals, he is bound by meticulously defined rights and duties.[1]

This passage has led me to the Kelantan Syariah Criminal Code (II) of 1993 because it is a perfect focus for the issues raised by Kessler. In a very real sense, the Code is an attempt to translate an individual's obligations to God into a social duty enforced by the state and thus make manifest Revelation in the temporal world of the twentieth century. The Code is the formal structure, chosen by the Kelantan government, through which the dictates of Revealed obligation can be implemented — made "real" in Muslim society. Here is the first real difficulty; there is no necessary connection, causal or otherwise, between Revelation and a Code. Indeed, they are quite distinct and separate conceptions of obligation. This is true in theory but, as we all know, the past 200 years have seen selections from the Syariah (Muslim law) restated in European forms. The state, with its authority, selects whatever passages from Syariah it deems appropriate, simplifies, and reformulates them into the language and legal concepts felt to be appropriate to the time and place.

The result is that, with few exceptions (in Saudi Arabia and perhaps some other countries), there is not now a "pure" Syariah. Instead, we have "laws for Muslims", the authority for which rests on state fiat, not in Revelation. The former is decisive and this has one very important implication: it is that any criticism of this form of "Islam" is also a criticism of the state. Those elements of the Syariah which are selected (family law, trusts) express state policy towards a form of Islam. Of course, the Syariah is diminished by this but that is the price demanded by the state in return for a certainty of administration.

The Constitution of Malaysia illustrates the comment just made. In the Ninth Schedule (List II, the State List), it sets out those subjects of Islamic law over which the States in the Federation have jurisdiction.[2] The jurisdiction is limited and is defined by the Constitution, and those matters not specified are excluded. Thus, "[the religious courts] shall have jurisdiction ... in respect only of any of the matters included in this paragraph". The result has been that each of the States has Islamic (or Muslim) law enactments of varying degrees of complexity but all include a) provision for a Majlis Islam, b) a Syariah court system, c) detailed provisions on family law, and d) a description of and penalties for offences against religion. All these subjects are strictly defined in the Ninth Schedule. In addition, Article 121 (1A) reserves jurisdiction in the defined Islamic matters for the Syariah court (see also below).[3]

The Kelantan Code, the subject of this chapter, attempts to expand considerably the jurisdiction of the Syariah courts to include a much wider range of punishments than is permitted in the Ninth Schedule. These include death and mutilation as well as imprisonment and fines; in short, it is intended to replace the existing criminal law (for Muslims) by extending the jurisdiction of the Syariah courts and redefining the criminal law. This, of course, requires an amendment to the Constitution, which has not been made. The Code is inoperative but it remains in the public domain and is a potent focus in the debate about the nature and place of Syariah in contemporary Malaysia.

Understandably, the politics of the Code have been much debated[4] but in this chapter, I take the Code itself as a text which has as its purpose the creation "of a good society as envisaged by Islam ... [in which] the individual is inspired to good by his submission to Allah ... to whom he is bound by meticulously defined rights and duties".[5] Can a Code actually do this by abstracting penalties devised in seventh-century Arabia? To answer the question, we must take the context, content, form and rationale of the Code.

Contexts

There are two contexts, the Federal Constitution and the State legislation, both briefly mentioned above. Between them, they have the function of determining respective Federal and State Islamic jurisdictions. Punishment for criminal offences remains in the Federal prerogative, except to the extent allowed in the Constitution. Other matters are distributed between the two.

The Malaysian Constitution and Islam

Article 3 of the Constitution declares Islam to be the religion of the Federation, and it also says that all religions may be practised in peace and harmony (Art. 3 (1)). All persons may freely practise their religion, and discrimination on the basis of religion is forbidden (Arts. 11–12). So far as Islam itself is concerned, Article 74 directs attention to the Ninth Schedule — the matters reserved for the States — and this gives the States in the Federation power to make laws on matters of Islam. The main subjects are family law and trusts and a list of offences against religion. The last does not include general criminal law, nor was such a conclusion envisaged in the Kelantan enactment. Finally, Article 121 (1A) provides that the secular courts have no jurisdiction over matters within the competence of the religious courts.

Article 121 (1A) has given rise to considerable litigation but that litigation is conducted in the secular courts *not* the religious courts. It is the former which decide the jurisdiction. The State religious courts do not have this capacity because they are inferior courts established only by State legislation, and this is dependent on the schedules in the Constitution. There are two decisions from the Malaysian Supreme (now Federal) Court which emphasize this point. Both[6] cases are on difficult and controversial points of law (respectively, marriage and apostasy) and for both, Article 121 (1A) is read as confirming religious court jurisdiction. The reason in both cases is that the interpretation of Article 121 (1A) requires it. The reading of the Article has nothing to do with Syariah but relies wholly on the constitutional laws of Malaysia. While the actual result in each case has been greeted with satisfaction by the Islamic side and dismay by feminist and human rights groups, none of these various interests seems to realize that we are not talking about the victory or defeat of an ideology. The real demonstration is a) that the Constitution, not Syariah, defines law, and b) the principles on which constitutional law is stated are secular, English (derived) and Malaysian, not Syariah.

State Legislation on Islam

This is the second context for the Kelantan Code. In common with all the States of Malaysia, Kelantan has an extensive volume of legislation on Islam. These pieces of legislation are modelled on the colonial enactments[7] but have been much elaborated from the 1980s. The problem with the colonial legacy has been the lack of clarity with respect to jurisdiction, and it is this which Article 121 (1A) attempts to solve.[8] The post–1980s elaborations do seem now to represent a change of emphasis in the Syariah legislation. While the earlier models[9] were concerned with Majlis Islam, religious courts, family law, and basic offences against religion, the post–1980s legislation has tended to be more expansive in the direction of the politics of law. There are two examples.

First, all the Malaysian States have legislation forbidding the propagation of non-Muslim doctrine among Muslims. While this is a continuation of past practice, recent elaborations forbid the use of Arabic phrases or words relating to Islam in general published materials. The rule is related to the prohibition on the teaching of Islam without a licence from the appropriate authority (the State Majlis) but its increased generalness has to do with political Islam in the 1980s. It is aimed at the Shi'a or perceived Shi'a, the Ahmadiya, and home-grown movements such as Al-Arqam and Nasrul Haq. Each of these classes, groups and movements is seen as a threat to State-sanctioned Islam. In fact, the State Departments of Religion keep lists of deviant theologies and groups. Al-Arqam is a particularly interesting example, because it was independent of governments, invented a small-scale but successful economy, and based itself on good theology. It was attacked and suppressed on the grounds of divisiveness in the Malay-Muslim community[10] — nothing at all to do with dogma. All legislation attempts to impose a unity of *umma*, by way of defining an Islam, which is the State definition. Dogma is a screen and is used only to justify a political position.

Secondly, a number, but not all, of the Malaysian States have legislation or bills relating to the renunciation of Islam. Kelantan, in fact, has incorporated provisions in the revised Council of Religion and Malay Custom Enactments of 1994. Other States also provide that the apostate, or person contemplating apostasy, be detained for re-education and rehabilitation. The provisions in Melaka, Kelantan, and Terengganu are remarkably similar, although the periods for detention vary: in the Kelantan case, it is up to three years, with monthly progress reports. Where the individual does not repent, then he or she is declared not to be a Muslim and his or her marriage is dissolved, his or her liabilities are determined according to Syariah, and then finally he or she is released. The constitutionality of these and similar provisions has not as yet been tested in any court but the detention provisions do seem to suggest that the detention does in fact count against the detainee as a new crime and is thus outside the competence of the State legislatures. In addition, Article 11, providing for freedom of religion, would also be an issue. That this amounts to more than mere speculation is demonstrated in the Perak Draft Bill (Crimes [Syariah]) of 2000, which proposes that a Muslim who declares himself or herself to be a non-Muslim is guilty of a criminal offence.

The context for the Kelantan Code is thus located in constitutional law and in States' legislation. Both are politicized to a degree not known until recently — the last decade or so. The Code is an example of the constitutional tensions. It attempts to force a new, wider context for Malaysian constitutional law, and must be read with this in mind.

Content

The content of the Code carries on the politicized theme: the content is wholly about punishment for ("Islamic") offences. The rationale is discussed below but should be kept in mind here in respect of the actual provisions.

The Code is in six parts followed by five schedules. Part I is *Ḥudúd*, defined as a) theft, b) robbery, c) unlawful sex, d) false or unprovable accusations of unlawful sex, e) consuming alcohol, and f) apostasy. The penalties include flogging, amputation, stoning, death, and imprisonment. Part II is *Ḳiṣāṣ*, which encompasses various forms of killing and wounding. Penalties are given in the form of *diya* (compensation), the basic measure of which is 4,450 grams of gold, "or such sums as may be fixed by HRH the Sultan". Part III sets out a simplified list of rules for evidence and is almost wholly concerned with the rules for proving sexual misconduct. Part IV describes punishments with reference to whipping and amputation. Parts V and VI are general provisions, including the establishment of Special Syariah Courts, and an Appeal Court. The five schedules provide a glossary and transliteration of Arabic terms,[11] tables of compensation for injury, and the regulations for whipping (such as the diameter and length of cane).

This short summary represents the contents of the Code, which is neither long nor complex. It is in fact a minimalist document.

The whole of the *fiqh* on crimes is condensed into fifty short sections. The obvious question, therefore, is whether such a text can ever be an accurate view of 1,400 years of legal thought. The answer must be no, because to isolate a "rule" from its jurisprudence is to ignore the justifications on which the rule depends. This can be illustrated in three examples but, before going on to these, some comment on the general noun *'adhāb*[12] is necessary. It has a range of meanings which include punishment (such as *ḥadd*, *ḳiṣāṣ*, discussed below) but also justice, which may also include forbearance, and this latter element is certainly a part of the formal classes of punishment. It is an important element because *ḥaḳḳ Allah* ("right" of God) and *ḥaḳḳ adāmī* ("right" of man) can never be clearly distinguished. The former looks to purification and mercy, the latter to recompense, but each contains elements of the other — only God *knows*. The former may be private but the latter is always public and so observable, and thus regulated. However, a separation of the two is a myth and all the great jurists of Islam are at one in this regard. The conclusion is that the absoluteness of prescription must be read in the context of the fluid boundaries of *'adhāb*. We can now take our examples.

Ḥadd (plural ḥudūd)

Ḥadd is a punishment which must be carried out for prescribed offences.[13] The Kelantan Code reproduces the offences in short form (see above). At first sight, the prescription is clear: there is no choice but to impose the given punishment; this is the accepted principle on which the Syariah is based. However, the Divine imperative and punishments for non-compliance rest on the assumption that there is always a general social acceptance that punishment is, in fact, appropriate. "Appropriateness" is decided at a time and a place; by whom is another matter. The history of Islam, like the history of Christianity, has many examples of abuses of punishments for non-compliance with a Divine imperative. The proponents of *ḥudūd* in Kelantan, therefore, must show that the punishment is "appropriate" for that place at that time, in the context of *'adhāb*. The Code does not demonstrate any attempt at all in this respect. Clearly, this is the result of an excessive minimalism.

Ḳiṣāṣ, ("qisos" in the Kelantan Code)

In the area of *ḳiṣāṣ*, namely, retaliation for killing and wounding, the offences and penalties derive from Qur'an XVII:33, XXV:68 and VI:151. The Kelantan Code sets out a summary from the standard *Shāfiʿī* texts, including the appropriate rates for compensation (*diya*). The rules are clear and the summary in the Code (3S. 24–38) is accurate. However, Malaysia in 1993 is not Arabia in the seventh century and, while the crimes in *ḳiṣāṣ* are common to both, the respective social systems are not. Allah did create mankind in all its variousness. The Kelantan Code denies variousness and, hence, practicality. Modern scholars of Islam from within Islam stress the value of variousness.[14] On practicality, the tribalism of the Hejaz is not the same as Kelantan or Minangkabau or Aceh or Batak or Javanese social structure. Allah created these societies as well as the Arab and the *Djāhilīya*. Again, it is a question of appropriateness in *ʿadhāb* and this is not addressed.

Shāhid

Shāhid means "to witness" but, for the current discussion, it is evidence to prove an offence against religion. *Shāhid* constitutes Part III of the Kelantan Code, divided into nine sections. The basic principles are the classical ones: that direct observation or confession are required to prove an offence. Confession is most trustworthy, even though it may be withdrawn at any time. Circumstantial evidence is specifically excluded, except for consumption of alcohol and, in the crime of unlawful sex (*zinā'*), pregnancy may be taken as evidence sufficient to convict. Section 40 requires four witnesses for *zinā'*, who must be male, just, with "a sense of honour", each of whom must see the act of "copulation". This evidence, however, may be withdrawn, in which case *zinā'* cannot be sustained. The "best" evidence is confession (S. 44) but this may be retracted. There also a reference to the Syariah Courts Evidence Enactment (1991) from which these provisions are taken. The most difficult factor in these rules is establishing *ʿadāla* (uprightness, integrity) of the witnesses. There is a vast difference between establishing this in the small tribal communities of seventh-century Arabia and a modern state in the fifteenth/twenty-

first century. The difficulty is not a new one and, in the history
of Islam, from the second/eighth century there was considerable
discussion on professional or permanent witnesses.[15] The subject
most frequently discussed was the corruption, which inevitably
occurred. Kelantan does, in fact, have a corps of "religious police"
against whom accusations of corruption and partiality are
frequently levelled. Their main activity seems to be searching out
zinā'. Much of the discussion in Malaysia revolves around the
changed circumstances — from first/seventh century Arabia to
fifteenth/twenty-first century Malaysia — in which *fiqh* now finds
itself.[16] The rules for evidence are the often-cited examples, and are
criticized from feminist, sociological, and political perspectives.
The general view from these perspectives is that one cannot
transpose rules, which have remained unaltered from the first/seventh
century to the fifteenth/twenty-first century. It is not just a-historical
but perverse.

From the legal point of view, there is much to be said for this
position. In Malaysia, the *fiqh* is constitutionally dependent, the
individual is primarily a citizen and then secondarily, a Muslim. The
primary context is the nation-state and the primary point of reference
in the state is citizenship, not religion. The Code attempts to reverse
this for the Kelantan Muslim, but this is not a possibility in criminal
law under the Malaysian Constitution.

Returning to a-historical and perverse, there is one further
comment. It is that to confine *shāhid* to *zinā'* is to ignore the
complexity of *shāhid* in Muslim legal thought. It is highly debatable
in theory and in practice throughout the Muslim world, and it is not
open to an individual or state (government) to select whatever it likes
for its own purposes. Any reading of the *fiqh* texts on the subject will
show the complexities and inconsistencies which exist. Again, the
Kelantan Code is a minimalist text in this respect.

As far as context is concerned, the Code does not tell us how
and why the prescriptions set down have been selected. Minimalism
is all very well but canons for selection must also be demonstrated.
We can infer, perhaps, a desire for a return to some original purity.
But for what purpose? For the individual, a society, or because
God demands it? The theme of minimalism is continued in the next
section.

Form

The Kelantan Code is in English statute form. The "statute" is always a minimalist text, the aim of which is a) clarity, and b) consistency of phrasing, so as to c) correctly express the intention of the legislature on d) a specific point of law. From the technical point of view, a certain standard of construction and drafting must be achieved if the statute is to be workable without excessive litigation. There will, of course, be litigation but it must be minimal. This way of writing a law has its own rules of construction and interpretation. The Kelantan Code thus presents us with two views of minimalism. From the Syariah side, it means selections from 1,400 years of *fiqh*; from the formal (English law) side, it should show an internal coherence, such that the text can be construed to give an unambiguous result without internal inconsistency. This is the test which the Kelantan Code must pass in respect of form.

Selection and Criteria for Selection

The result of taking a minimalist selection of rules from one system of jurisprudence and putting it into a minimal text from another is to deny, or at best, to seriously diminish the former. The colonial "Islamic law" legislation in Malaya is an obvious example, as is the later legislation in contemporary Malaysia. It is first a trivialization of *fiqh* because of the minimal nature of its content and, secondly, the new form requires a new way of legal thinking, which is determined by a form which is foreign to *fiqh*. For example, the glossary of Arabic words (Schedule I) is minimal and the English transliteration leaves much to be desired. This is not to say that one cannot understand them; they are clear enough. However, they do not reflect *contemporary Muslim thought*. Selection is thus without a stated criterion. It is, therefore, without context whether sociological, historical, or legal. However, these are precisely the parameters which must be demonstrated. The "Explanatory Statement" attached to the Code appears to recognize this but does not in fact come anywhere near achieving it. The Statement gives only the content of each section in short form, nothing else. It is not an explanation, let alone a statement of principle for establishing criteria. The result is that it is impossible to construe the *fiqh* content, *as it now appears in the English form.* This means that we cannot understand the text of the Code *except by English legal reasoning.* It is obvious that the Kelantan legislature did not understand this.

Structural Inconsistency

Structural inconsistency in the Code derives from the issues raised in the comments just made. The phrase means inconsistencies internal to the Code; these are the draftsman's bane. There are at least three obvious examples in the Code.

1.   First, in the interpretation section (S2 [3]), there is a direction to the state Interpretation Enactments of 1948 and 1967. These may be referred to "if not contrary to Syariah law". The reference introduces a number of difficulties. For example, and fundamental to the interpretation of the Code, the Interpretation Enactments are based directly on English legal reasoning. This consists of the known canons of construction as expressed in judicial precedent. This method of ascertaining the meaning of a statute has nothing in common with *fiqh*. By what means is a quite complex subject to be known to, and applied by, Qāḍī in the religious courts, bearing in mind that the principles of legal reasoning are not part of his own concept of law? It is an impossible burden to lay upon him, but this is what is being indicated. The point is that the Evidence Enactments open up the whole of the Kelantan Code to two hundred years of precedent on statutory interpretation. Additionally, the laws of statutory interpretation are among the most complex in the English/ Malaysian legal system.

There is one further point; the saving provision, "if not contrary to Syariah law", merely compounds the difficulty. What Syariah law? Is it the classical texts and, if so, which ones? Is it the jurisprudence in the *Jernal Hukum* or the State Appeal Board? If either, then we are again in the realm of English legal reasoning, which inevitably takes one back to the Anglo-Muslim jurisprudence. The problem here is that this was supposedly to have been excised by Article 121 (1A) of the Federal Constitution.

The experience of the Malaysian Appeal Boards demonstrates the confusion and difficulty which can arise.[17]

To narrow the argument to the Interpretation and General Clauses Enactments, how do these relate to the Syariah Evidence Enactment? Theoretically, the Enactments are separate and have respectively discrete competences. However, even a brief glance is enough to show that in practice this will be impossible to maintain. While the Interpretation and General Clauses Enactments are incorporated into the Kelantan Code, the draftsman does not appear to have read them carefully, if at all. To be sure, the draftsman has provided a list of words and expressions to be interpreted, and provisions for schedules. However, repeals, amendments, construction of amendments, construction of subsidiary rules, and terms of subsidiary rules are not defined. There is no mention of judicial notice of subsidiary legislation; the authority to make rules is assumed but not specified. There is no provision for saving rights, or acts binding on the government.

This is an impossible position for both the Syariah Court judges and (eventually) the Federal Court judges. All legislation must deal with the technical matters indicated immediately above. These are part of the law. I doubt if the *Qāḍī* would know this. Even the High Court and Federal Court judges, trained in the secular system, will have to exercise judicial "innovation", and what the results of this might be are totally unpredictable. This is bad drafting because unpredictability must be excluded from a statute as far as possible.

The Kelantan Code gets more minimalist by the section, to the point of unworkability, and there is a well-known High Court decision which demonstrates this. The case is *Samivellu* v *Public Prosecutor* [1972] 1MLJ 28 on the Interpretation Enactment and the Evidence Enactment. The subject has nothing to do with Syariah and space does not allow a full description, but briefly it says that the Evidence Enactments must be read with the Interpretation and General Clauses Ordinances/Enactments. The basic reference is to "written law" but, in the case of Syariah, we do not know how far this extends outside statute and precedent. The Kelantan Code is hence becoming a real invitation to unnecessary litigation.

2. The second example is Section 62 of the Kelantan Code, which can be read as an extension of the comments just made. The section says:

> 62. (1) All offences under this Enactment and the provisions relating thereto shall be interpreted according to the Syariah law and the *precedents* found therein; and reference to such law shall be made *in respect of any matter not provided for in this Enactment*.
>
> (2) If any doubt of difficulty arises in the interpretation of *any word, expression* or term relating to Syariah law, the Court trying the case shall have jurisdiction to give meaning to such word, expression or term [emphasis added].

Subsection (1) repeats in short form the comments made immediately above but the phrase in italics attempts to widen significantly the scope of the Code. What "any matter" actually means has become problematic. We have already seen that "precedents" is uncertain and to this uncertainty can be added the status of *fatāwā* given by the Kelantan Majlis. Subsection (2) is a catch-all, and, while it can be construed as confined to the Code, the phrasing is so wide as to raise doubt. Even assuming a catch-all, the phrase "any word, expression" reinforces doubt. For example, theft is defined in the Code, but if we take theft in relation to *wakaf* we are again forced back to English forms because *wakaf* is already defined in other Kelantan Islamic legislation[18] as "charitable trust". The Syariah does not know charitable "trust" in the English law sense, but *wakaf* has now been assimilated to it. What law applies then and do the *Qadi* know the answer; do they know what *wakaf* in the sense of charitable trust means in law?

3. Finally, we can mention *irtidād* (*ridda*) in Section 23, the offence of apostasy. The penalty is death, a punishment clearly drawn from *fiqh* and *hadith*, not, it should be noted, from the Qur'an (XVI:106; III:86f). Section 23 is debatable at several levels. One could speak in terms of *taqlīd* and *ijtihād* but that debate is never ending. More germane here, perhaps, is the fact that the Kelantan Code arrogates to the state authority the exclusive right of judgement and hence the social and

legal consequences for *irtidād*. This is not new in the history of Islam. The problem is that the last 1,400 years of legal commentary is ambivalent and, while there is certainly authority to support capital punishment, there is equally authority which denies it.[19] Other provisions in Section 23 are equally vague and so general as to almost constitute an incoherence (for example, the uses of *ḥarām*, *ḥalāl*, *rukun īmān*, *rukun Islam*).

In short, from the point of view of form, the Code leaves much to be desired. It certainly opens the gate to litigation, and the draftsman must be ashamed of himself for having put forward such a sloppy piece of work. From the formal point of view, the Code is incompetent.

Rationale

The reason or rationale for any piece of legislation takes us into the uncertain waters of motive, politics, and ethical justification, and these bring us back to the issues raised by Clive Kessler at the beginning of this essay.

While rationale is always debatable, the traditional view of a statute is that its meaning must be found from within the text itself; it must stand or fall on its own terms. This view values certainty above all else and has much to commend it. On the other hand, it can be overly restrictive for the judiciary, particularly where moral issues are concerned. The Kelantan Code falls clearly into this latter category. Proponents of the Code put forward four arguments to justify it.

1. The *ḥudūd* are mandatory for Muslims

The authority usually cited is Q V:50 and the preceding and following *ayat* (47–49 and 51–53) relate the history of Revelation to Jews and Christians and restate the duty of obedience to God's commands. To fail in this duty is to fall into rebelliousness. However, the citation is not conclusive when read with Q XVI:106, and III:86. On the other hand, *hadīth* from the six *ṣaḥīḥs* do show that apostasy is punishable by death but, even in this source, there is also evidence (Nasā'ī, *Taḥrim al-dam*, Abu Dāwūd, *Ḥudūd*, and Tabarī, *Tafsīr*) that the Prophet forgave apostates. It is only in the later *fiqh* texts that *ḥadd* is fully elaborated, leaving aside clear *naṣṣ*. Muslims in Kelantan are being asked to accept the authority of the *fiqh* texts, in which the answer appears decisive in the standard *Shāfiʿī* works. But is this conclusive? Yes, if one accepts *taqlīd*, but even within it there are shades of emphases over the centuries of Muslim scholarship. Given the circumstances of the *umma* in the fifteenth/twenty-first century (colonialism, post-colonial nation-states), it is quite wrong to ignore variable practices. Such is a-historical and is not an option for any of the three monotheisms, and certainly not for Islam in contemporary Kelantan. In short, while the proposition may appear unanswerable, it is nevertheless open to debate. There is no evidence that this debate, *in the terms of modern Arabic language scholarship*, has even been considered (see below).

2. God's laws are certain, man's are not

This proposition is, at best, disingenuous; "certain" is not a class in either Syariah or Malaysian law. To suppose otherwise is to seriously misunderstand the jurisprudence of both. If "certain" means the Qur'an and Sunna, then the proposition has a meaning because these are Revealed sources. However, if it also means *fiqh* then there is a real difficulty which we all know. It is that the whole body of *fiqh* is open to debate and is constantly debated. Being made by men it can never be certain unless, of course, one wishes to surrender to a blind *taqlīd*. Such surrender has never been a practical proposition and is certainly not viable in the fifteenth/twenty-first century. Furthermore, are the contemporary forms of *fiqh* in Kelantan and the other states of Malaysia "certain"? The answer is no, they are not, and the reason is that they are in statutes which can be changed from time to time, and *this is exactly what the Kelantan Code proposes to do*. There is no principle of "certainty", and the Code itself is an example of this.

The proposition is illogical, but it has a further dimension. This is that it attempts to shut off *ijtihād*; it is, in fact, regressive. As Farish Noor's chapter in this volume demonstrates, an arrogation of "truth" to oneself, as in the Code, is to claim certainty of doctrine. What the Code demonstrates is the impossibility of a practical and workable *implementation*.

Ijtihād cannot be denied because its whole purpose is to deal with uncertainty. The Code attempts to arrive at a certainty through a historical reference, the application of which cannot be known (for certain, if at all) in contemporary Kelantan.

3. The *ḥudūd* laws will achieve a greater degree of public order

This is an appeal to the belief that a law on its own can succeed in changing individual behaviour for the better and thus create a better society. In fact, law cannot do this as thousands of studies in Western and non-Western societies have shown.[20] Law may be an instrument of social engineering but that is the limit of its efficacy. The example cited by the Kelantan government — that Saudi Arabia is crime-free because of *ḥudūd* — is specious. It is no more crime-free than any other country. Contrary examples, such as Pakistan and Sudan, show that state-sanctioned violence in the name of Islam does not reduce crime rates. Indeed, it has led to a corruption of the social justice ideals of Islam.

4. *Ḥudūd* will be freely accepted once known

This justification is confused. It appears to mean that objection to *ḥudād* laws is based on a) the lack of knowledge and/or b) the influence of immoral and anti-Muslim Western thought. Both can be cured by education in Islamic values. This proposition is without merit.

Of the four rationales, only the first has any intellectual respectability; but it is also open to debate.

Conclusion

What then do we make of the Kelantan Code? Is it truly submission to Allah in the sense used by Clive Kessler — "inspired to good by submission"? But submission to what? The Code is not in force, but whether it will be or not is not the point. It represents a certain sort of thinking about Islam and law which is characteristic of the contemporary Muslim world. It says, in short, that the duty to submit to Allah can and must be enforced by the state — this is what the Kelantan Code means. The issue is solely one of authority; to determine who has the authority to define an Islamic society, and to put in place the means to achieve it.

The body of this chapter has looked at how successful or otherwise the Code is in achieving this purpose. As we have seen, it is seriously deficient and almost certainly unworkable. The constitutional context, in fact, makes it impossible, at least for the time being; the contents are debatable given the lack of criteria; the formal drafting is poor; and the rationale is non-existent or weak. Sociological implications are not even considered.

There is one further weakness, and it is a considerable one. There is no indication that contemporary Muslim thought on state, authority, or law is present in the debates surrounding the Code. It certainly does not appear in the Code itself. Thus, the so-called "religious utilitarians"[21] who include 'Abd al-Wahhab (d. 1456), 'Allal al-Fasi (d. 1973), and Hasan Turabi, promote an "expansive" maslaha. In contrast, another group, the "religious liberals"[22] including Sa'id Ashmawi, Fazlur Rahman (d. 1958), and Muhammad Shahrur, deny that traditional religious interpretation is either faithful to Islam or of any practical use. These are debates from within Islam and they are vital to any discussion of the sociology of law in contemporary Islam. There seems to be no evidence that the issues raised in these debates (in Arabic) have been considered in Kelantan.

The issues raised by Clive Kessler in 1973 remain unresolved; one might even say not approached in a serious, informed way. That is why "Submission to Allah" remains highly problematic.

Notes

1. Kessler (1977), pp. 211–12.
2. Except with respect to the Federal Territories of Kuala Lumpur and Labuan, Islamic law and personal and family law of persons professing the religion of Islam, including the Islamic law relating to succession, testate and intestate, betrothal, marriage, divorce, dower, maintenance, adoption, legitimacy, guardianship, gifts, partitions and non-charitable trusts; Wakafs and the definition and regulation of charitable and religious trusts, the appointment of trustees and the incorporation of persons in respect of Islamic religious and charitable endowments, institutions, trusts, charities and charitable institutions operating wholly within the State; Malay customs; Zakat, Fitrah and Baitulmal or similar Islamic religious

revenue; mosques or any Islamic public places of worship, creation and punishment of offences by persons professing the religion of Islam against precepts of that religion, except in regard to matters included in the Federal List; the constitution, organization and procedure of Syariah courts, which shall have jurisdiction only over persons professing the religion of Islam and in respect only of any of the matters included in this paragraph, but shall not have jurisdiction in respect of offences except in so far as conferred by federal law, the control of propagating doctrines and beliefs among persons professing the religion of Islam; the determination of matters of Islamic law and doctrine and Malay custom.

3. This Article is not without its own difficulties. See Hooker (1999).
4. See Norani Othman (1994), especially pp. 147 ff. See also Rose Ismail (1995).
5. Kessler (1977), p. 1.
6. *Mohamed* v *Faridah* [1992] 2MLJ 793, *Soon Singh* [1994] 1MLJ 690.
7. See Hooker (1984).
8. See, for example, the Federal Court's comments in *Dalip Kaur* v *Pegawai Polis* ... [1991] 1MLJ 1.
9. See Hooker (1974), p. 7.
10. See Meuleman (1996), pp. 43–78.
11. In passing, it should be noted that the transliterations are a mess; they show absolutely no grasp of either Arabic or English orthography. This is obviously a matter of considerable concern, particularly when one is dealing with a *law* text where correctness and exactness are fundamental.
12. The noun is not in the glossary of the Kelantan Code.
13. s.v. *ḥadd* in EI².
14. A. Hasan (1983), pp. 71–90.
15. s.v. *shāhid* in EI².
16. See the contributions in Rose Ismail (1995).
17. See Hooker (1999), pp. 68–74.
18. Kelantan Council of the Religion and Malay Custom Enactment, 1994.
19. s.v. *murtadd* in EI².
20. See Hooker (1975).
21. The phrase is Professor Wael Hallaq's; see Hallaq (1997).
22. Ibid.

References

A. Hasan. "Modes of Reasoning in Legal Cause". *Islamic Studies* 22, no. 1 (1983): 71–90.

Hallaq, Wael. *A History of Islamic Legal Theories: An Introduction to Sunni usul al-fiqh*. Cambridge: Cambridge University Press, 1997.

Hooker, M. B. *Legal Pluralism: An Introduction to Colonial and Neo-colonial Laws*. Oxford: The Clarendon Press, 1975.

————. *Islamic Law in Southeast Asia*. Singapore: Oxford University Press, 1984.

————. "*Qadi* Jurisdiction in Contemporary Malaysian and Singapore". In *Public Law in Contemporary Malaysia*, edited by M. A. Wu, pp. 57–75. Kuala Lumpur: Longman, 1999.

Kessler, Clive S. *Islam and Politics in a Malay State: Kelantan 1838–1969*. Ithaca, London: Cornell University Press, 1977.

Meulman, J. H. "Reactions and Attitudes Toward the *Darul Arqam* Movement in Southeast Asia". *Studia Islamika* 3, no. 1 (1996): 43–78.

Norani Othman, ed. *Syariah Law and the Modern Nation State*. Kuala Lumpur: Sisters in Islam, 1994.

Rose Ismail, ed. *Hudud in Malaysia: The Issues at Stake*. Kuala Lumpur: Sisters in Islam, 1995.

PART II

Society

6

THE MALAY WORLD
The Concept of Malay Studies and
National Identity Formation

SHAMSUL A. B.

In his ground-breaking study of the interplay of religion and politics within the processes which groups use to define themselves and their place in the world, Clive Kessler (1978) focused on a community of Malay peasants in Kelantan, Malaysia. He was interested especially in the need to understand the articulation of Islam within this community, not in a context of "a mysteriously disembodied presence" but as "an idiom whereby people may shape and express their own experience of themselves both as the products and the producers of their society's history" (Kessler 1978, p. 244). This chapter takes Kessler's insight as a starting point (Kessler 1978, pp. 17–20), much as I did previously in my own community-based study of local politics (Shamsul 1986). The present chapter, however, looks at a different sector as the prism through which to examine a group as both the creator and the object of its identity formation activities. The selected collectivity for this chapter is the élite community in Malaysia (and previously, Malaya) of "knowledge constructors" or the "intelligentsia", such as colonial administrators, travellers, scholars, politicians, nationalists, and government officials. It is these people who, over time, have been responsible for providing an "idiom" or "ruling idea" that has shaped the way Malaysians express their experience, write history, and present knowledge and truth, as well as sustain mystiques and prolong myths.

As noted above, if Kessler was interested in a community of Malay peasants, I am interested in a loosely-structured community of intelligentsia (of local and foreign membership). Both groups, however, play the same role in society but at different levels, as producers and products of the society's history. If, on the one hand, the peasants survived on an open system of wisdom-making, the intelligentsia, on the other, survives on constructed "ruling ideas". Both the peasants and the intellectuals have shown themselves as powerful influences and have had lasting impacts upon the surrounding society at large.

Malay Studies and Malay World Studies

The arena in which, over time, the intelligentsia in Malaysia has pursued its activities in knowledge formation is broad and varied, covering areas in politics, economics, the arts, religion, and a host of other social areas. Of necessity, therefore, this chapter focuses on a delineated field, namely, the subject of "Malay Studies" and its development and vicissitudes over time. Malay Studies, and the offshoot "Malay World Studies", provide a rich source of material for the examination of the intelligentsia's role in knowledge and identity formation. A central aspect of this chapter, therefore, will be to sketch the location of "Malay Studies" and "Malay World Studies" within the larger canvass of colonialism and colonial knowledge construction, and subsequently in the formation of the Malaysian post-colonial state.[1] As an illustration of the journey from Malay Studies to Malay World Studies, the chapter concludes with an outline of a recent project being conducted on the latter area.

Knowledge and Nation Formation

Before turning to the specific discussion of Malay Studies, it is important to provide a backdrop against which such an investigation can be pursued. The origins of Malay Studies and the field's construction and redirection over time cannot be considered in a vacuum but must be seen as an example of knowledge construction in cultural and nation-state formation.

In recent literature on nationalism and nation-formation, there appear to be few attempts to explore the relationship between nation-formation and the social sciences, except in the most oblique manner (Hutchinson and Smith 1994; Guibenau 1996; and James 1996). This paucity occurs, despite the widely acknowledged fact that the beginnings of the social sciences in a locality are closely related to the multiple circumstances leading to the birth of the nation. For instance, Giddens has argued that the modern nation-state and social science, particularly sociology as a social scientific discipline, are intimately linked (Giddens 1995, 1996). This is not at all surprising because the self-understanding of a national community as a culturally homogenous and spatio-temporally delimited entity, or as "the nation", especially in eighteenth-century Europe, provided the model, under the conditions of modernity, for a distinct sphere of "the social". This new understanding of "the social" as a theoretical category made social science possible.

It is apparent that the close links which the social sciences have with the nation-state were forged at a time when European nation-states were engaged in establishing a new global order. Imperialism, and later colonialism, required that the main Western powers reach an understanding for an efficient exploitation of their resources. The global economy then demanded the increasing co-ordination of transnational regions of production, exchange, and consumption. This required a basis of consensus beyond the nation, which was provided by the transnational community of scholars, namely, the social scientists, who then provided the much-needed ideals of a universal and empirical (social) science.

It is also important to recognize that both the nation-state and the social sciences are modern inventions and an acknowledged feature of modernity is the crucial role of knowledge for the expression, maintenance, and reproduction of power. While knowledge represents a form of power, certain modes of power, such as policing and crowd control in the conditions of modernity, can only be expressed through their relationship with knowledge, such as the activity of spying and surveillance. The social sciences, however, are not the "slave of the nation-state". Even as social science requires the resources of the modern nation-states for its teaching and research needs, especially in the post-colonial context, it is equally dependent on a vigorous civil culture distinct from the state, lest the state conflates its interests (particularly in "nationhood") with (civil) society at large. In other words, knowledge is not only a relationship of power; power also requires new forms of knowledge, such as social science, for its effectiveness in modern society. Hence, as many have argued, a critical social science is necessary to counterbalance modern society's functional goals because social science has emancipatory as well as instrumental goals (Atal 1974, pp. 2–5; Shamsul 2001c).

There has, therefore, been an established relationship between nation-formation and social science, both in the past and at present. In spite of "globalization" and the "borderless world", the nation-state remains arguably the single most important political unit, both as a polity and as an analytical category, which frames global social conduct. This affects the way the social sciences develop the approach to research and its teaching as a corpus of knowledge. While one could claim its universality, for many reasons social science, together with its practice, nonetheless remains trapped in its "dividedness" and its organization, usually within "the nation-state". For instance, in bureaucratic terms, the teaching of social science has always been divided along disciplinary lines and has rarely been taught as a single knowledge entity. The integrated core of the social sciences has been driven by its capacity to be divided up, in bureaucratic and organizational terms, into departments, institutes, centres, and faculties (faculty of economics, faculty of arts, and so on).

Nonetheless, however fragmented the organization of the teaching and research and the exercise in finding presentation and publication within the social sciences may be, the divided parts are often "united" or "grouped" under the umbrella of the "nation-state", under or within an organization such as a "national social science commission" or "social science research council" or "national liaison committee for social science" or "social science academy" or "national social science association". It is in this context that social science and its practice become intricately linked with the interests of the nation-state because, almost without exception, nation-states in the world today are run and governed by social scientists, who, in turn, often have prominent social scientists, local and foreign, as their advisers (Shamsul 1993, 1995a, 1995b, 2001c). Such situations have given rise to what could be called "methodological nationalism", in which universal social issues are studied in the micro-context of a nation-state, not as universal social issues unimpeded by the physical and ideational boundaries of historically created nation-states.

The academic social scientists often find this situation difficult to cope with, especially if they are employed in state-sponsored universities and yet want to voice dissenting views on social issues that could be perceived as "criticizing the government" or, worse still, as "threatening national security and political stability". This gag on open discussion was also present during the colonial era, when independence fighters and nationalists, most of whom were social scientists employed in various occupations and at various levels, were put behind bars for "anti-establishment" activities. Draconian laws and regulations were often introduced to prevent these activists from "poisoning" people's minds. In other words, there is embedded within social science a potentially "explosive" political element, one that is viewed by the powers that be as having the capability to subvert the nation-state. It is therefore inevitable that the nature of the relationship between nation-state and social science had, in the past, always been a contentious and dialectical one.

It is useful to bear in mind this linkage between the social sciences and the vicissitudes in the formation of nation-states as we turn to examine the history and development of what is now known as "Malay Studies", consisting of a corpus of social scientific knowledge on Malaysia.[2] Critical in such an investigation is the need to establish the role and influence of "colonial knowledge" in providing what could be termed as "baseline knowledge" in the subsequent exercise of creating ethnographies, official reports, analyses and descriptions on the whole society and culture of Malaysia, or in the production of a mass of, almost uncontested, so-called "facts" on Malaysia.[3]

The Making of Colonial Knowledge: The "Epistemological Space" Conquered

Over the centuries, a number of influential thinkers have, through their novel constructions of the world outside the European cultural mainstream, changed the ways in which the cultures of what was then the "new world" were regarded. Jean Jacques Rousseau, with his idea of the "noble savage" (1915) is one such watershed. Within our own times, Edward Said's *Orientalism* (1978) has had far-reaching effects, outlining the West's imposition of a form of knowledge, and hence power, which designated the culture of the non-West as "other", as exotic and irrational, labelling it "Orientalist". Said also pointed out the disparate nature of the overall concept of Orientalism, analysing the different aspects of, for example, the British and French forms of Orientalism which informed the variations in their activities, from research to colonial policies (Said 1978, pp. 264–66).

In the 1950s and the 1960s, long before Michel Foucault (1980) made "knowledge" a term inseparable from the term "power", and before Edward Said further opened the discussion of the relations between power and knowledge in colonial discourses and orientalist scholarship, Bernard Cohn, an American anthropologist specializing in the study of India, had begun to apply an anthropological perspective to the history of colonialism and the form of knowledge which it propagated. Cohn's path-breaking essays are now published in two separate volumes (Cohn 1986, 1996).

The most important concept introduced by Cohn to describe the nature, depth, breadth, and extent of European domination is explained in the following passage.

> In coming to India, they (the British) unknowingly and unwittingly invaded and conquered not only a territory but an *epistemological space* as well. The 'facts' of this space did not exactly correspond to those of the invaders. Nevertheless, the British believed they could explore and conquer this space through translation…. The first step was evidently to learn the local languages…. The knowledge of languages was necessary to issue commands, collect taxes, maintain law and order, and to create other forms of knowledge about the people they are ruling… to classify, categorize, and bound the vast social world that was India so that it could be controlled (Cohn 1996, p. 4–5; emphasis added).

The concept of great explanatory power introduced by Cohn was that of "epistemological space". Cohn was to work on this concept further as his life-long intellectual project, examining in detail how the invasion and conquering of this space became so important to the British — as important as, if not more than, the invasion and conquering of the territorial or physical space itself. In popular parlance, colonizing the mind had equal importance with colonizing the territory. Cohn detailed how the colonizing of the epistemological space was developed and systematized within the British colonial project and how the system subsequently dismantled, reconstituted and replaced, almost completely, the indigenous thought system. Extending Cohn's argument, it would be feasible to say that, when a British colony, such as Malaya, obtained its independence, it regained only its territorial space (perhaps partially) but not its epistemological space. The latter, in fact, had been totally transformed, reconstituted, and reshaped.

In pre-modern Southeast Asia, power was made visible through theatrical displays, such as processions, royal entries, coronations, weddings, funerals, and other rituals. These activities, often managed by priests, court historians and genealogists, artists and artisans, became a visual and abstract legitimation of the rulers over the ruled (Wolters 1999). When European domination finally took root in the region in the nineteenth century, the indigenous power made visible through ritual performance and dramatic display was soon replaced by the colonial power through its "officializing procedures" that spread to many areas, both geographically and culturally. The colonists took control of the epistemological space by defining and classifying physical and social space, making separations between public and private spheres, replacing religious institutions with agencies such as the registrar of births, marriages and deaths, and by standardizing languages and scripts. The colonial state considered some activities as legitimate, for which it therefore gave licences, while other activities were considered illegal and suppressed. The advent of public education and its rituals helped to foster and homogenize "official beliefs" in how things are and how they ought to be. The schools became the critical "civilizing" institutions that were charged with producing moral and productive citizens.

It could therefore be said that when the colonialists came to Southeast Asia, they were entering "a new world that they tried to comprehend using their own forms of knowing and thinking" (Cohn 1996, p. 4). Not unlike present-day prerequisites for attaining ISO

9000 (a detailed quality assurance measurement set by International Standards Organization [ISO] in which documentation is basic and critical) the colonial state also had to meet certain preordained standards imposed from outside. The documentation that was developed to accompany and facilitate these changes actually created and normalized a vast amount of information, which in turn became the foundation of the colonists' machinery of government. The documents included annual reports, the census, and statistical data on finance, trade, health, demography, crime, education, transportation, public work, agriculture and irrigation, and industry. The data thus created became "facts" that required interpretation by trained bureaucrats with specialist knowledge of local indigenous culture.

Cohn outlined, in some detail, the set of "investigative modalities" that helped to gather and create the "facts" (1996, pp. 5–11). By "investigative modality", he means "... the definition of a body of information that is needed, the procedures by which appropriate knowledge is gathered, its ordering and classification, and then how it is transformed into usable forms, such as published reports, statistical returns, histories, gazetteers, legal codes, and encyclopedias." There were at least six major investigative modalities invented by the British during their rule in India, according to Cohn, namely, the historiographic, the travel, the survey, the enumerative, the museological, and the surveillance modality. Each modality defined and gathered a specific set of information, which in turn was classified and categorized in a particular manner suited to colonial bureaucratic and policy needs.

It is not surprising therefore that, in this context, post-colonial states were also perceived as "the natural embodiments of history, territory and society" (Cohn 1996, p. 3). In fact, the establishment and maintenance of the post-colonial nation, after the period of European rule, depended upon determining, codifying, controlling and representing the past by repeating the techniques of the construction of "facts" and "knowledge" already set in place by the colonialists. It must also be noted that social scientific disciplines, such as anthropology, also played an important role in the invasion of the epistemological space. The setting up by the colonial state of tertiary educational institutions, such as universities, shaped in the orientalist mould, meant that the academic departments within these institutions necessarily became the logical extension of the epistemological invasion.

For instance, in Malaysia during the colonial period (1819–1957), anthropology as a medium of intellectual discourse and as a method of knowledge accumulation was an integral part of the administrative science of the colonial state. This anthropological method was instrumental in the construction of the colonial imagination and knowledge about the "natives" of Malaysia, a process deeply rooted in "British orientalism". At that time, anthropological knowledge was perceived as critical in the implementation of the British policy of "indirect rule", that is, the formal delegation of power to native authorities and native courts. The policy made knowledge of indigenous Malayan and Bornean political and legal institutions, particularly those of the Malays, an important prerequisite for colonial administrators in the course of their duties. The British preferred to do the teaching of anthropology for their officers, rather than putting up with the idiosyncrasies of anthropologists outside the system of colonial rule whose interests were not always in line with those of the administration.[4]

Consequently, the anthropologically-conscious colonial officers took up the added role of researchers. They began to publish extensively on various aspects of Malay culture and history, mostly in the publications of the local branch of the London-based Royal Asiatic Society, such as the *Journal of the Straits Settlement Branch of the Royal Asiatic Society (JSSBRAS)*, which later became the *Journal of the Malayan Branch of the Royal Asiatic Society (JMBRAS)*. The Society, too, published numerous monographs on the culture and history of the various native groups. The two most prolific colonial administrator-scholars were R. J. Wilkinson and R. O. W. Winstedt, whose works on Malay history, literature, and customs are still cited today (Wilkinson 1971; and Winstedt 1988).

"Malay Studies" as a field of study emerged and developed within this environment (Mohd. Taib Osman 1991; and Shamsul 1993). The establishment of the Department of Malay Studies, the Department of Chinese Studies, and the Department of Indian Studies at the University of Malaya (Malaysia's first university, set up in 1949) was in fact modelled on the School of Oriental and African Studies, London. This copying illustrates the colonial invasion of the epistemological space, virtually unimpeded. In fact, this instance of colonial cultural dominance was publicly endorsed and became consolidated intellectually with the presence of the university and the said academic departments.

Perhaps the most important invasion, and one which is often not considered seriously enough, is the entry of social categories such as "race" (both its biological and social component and meanings) and "nation" into local cosmology and world-view through colonization. This conquest of the indigenous epistemological space contributed significantly to the slow dismantling of the traditional thought system over time, and its displacement by the Western-based system. The introduction of such social categories had a humble and unnoticed beginning. For instance, what seemed to be a "harmless" bureaucratic practice of census-taking actually helped to invent, evolve, and consolidate "racial categories", such as Malay, Chinese, and Indian in Malaysia, with the birth of terms such as "Census Malay", "Census Chinese", and so on.[5] The introduction of legislation such as the Malay Reservation Enactment 1913, the setting up of a Department of Chinese Affairs, and the special government-approved toddy shops for the Indians during the British rule drove home the point further, at the everyday level, to the people at the grass-roots that racial categories such Malay, Indian, and Chinese mattered very much, if one was to avoid the colonists' wrath. Hence, being a "Malay", a "Chinese", or an "Indian", in the colonialist way, was critical for everyday existence, formally and informally (Swift 1962).

The evolution and consolidation of these racial categories were accompanied by a growing political consciousness, through colonial bureaucratic practices and race-specific socialization, particularly via a pluralistic Western-oriented vernacular education system. It was in such a context that the racial categories, once consolidated and meaningful to the social actors, developed into racial-based notions about nation and hence, about issues of identity and their economic and political implications. There was a two-way exchange in the appropriation exercise during the colonial period; not only were the colonists appropriating what the locals had to offer culturally but the locals too were selecting, appropriating, and internalizing what the colonialists offered them, both through coercion and by other means. For these reasons, "difference" as a defining mode of everyday existence, in contrast to the top-down "homogenizing schemes", dominated the minds and everyday existence of the populace. Being a "Malay" or "Chinese" or "Indian" and demanding a "Malay nation", or "Chinese nation", or "Indian nation", historically, was not the result of a simple diffusion process called "derivative modernity discourse", as argued rather simplistically, even by a number of serious researchers (Iklmal Said 1992; and Kahn 2001).

Examinations of the epistemological space imposed by the Europeans on their colonies are not confined to Said and Cohn. Several other thinkers also turned to this crucial area of research, among them two prominent non-European social scientists, Anouar Abdel Malek (1983) and Syed Hussein Alatas (1977). They worked on related themes which offered a stringent critique of Western knowledge on non-Europeans — the former on "orientalism" and the latter on the "myth of the lazy native".

The all-important epistemological space that remains to be looked at in the examination of social transformation in Malaysia is the origin and nature of social scientific knowledge on Malaysia.[6] It was through the invasion of this space by colonialism that Western notions were introduced and became embedded and internalized as "facts" within the local thought system. Concepts such as "race", and "nation", have already been referred to, but even less loaded terms, such as "museum", "map" and even *kampung*, became accepted as given. Yet, the word *kampung,* for example, in its official usage refers to a physical area within which one usually finds a cluster of smaller *kampungs*, and in its daily vernacular language could refer to a compound around a house or the homestead. In other words, the problematic nature of terms like *kampung* and others have been disguised because they became integral to the discourse of nation-building. In fact, terms like these have been perceived as the "basic essentials" for identity formation in Malaysia. Various endeavours in the social sciences in Malaysia have taken the colonial version of the epistemological space – from the macro-level construction of research endeavours to the specifics of terminology — as their defining locus.

From time to time, there have been attempts to roll back the colonial definition of the scope of the social sciences in Malaysia, and to undertake scholarly work whose basis is defined in post-colonial terms. One such endeavour is a project, described below, which can be viewed as a case study to demonstrate how one research institution in Malaysia is attempting to re-evaluate itself and its future direction by a process of self-examination conducted through its research projects and, especially, the present project on "the construction of knowledge about the Malay world by others".

ATMA's Past Experience and Recent Reorientation

The Institute of the Malay World and Civilization, known by its Malay acronym ATMA, has an interesting history. Established in 1970 as the Department of Malay Language and Literature, it was upgraded in December 1972 to an academic institute called The Institute of Malay Language, Literature and Culture, known by its Malay acronym, IBKKM. In 1993, IBKKM was renamed anew as the Institute of the Malay World and Civilization (ATMA).

ATMA's declared core business is the promotion of Malay Studies, for both "academic analyses" and "public advocacy". Malay Studies has roots in the colonial epoch and provides another instance of the colonial invasion of the epistemological space, discussed above. Syed Naguib Al-Attas, the founding director of IBKKM, held the view that Malay Studies began with Stamford Raffles, a merchant-scholar and "Agent to the Governor-General with the Malay States", who in the first decade of 1800 visited Malacca to collect old Malay manuscripts and subsequently mooted the idea that an educational institution for the natives of the Malay world should be established. In Raffles' words, as quoted by Al-Attas (see *Buku Panduan* 1972, p. 14):

> (An educational) institution of the nature of a Native College which shall embrace not only the object of educating the higher classes of the native population, but at the same time that of affording instruction to the officers of the Company in native languages and of facilitating our more general researches into the history, condition and resources of these countries... It is from the banks of the Ganges to the utmost limits of China and Japan and to New-Holland that the influences of our proposed Institution is calculated to extend.

Raffles even suggested the appointment of "native professors" to teach Malay, Bugis, and Siam language, with supporting staff to teach Chinese, Javanese, Burmese, Pali, and Arabic. The idea of Malay Studies had an influence on Raffles' thinking over a considerable period while he was in the Far East (Chelliah 1940, pp. 11–33).

It was, however, not until one hundred years later in 1919, that a college not exactly like the one envisaged by Raffles, was established. Appropriately, it was named after him, "Raffles College". It functioned as a "University College", like those that were affiliated to the University of London, running a three-year undergraduate degree course, teaching English, geography, history, economics, mathematics, physics, and chemistry, with the notable absence of Malay Studies, a field of studies dear to Raffles.

In 1949, Raffles College, together with King Edward VII College of Medicine, was jointly upgraded as the University College of Malaya. In this new organizational structure, Malay Studies finally found its space, with the setting-up of a Department of Malay Studies, together with a Department of Chinese Studies, and a Department of Indian Studies. Za'aba, or Zainal Abidin Ahmad, an eminent scholar, was its first Head of Department.

About a decade later, in 1957, the year of the independence of the Federation of Malaya, the Faculty of Arts, University of Malaya, previously located in Singapore, was shifted to Kuala Lumpur. That Department of Malay Studies was then expanded in scope and coverage to include the study of culture, modern and classical Malay literature, and modern linguistics.

In 1970, when the Malay language became the sole medium of instruction in government-funded national schools and UKM (Universiti Kebangsaan Malaysia) was established in the same year, the role of ATMA became critical in furthering the Malay-oriented post-independence "nationalist/ethnic cause". Thus, ATMA was created, based on a political agenda quite different from that of the Department of Malay Studies, University of Malaya. It could be argued that ATMA was indeed a post-independence Malay ethnic project mainly to promote Malay language-based knowledge and consolidate "Malayness", as it were. The Department of Malay Studies, University of Malaya, on the other hand, was established clearly as part of a colonial project. However, the "nationalist" Malay academics within the latter institution were also members of the group that initiated the establishment of UKM — hence, the political-historical connection between the two institutions.

In this way, Malay Studies, a colonial construction in epistemological terms, quickly became an integral part of a post-nationalist project. Malay Studies thus became a critical element in the political aspect of nation-building in Malaysia, particularly in defining a Malay-based "national culture", "national language", "national education system", "national identity", "national integration", and so on. This phenomenon was not unrelated to the launching of the pro-Malay affirmative action policy called the New Economic Policy of 1971–90, the economic component of the long-term strategy of nation-building (Shamsul 2000).

ATMA's participation in the post-nationalist project intensified when it became involved in a number of programmes initiated together with the Malay literary non-governmental organizations (NGOs), such as GAPENA (Gabungan Penulis Nasional or National Writers Union, a loosely organized, nationally-based writers' association) and some quasi-government bodies in charge of Malay language and its development (such as Dewan Bahasa & Pustaka). ATMA's major role was to be the academic platform to organize international conferences and meetings about the Malay world and overseas "educational and study" trips to visit "Malays" in various parts of the world — the "Malay diaspora". A further role for ATMA was to publish materials aimed at enhancing both popular and academic knowledge about the Malays as an ethnic group. Slowly, Malay Studies in the 1970s and 1980s became the study of the "ethnic Malays" instead of the "Malay world", particularly Malays in Peninsular Malaysia and not Malays in East Malaysia or in Brunei, Indonesia, and Singapore. The topic of Malays in Singapore was under the purview, so to speak, of the Department of Malay Studies, National University of Singapore, and the study of Malays in Brunei constituted the academic and research domains of the Academy of Brunei Studies, Universiti Brunei Darussalam.

Such parcelling of knowledge, both in terms of "methodological nationalism" as well as "ethnicization of knowledge", narrowed down the focus of Malay Studies on the "Malay ethnic". It soon became apparent, especially to the UKM academic leadership, that there was a significant academic and intellectual need to shift from this narrow focus of "Malay Studies as an ethnic study" to "Malay World Studies as an area study", characterized by its rich diversity and pluralism.

In the latter construction, the word "Malay" is used to refer to a historical, geopolitical reality used by locals and foreigners and not to represent a particular ethnic group. This applies, even though there is such an ethnic group in the region whose language has become the lingua franca of the region and whose identity has furnished the major element in giving the region a conceptual unity labelled the "Malay world".

For a long time, the colonial-created concept of "Malay Studies" has been influential, not only in academic circles around the world but also in Malaysia's own domestic political arena. Indeed, in post-colonial Malaysia, Malay Studies has always been associated with Malaysia's ethnic Malay-centred post-nationalist ideology. As noted above, this definition of the subject has led to the narrowing of the empirical focus of Malay Studies, especially in the context of research, to Malays in Peninsular Malaysia. While it can be argued that such a focus has been important for political reasons, it nevertheless has a limiting effect upon the scope and activities of the academic enterprise in this area. However, the debate on what "Malay Studies" should constitute remains alive.[7]

For instance, even though ATMA has been actively involved in promoting the concept of the "Malay diaspora" in the context of "Malay Studies" since the late 1980s (for example, work on our "lost cousins" in Sri Lanka, Vietnam, Champa, South Africa, Madagascar, Western Australia, Saudi Arabia, and elsewhere), there is nonetheless a clear absence of a rigorous academic debate on the theme of the "Malay diaspora", despite the research and publications emanating from the journeys to those places.

The research journeys and the findings have been dominated, and therefore limited, by what could be called a "litmus test" approach, in which each journey became an exercise of testing, as it were, the level of "Malayness" of the people being studied, when compared with Malays in Malaysia. Some of the findings may shore up a notional standard of Malayness as a benchmark for use in a range of political as well as academic exercises and may also have led to an increase in publications on Malays around the world. This approach, however, does not help to further the serious academic pursuit of the study of the Malay world and civilization. This shortcoming is particularly noticeable when it occurs within the precincts of a university-based research institute with the title, the "Institute of the Malay World and Civilisation", which happens to be the only fully-fledged research institute on this subject in the Malay world.

In April 1999, ATMA, in redefining its directions, decided that it needed to return to the fundamental concept in Malay Studies, involving a return to the term and concept of "the Malay world", rather than "Malay ethnic", as a guide to the Institute's academic endeavour. Although the analogy is not a perfect fit, as Wolters (1999, pp. 42–45) has pointed out, it is still useful to define the Malay world as a "Mediterranean", in the sense that the Malay world is an abstract, intellectual space as well as a physical location, not unlike the Mediterranean, where a number of civilizations came to meet over time.[8] In the Malaysian case, it is the space and location where the Chinese, Indian, Arabian, European, and other world civilizations, for various reasons and under differing circumstances, met. The dialogues among the civilizations of the Malay world produced a diverse yet integrated culture, exemplifying the concept of pluralism, long before the term was coined.

For this reason, the Malay world, like the Mediterranean, has been a significant contributor to developments in the fields of both the physical and the social sciences. Among examples which readily come to mind are the contribution of Alfred Wallace and his letters to Charles Darwin before Darwin's *Origin of Species* was published in 1859; the theory of "economic dualism" by the Dutch economist, Boeke; the theory of the plural society by Furnivall; cultural aspects of anthropology by Clifford Geertz; and a critique on orientalism by Syed Hussein Alatas, author of the famous book *Myth of the Lazy Native* (1977), and his brother Syed Naguib Alatas.

Encouraged by the significance of the contributions of the Malay world, ATMA's personnel reached the view that it would be an appropriate time to embark on a project to investigate further the process of theory construction, in both the natural sciences and the humanities and social sciences, relevant to the Malay world. To that end, ATMA embarked on a long-term project called "The Construction of the Malay World by Others", aimed at examining closely the writings of non-Southeast Asian writers, academics, and others about this region, from as early as possible. The project also sought to examine the way the writers viewed and analysed their own societies, in the course of their experiences of the Malay world, as well as looking at their perceptions and descriptions of the Malay world itself.

Organizationally, this project has taken the form of a series of international colloquia, which began in November 2000. Successive colloquia have examined "Dutch scholarship and the Malay World" (November 2000); "French scholarship and the Malay World" (April 2001); "Nordic scholarship and the Malay World" (November 2001); and "Germanic scholarship and the Malay World" (March 2002). Plans for future events include "Japanese scholarship and the Malay World"; "Chinese scholarship and the Malay World"; "British scholarship and the Malay World"; and "Natural Science and the Malay World".

The series is aimed at demonstrating the Malay world's significant contributions to knowledge construction around the globe in numerous fields but, more importantly, at stimulating scholars in the Malay world itself to match the outstanding research by "the Others" through conducting their own serious research. This is a crucial and not impossible task. It demands, on the part of the local scholars, a great deal of rethinking, self-reflection, and self-criticism on the development and maintenance of high quality scholarship and research.

In 2000, a "Malay World Database" was established by ATMA. The database constitutes a collection of single-article texts, already indexed and catalogued according to author, title, source, and keywords, by ATMA's information technology experts. The catalogue is available, both in print — in photocopy form and as a specialist collection in ATMA's library — and on-line. There are now about 20,000 articles in the collection and it is hoped that at least 50,000 articles will comprise the collection by the end of 2003. That magnitude will make the database the largest single database on the Malay world available globally, accessible from anywhere on-line (Website: *www.atma.ukm.my*). From this database, plans are that a larger database, indeed a portal, called the "Malaycivilization.com" portal will be developed by 2004. Substantial funding has been received for this venture, which will enable ATMA, using information and communications technology, to move beyond the academic and research sphere into the private-sector sphere, promoting the database and attracting interested parties (academic, research, commercial, and others) to use the database for work on the entire field of the

Malay world, for both academic and non-academic purposes. "Malay world studies" is at the core of this major endeavour. Just as the Malay region interacted with the rest of the world through trade in the fifteenth century, it is hoped that continuing contacts and exchanges will take place between the Malay world and the rest of the globe by means of Internet contact in the twenty-first century.

Conclusion

This chapter has described a significant project on the Malay world, established by ATMA, as a systematic beginning to the transition from purely economic transactions, in the form of sea trade, to cultural and intellectual transactions via information technology. The origins of the project have been briefly traced, examining ATMA's directional change towards a renewal of a broad and encompassing concept of Malay Studies. This new direction moved away from the narrower view, which had previously dominated academic endeavours, and had in turn arisen as a response to the demands of certain sections of the academic and political communities, in their quest for a tool for post-colonial nation-building.

It is also important to note that the establishment of ATMA signalled a crucial and significant epistemological shift in Malay Studies in Malaysia. The one introduced and expanded in the Department of Malay Studies, University of Malaya, both in its Singapore and Kuala Lumpur campuses, had a colonial origin. Hence, its subsequent expansion remained within the epistemological space of colonial knowledge, as has its newer ontological representation in the present form of the Academy of Malay Studies, University of Malaya. ATMA, on the other hand, took on a different epistemological stance. Although the major part of the corpus of knowledge on Malay Studies that ATMA taught and developed was also colonial in origin, its evolution continued on a different path. The change occurred within ATMA from a conscious, continuous and consistent attempt to shed the colonial influence on the image of Malay Studies, a development not unrelated to the post-independence mood. In a changing post-independence context, ATMA was open to other epistemological orientations, such as the "Islamic one" propagated by its founding Director, Syed Naguib Al-Attas, in the 1970s. Later, in the 1980s and 1990s, ATMA embarked on the "Malay diaspora" project, in a conscious attempt to redefine "colonial" Malaya-centred Malay Studies and to turn it into a "national" Malay ethnic-based Malay Studies. It is not surprising, therefore, that since 1999 Malay Studies has been undergoing another epistemological shift, mainly in response to both national and global changes. This change seems to have bypassed the version of Malay Studies within the University of Malaya, arguably still trapped in the colonial knowledge parameters.

The two main versions of Malay Studies sketched out in this chapter — the post-colonial construction, limited in scope, and the broader, Malay-world concept championed by ATMA — in turn were developed within the framework of various renderings of the epistemological space. This space has from earliest times been a battle-ground, vied over by the historical forces and powers which, jockeying for domination, held sway over the Malay peninsula for centuries. Now that Malaysia is a mature nation, with significant efforts at nation-building on record, it seems that the ATMA project is a fitting symbol of Malaysia's arrival at a point of national academic and political maturity. The project does not deny the significant contribution of Malay Studies in the various conceptualizations that existed at different times in the region's history. The present stage, encapsulated by the ATMA project, builds on the diverse constructs of Malay Studies over time and brings into being a new phase, focused on the breadth of the Malay world and consistent with Malaysia's current standing globally.

Notes

1. See the interesting recent works of Philpott (2000) and Abidin (2000) on Indonesia, and Parera (1999) on Sri Lanka for comparison.
2. A number of useful comments on Malaysian social science has been made by Ramasamy (1983), Rustam A. Sani and Norani Othman (1991), Tham (1981), and Shamsul (2001b). A useful historical report was written by Firth (1948). But it is the so-called confidential report by Glazer et al. (1970), prepared under the sponsorship of the Ford Foundation, that should be of interest to Malaysianists. It came soon after the 13 May 1969 race riots; see, Funston (1975) for a useful survey of writings on the tragic event.

3. I have written a series of essays on "colonial knowledge" in the context of identity formation in Malaysia and they are as follows: Shamsul (1998), (1999a), (1999b), (2000a), (2000b), (2000c), (2001a) and (2001b).

4. There has been much written on the role of anthropology in Western imperialism; the recent ones are by Moore (1994), Kuklick (1991), and Thomas (1994). On the role and influence of anthropology in Malaysia, see, Hanapi Dolah (1997), Shamsul (1995b), Wazir (1993), (1994), (1995), and (1996).

5. There are numerous published materials on race relations in Malaysia and aspects of it, such as by Hirschman (1986), (1987); Milner (1995); Ariffin Omar (1993); Swift (1962); Abdul Rahman Embong (1974); and Nash (1989). The best but rather dated bibliography on race relations in Malaysia is by Tan Chee Beng (1992).

6. The two most important volumes on Malaysian Studies for Malaysianists are those edited volumes by Lent (1979) and Lent and Mulliner (1986). A number of important bibliographies that would help us to trace the trajectory of the development of Malaysian Studies and the range of published materials available are those of Freedman and Swift (1959); Brown and Ampalavanar (1986); Tan (1992); and Ooi (1999).

7. From 22 March to 2 April 2001 there was a furious debate in the Malay daily, *Berita Harian*, almost every day, regarding the future of the Jabatan Persuratan Melayu (JPM or Department of Malay Letters) at Universiti Kebangsaan as a result of the restructuring of three "arts-oriented" faculties at UKM, namely, the Faculty of Social Sciences & Humanities, the Faculty of Language Studies, and the Faculty of Development Science. There were unfounded accusations thrown at the UKM top leadership from the self-proclaimed "Malay post-nationalists" from JPM and their supporters that JPM would be relegated to a mere Programme within one of the six new Centres of the new combined faculty. On 15 November 2001, when the new faculty was launched officially, JPM was actually expanded to become one of the six Centres but not before UKM's top leadership was publicly cited as "anti-Malay" and "traitors". The absence of their scholarly contributions, particularly, in English is very obvious; see, for instance, Chapter 10, "Society and Genre", pp. 349–74, of Hooker (2000).

8. See Braudel (1972–73).

References

Abdul Rahman Embong. "A Comment on the State of the Sociology of Race Relations and Political Sociology in Malaysia", *Jernal Antropologi & Sosiologi* 3 (1974): 63–68.

Anouar Abdel Malik. *Civilisaton and Social Theory*. London: Macmillan, 1983.

Anwar Ibrahim. *Asian Renaissance*. Kuala Lumpur: Pelanduk, 1996.

Ariffin Omar. *Bangsa Melayu: Malay Concepts of Democracy and Community 1945–1950*. Kuala Lumpur: Oxford University Press, 1993.

Atal, Yogesh, ed. *Social Science in Asia*. New Delhi: Abhinav Publications, 1974.

Braudel, Fernand. *The Mediterranean and the Mediterranean World in the Age of Philip II*, translated by Sian Reynolds. London: Collins, 1972–73.

Brown, Ian, and R. Ampalavanar, compilers. *Malaysia*. World Bibliographical Series No. 12. London: Clio Press, 1986.

Buku Panduan: Jabatan Bahasa dan Kesusasteraan Melayu. Kuala Lumpur: Universiti Kebangsaan Malaysia, 1972.

Chelliah, D. D. "A History of the Educational Policy of the Straits Settlements with Recommendations for a New System Based on Vernaculars". Ph.D. thesis, University of London, 1940.

Cohn, Bernard. *Colonialism and Its Forms of Knowledge: The British in India*. Princeton, New Jersey: Princeton University Press, 1996.

——— . *An Anthropologist among the Historians and Other Essays*. Delhi: Oxford University Press, 1986.

Freedman, Maurice, and Michael Swift. "Rural Sociology in Malaya". *Current Sociology* 12, no. 2 (1959): 1–15.

Firth, Raymond. *Report on Social Science Research in Malaya*. Singapore: Government Printer, 1948.

Foucault, Michel. *Power/Knowledge: Selected Interviews and Other Writings, 1972–77*, edited by Colin Gordon. Brighton, Sussex: Harvester Press, 1980.

Funston, John. "Writings on May 13". *Akademika* 6 (1975): 1–16.

Glazer, Nathan, Samuel Huntington, Manning Nash, Manning and Myron Weiner. *Social Science Research for National Unity: A Confidential Report to the Government of Malaysia*. New York: Ford Foundation, 1970.

Giddens, Anthony. "In Defence of Sociology". In *In Defence of Sociology: Essays, Interpretations and Rejoinders*, edited by Anthony Giddens, pp. 1–7. Oxford: Polity, 1996.

——— . "Epilogue: Notes on the Future of Anthropology". In *The Future of Anthropology and its Relevance to the Contemporary World*, edited by Akber Ahmed and Chris Shore. London: Athlone, 1995.

Guibenau, Montserrat. *Nationalisms: The Nation-State and Nationalisms in the Twentieth Century*. Oxford: Polity, 1996.

Hanapi Dolah. "Beberapa Teori Antropologi dan Sosiologi: Penerapan dalam Pengajian Melayu". In *Pembangunan Seni dan Sastera*, compiled by Mana Sikana. Bangi: Jabatan Persuratan Melayu, Universiti Kebangsaan Malaysia, 1997.

Hirschman, Charles. "The Meaning and Measurement of Ethnicity in Malaysia: An Analysis of Census Classification." *Journal of Asian Studies* 46, no. 3 (1987): 555–82.

————. "The Making of Race in Colonial Malaya: Political Economy and Racial Category." *Sociological Forum* (Spring 1986), pp. 330–61.

Hooker, Virgina Matheson. *Writing a New Society: Social Change Through the Novel in Malay*. Sydney: Allen & Unwin, 2000.

Hutchinson, John, and Anthony D. Smith, ed. *Nationalism: A Reader*. Oxford: Oxford University Press, 1994.

Iklmal Said. "Ethnic Perspective of the Malay Left". In *Fragmented Vision: Culture and Politics in Contemporary Malaysia*, edited by Joel S. Kahn & Francis Loh, pp. 254–81. Sydney: Allen & Unwin, 1992.

James, Paul. *Nation-Formation: Towards a Theory of Abstract Community*. London: Sage, 1996.

Kahn, Joel. *Modernity and Exclusion*. London: Sage, 2001.

Kessler, Clive. *Islam and Politics in a Malay State: Kelantan 1838–1969*. Ithaca, NY.: Cornell University Press, 1978.

Kuklick, Henrika. *The Savage Within: The Social History of British Anthropology, 1885–1945*. Cambridge: Cambridge University Press, 1991.

Kusno Abidin. *Behind the Postcolonial: Architecture, Urban Space and Political Cultures in Indonesia*. London: Routledge, 2000.

Lent, John, ed. *Malaysian Studies: Present Knowledge and Research Trends*. Occasional Paper No. 7. Dekalb, Illinois: Center for Southeast Asian Studies, Northern Illinois University, 1979.

Lent, John, and K. Mulliner, eds. *Malaysian Studies: Archaeology, Historiography, Geography and Bibliography*. Occasional Paper No. 11. DeKalb, Illinois: Center for Southeast Asian Studies, Northern Illinois University, 1986.

Milner, Anthony. *Invention of Politics in Colonial Malaya*. Melbourne: Cambridge University Press, 1995.

————. "Colonial Records History: British Malaya". *Kajian Malaysia* 4, no. 2 (1986): 1–18.

Mohd Taib Osman. *Pengajian Melayu Sebagai Bidang Ilmu di Universiti*. Inaugural Lecture for the Chair of Malay Studies. Kuala Lumpur: Universiti of Malaya Press, 1991.

Moore, Salley Falk. *Anthropology & Africa: Changing Perspectives on a Changing Scene*. Charlottesville & London: The University Press of Virginia, 1994.

Nash, Manning. *The Cauldron of Ethnicity in the Modern World*. Chicago: Chicago University Press, 1989.

Ooi Keat Gin, compiler. *Malaysia*. Revised edition. World Bibliographical Series No. 12. Denver, Colorado: Clio Press, 1999.

Perera, Nihal. *Decolonising Ceylon: Colonialism, Nationalism and the Politics of Space in Sri Lanka*. Delhi: Oxford University Press, 1999.

Philpott, Simon. *Rethinking Indonesia: Postcolonial Theory, Authoritarianism and Identity*. New York: St. Martin's Press, 2000.

Ramasamy, P. "The State of Social Sciences in Malaysia: A Brief Historical Overview". *Ilmu Masyarakat* 4 (1983): 67–69.

Rousseau, Jean Jacques. *Political Writings*, translated by G. D. H. Cole. Cambridge: Cambridge University Press, 1915.

Rustam A. Sani, and Norani Othman. "The Social Sciences in Malaysia". *Akademika* 38 (1991): 5–28.

Said, Edward. *Orientalism*. Hammondsworth: Penguin, 1978.

——— . *Covering Islam*. New York: Pantheon, 1981.

——— . *Culture and Imperialism*. London: Chatto, 1993.

Shamsul A. B. *From British to Bumiputera Rule: Local Politics and Rural Develoment in Peninsular Malaysia*. Singapore: Institute of Southeast Asian Studies, 1986.

——— . *Antropologi dan Modenisasi: Mengungkapkan Pengalaman Malaysia*. Professorial Inaugural Lecture. Bangi: Penerbit UKM, 1993.

——— . "Malaysia: The Kratonisation of Social Science". In *Social Science in Southeast Asia: From Particularism to Universalism*, edited by Nico S. Nordholt and Leontine Visser, pp. 87–109. Amsterdam: VU University Press, 1995a.

——— . "The State of Anthropology and Anthropology and the State in Malaysia". *Minpaku Anthropological Newsletter* (Osaka) 1, no. 1 (1995b): 5–6.

——— . "Nations-of-Intent in Malaysia". In *Asian Forms of the Nation*, edited by Stein Tonnesson and Hans Antloev, pp. 323–47. London: Curzon and Nordic Institute of Asian Studies, 1996a.

——— . "Debating about Identity in Malaysia: A Discourse Analysis". *Southeast Asian Studies* 34, no. 3 (1996b): 566–600.

——— . "The Construction and Transformation of a Social Identity: Malayness and Bumiputeraness Re-examined". *Journal of Asian and African Studies* (Tokyo) 52 (1996): 1–19.

——— . "Redefining Cultural Nationalism in Multiethnic Malaysia: A Recent Observation". *Inter-Asia Cultural Studies* 1, no. 1 (2000a): 169–71.

————— . "Ethnicity, Class, Culture or Identity? Competing Paradigms in Malaysian Studies". *Akademika* 53 (July 1998): 33–59.

————— . "Colonial Knowledge and the Construction of Malay and Malayness: Exploring the Literary Component". *Sari* 17 July (1999a): 3–17.

————— . "Identity Contestation in Malaysia: A Comparative Commentary on 'Malayness' and 'Chineseness'". *Akademika* 55 (July 1999b): 17–37.

————— . "Colonial Knowledge & Identity Formation: Literature and the Construction of Malay and Malayness". *Asian Culture Quarterly* 28, no. 1 (2000a): 49–64.

————— . "Ilmu Kolonial dan Pembinaan Fakta mengenai Malaysia". In *Masyarakat, Budaya dan Perubahan*, edited by Rahimah Aziz and Mohamed Yusoff Ismail, pp. 189–201. Bangi: Penerbit Universiti Kebangsaan Malaysia, 2000b.

————— . "Ilmu Kolonial Tunjang Pembinaan Ilmu Sains Sosial: Satu Tinjauan Kritis". *Jurnal Pengajian Umum* 1 (December 2000c): 1–16.

————— . "'Malay' and 'Malayness' in Malaysia Reconsidered: A Critical Review". *Communal/Plural* 9, no. 1 (2001a): 69–80.

————— . "Colonial Knowledge and the Shaping of Europe-Asia Relations: A Critical Evaluation". In *Asia-Europe on the Eve of the 21st Century*, edited by Suthipand Chirathivat et al., pp. 29–41. Bangkok & Singapore: Centre for European Studies, Chulalongkorn University, and Institute of Southeast Asian Studies, 2001b.

————— . "Social Science in Southeast Asia Observed: A Malaysian Viewpoint". *Inter-Asia Cultural Studies* 2, no. 2 (2001c): 177–98.

Sweeney, Amin. *A Full Hearing: Orality and Literacy in the Malay World*. Berkeley: University of California Press, 1987.

Swift, Michael G. "Malayan Politics: Race and Class". *Civilizations* 12 (1962): 237–45.

————— . *Malay Peasant Society in Jelebu*. London: Athlone, 1965.

Syed Farid Alatas. "On the Indigenization of Academic Discourse". *Alternatives* 18, no. 3 (1993): 307–38.

Syed Hussein Alatas. *The Myth of the Lazy Native*. London: Frank Cass, 1977.

Syed Naguib Al-Attas. *Preliminary Statement on the General Theory of the Islamization of the Malay-Indonesia Archipelago*. Kuala Lumpur: Dewan Bahasa & Pustaka, 1969.

Tan Chee Beng. *Bibliography on Ethnicity and Race Relations in Malaysia*. Kuala Lumpur: Institut Pengajian Tinggi, Universiti Malaya, 1992.

Tham Seong Chee. *Social Science Research in Malaysia*. Singapore: Graham Brash, 1981.

Thomas, Nicholas. *Colonialism's Culture: Anthropology, Travel and Government.* Princeton, NJ.: Princeton University Press, 1994.

Wazir Karim Jahan. *Women and Culture: Between Malay Adat and Islam.* Boulder, Colorado: Westview, 1992.

————— . "Epilogue: The 'Nativised' Self and the 'Native'". In *Gendered Fields: Women, Men, Ethnography*, edited by Diane Bell, Pat Caplan and Wazir Karim Jahan, pp. 249–51. London: Routledge, 1993.

————— . "Do Not Forget Us: The Intellectual in Indigenous Anthropology". Public Lecture, Universiti Sains Malaysia, 22 January 1994.

————— . "Introduction: Genderizing Anthropology in Southeast Asia". In *Male & Female in Developing Southeast Asia*, edited by Wazir Karim Jahan, pp. 11–74. Oxford: Berg, 1995.

————— . "Anthropology Without Tears: How a 'Local' sees the 'Local' and the 'Global'". In *The Future of Anthropological Knowledge*, edited by Henrietta Moore, pp. 115–38. London: Routledge, 1996.

Wilkinson, R. J. *Papers on Malay Subjects.* Selected and introduced by P. L. Burns. Kuala Lumpur: Oxford University Press, 1971.

Winstedt, R. W. *The Malays: A Cultural History.* Revised and updated by Tham Seong Chee. Singapore: Graham Brash, 1988.

Wolters, O. W. *History, Culture, and Region in Southeast Asian Perspectives.* Revised edition. Singapore: Institute of Southeast Asian Studies, 1999.

7

(RE)FRAMING WOMEN'S RIGHTS CLAIMS IN MALAYSIA

Maila Stivens

This chapter will explore briefly some of the dimensions of recent women's "rights" claims in Malaysia.[1] Its main focus is the complex and often tense relationships among a range of women's non-governmental organizations (NGOs), the "soft-authoritarian"[2] state, and the powerful cultural particularisms embedded in the Malaysian modernity project. Across the region, recent social transformations have seen political claims of many kinds erupting, especially a range of claims made in the language of "rights". In Malaysia, dramatic economic and political changes have produced a reshaping of the spaces within which women can act politically as gendered agents, with concerted activism relating to domestic and sexual violence. The last few years have seen a more proactive push by women's organizations, a change that one participant there has labelled a move from activism to political empowerment (Martinez 2000). In this initiative, rights claims on the state and on sections of "civil society" for a complex array of women's rights have become prominent within a wider momentum for reform, with an apparent growing willingness to make local versions of more "universal" rights claims. But, the pressures of ethno-nationalism and support for ideas about an alternative "Asian way" to becoming modern have produced especially complex terrains for such rights claims. This chapter is particularly interested in the ways in which such rights claims have been reconfigured, reframed, and reworked in the recent conjunctures, in complex dialogues with state, religion, and everyday practices.

Politics, Gender, and "Culture"

Claiming rights for women in contemporary Southeast Asia is a delicate business. Political scientist Shirin Rai suggests that, for women negotiating with authoritarian states, "the state and civil society [*sic*] are both complex terrains: fractured, oppressive, threatening [but] also providing spaces for struggle and negotiation" (1996, p. 32). Malaysia's state-driven move to modernity has produced dramatic new work, class, and political landscapes, but these transformations have not brought about the growing commitment to freedom, individualism, human rights and democracy that some commentators had predicted and hoped for.[3] Instead, there has been both a growing commitment to versions of religious and cultural particularism and a growing state authoritarianism,[4] in which the semblance of democratic legitimacy allows coercion to be used as an effective strategy by the state (Jesudason 1996, p. 128; and Means 1991). While a small section of the new middle classes[5] is involved in various reformist NGO activities, these classes are seen by key commentators such as Jesudason as constrained to an instrumental orientation to life by both the post-colonial and syncretic state (1996); the population is seen to support the ruling coalition as long as it delivers a measure of prosperity. It is suggested that political activities have often been channelled into state-sanctioned activities, with many of the prominent sites of "civil society", including the media, the universities, and Muslim religious institutions established by state design or funding (Othman 1998). Jesudason has proposed that opposition party ideologies, "the possibilities of alliance formation, the orientations and political activities of the middle classes, and the very identities of social actors" — for example, highly managed ethnic and religious identities — are refractions of

the state (1996, p. 135). While the *reformasi* (reform) movement
that arose after deputy Prime Minister Anwar Ibrahim's dismissal in
1998 mobilized some sections of the populace — although the
movement is in some disarray at the time of writing — significant
questions surround the continuing production of "compliance"
within Malaysian society. This is related in complicated ways to the
state's Islamization project since the early 1990s (see Nagata 1994; and
Camroux 1996).[6] More than twenty years ago, Clive Kessler's
pioneering study of Kelantan Islam pointed to the ways in which
Islamic discourse in Malaysia had acted as a powerful site of political
contest and a vehicle for forms of social protest (1978). His analysis
has continuing force today for understanding women's negotiations
with and within late twentieth and early twenty-first Malaysian state
and society: Islamic discourse and practice form a central locale both
of tensions within the women's movement and for reformist gender
politics. These will be discussed below.

Rodan argues usefully that contemporary political processes in
the region are better understood as the opening of political space
rather than as a struggle between "civil society" (conceived of as a
coherent entity) and state (Rodan 1996). This echoes important points
made by feminist critics of political science, who suggest that the idea
of a "civil society" pitting itself against a monolithic "state" overstates
the unitary character of both entities, from which gender relations
have often been analytically excluded — both have embodied sets of
assumptions about the political subject as male.[7] Ideas of a "state/civil
society" opposition, "state constraints," and "instrumentalist pragmatism"
offered by some of the hopeful writing on the "democratization"
process do not necessarily help in understanding how processes
producing spaces for dissent arise.[8]

Reflexive "Womanisms"/"Feminisms"

Some of the most successful women's campaigns in Malaysia have
involved intense activity by what the Filipino historian Reynaldo
Ileto has termed "scholar-activists":[9] he sees such people as playing
a pivotal role in Southeast Asian politics. Malaysian women scholar-
activists have made a number of highly reflexive explorations of the
relationships between feminist theory and practice and their own

location within global feminisms and local Malaysian activisms. This has produced a small but significant literature: a special issue of the local journal *Kajian Malaysia* devoted to "Feminism in Malaysia", edited by anthropologist Maznah Mohamad and literature scholar Wong Soak Koon (1994); and a number of articles and conference papers by Rohana Ariffin (1999), Lai (1999), Ng (1999) Ng and Chee (1996), Norani Othman (1998, 1999), Martinez (2000), and Maznah Mohamad (2001). As the *Kajian* collection noted, there has been a widespread avoidance of the term "feminist" by Malaysian women activists (Maznah Mohamad and Wong 1994). A prominent section of activists has long maintained a careful distance from "Western" "feminisms": it has eschewed what it sees as the universalist agendas of feminist global politics, and expressed grave anxiety about the derivative nature of much of women's movement's thought and action (for example, Maznah Mohamad and Wong 1994). (A prominent member of the Malaysian Sisters in Islam group, anthropologist Norani Othman [one of the editors of this book], for example, has in some public presentations argued that she prefers the term "womanist" to "feminist".). The reasons for this distancing have included a range of factors: a post-colonial wariness of the "alien" agendas of feminism(s), which has/have often been seen as the child of Western neo-colonial civilizing missions (cf. Mohanty et al. 1991); a distrust of the supposed emphasis on sexuality in "Western" feminisms, which is often construed as an anarchic sexual libertarianism (Lai 1999); and last but not least, a strategic move within a difficult political climate: in the tense relationship with a repressive state, the processes of self-censorship have worked powerfully to suppress the "too radical" in the carefully-orchestrated delicate negotiations with and within the state (Netto 1999).

These tensions have surfaced linguistically around the key terms for the political subject and object of recent campaigns and groups. Is it "woman" and/or "gender"? How are the terms "woman", "gender" and "rights" understood? Malaysian discussions in the early 1990s, for example, looked at the ways in which there were no Bahasa Malaysia terms for "woman" understood as a unitary political category (personal communication, Jomo Sundaram). Many women's organizations in Malaysia have adopted the term *Wanita* for "women", often producing neologisms based on this, such as *Tenaganita* (an organization working for women workers' rights, which combines the words *tenaga* [labour] and *wanita*) and *Puspanita* (a civil servants' organization).[10] The term "gender" was mostly adopted directly into Malay, but not without discussion of the problem of using an imported category. This question of the language within which rights claims are posed is a critical one: the Malay and Indonesian word for rights is *hak*, an Arabic term, which Ariel Heryanto has noted has a long history of usage in the region — for example, in relation to property rights: this can give it considerable legitimacy,[11] especially within Muslim circles.

The tensions about the meaning of "woman" are tied directly to the persisting disagreements within the advocacy groups about what is understood by women's "interests". Such disagreements have been deeply embedded within the cultural politics of identity, ethnicity, nationalism, and the state's Islamic modernity project. Women activists negotiating the complex contemporary Malaysian political landscape have had special problems in contending with the continuing ethnicization of Malaysian politics, with "ethnic" tensions as a constant within many women's organizations. The activists also have to contend with an elaborate body of ideas about the Asian "modern" that profoundly implicate "gender"; these include cultural contests about women's bodies and behaviour, which explicitly locate the "too modern" woman as "Western"[12] and ideas about "Asian values" and the "Asian family" which flourished in the years leading to the 1997 financial collapse.[13] Such contests have been especially acute for Malay women, who have had to negotiate a politicized Islam, within the ongoing Islamization of Malaysian society, but the contests have had an equally powerful if less overt impact on women of other ethnicities.

Histories

We have only a few sources for the history of the development of women's organizations in Malaysia. The main ones include books on the history of women in party politics by the "foreign" scholars Manderson (1980) and Dancz (1987); the special issue of the local journal *Kajian Malaysia* devoted to "Feminism in Malaysia", noted above (1994); and articles and conference papers by scholar-activists Rohana Ariffin (1999), Lai Suat Yuan (1999), Cecilia Ng (1999),

Cecilia Ng and Chee Leng Heng (1996), Patricia Martinez (2000), and Maznah Mohamad (2001).

There has been a long history of women's organizations in colonial and independent Malay(si)a working for political change, especially in anti-colonial nationalist struggles, within women's arms of parties, and in a welfarist capacity in campaigns for women's education, health and education, and around marriage and polygamy (Ng and Chee 1996). Many such organizations were strongly tied to state patronage.[14] Most writers feel that gender considerations were often subordinated to those of nationalism, ethno-nationalism, and class in much of this activity.[15]

From the 1970s, there was considerable interest in feminisms, which was given impetus by the development from the mid-1970s of a global feminist public around the United Nations Decade for Women and the world conferences on women. The influence of Indian feminists was especially marked.[16] By the mid-1980s, Malaysian women were joining women across the region in campaigning against issues such as sexual assault and domestic violence, and setting up a range of Women's Crisis Centres (WCC).[17]

The late 1980s and the 1990s saw a growing number of women's groups combining to lobby more ambitiously and proactively for policy change and action at the national and international levels. A coalition of women's organizations launched the Women's Manifesto in 1990, seeking to secure commitments from all political parties about improving the status of women in the areas of work, the law, and violence against women (Lai 1999; Martinez n.d.; and Women's Agenda for Change website, http://wa4change.tripod.com/english.htm. Malaysian women's groups were also energetically involved in the preparations for the Fourth World Conference on Women (see Jamilah Ariffin 1994) as well as the NGO Forum on Women in Beijing (http://members.xoom.com/wa4change/).

The mid-1990s also saw attempts by women's organizations to widen the issues of concern to include land, the environment, domestic workers' rights, sex workers, sexual harassment, and the wider issues of human rights, democracy, and corruption (Lai 1999; and Ng and Chee 1996).[18] A particular achievement has been the concerted campaign over nearly a decade for a Domestic Violence Act, finally resulting in its enactment in 1994, although there are continuing problems with its implementation.[19]

In 1999, a number of women's groups, in an overtly proactive move, built on the 1990 Women's Manifesto[20] to draft a detailed eleven-point document, the Women's Agenda for Change (WAC). This was presented to the government to obtain its commitment to women (see http://wa4change.tripod.com/english.htm). WAC represents a coalition of women's groups drawn from all the major ethnic groups and their respective organizations, including Jamaah Islah Malaysia (Wanita JIM), a Muslim women's organization; Sisters In Islam (SIS), a reformist women's group working for women's rights within Islam, which is discussed below; All Women's Action Society (AWAM); Persatuan Sahabat Wanita Selangor (PSWS, a support group for women workers); Malaysian Trade Union Congress (Women [sic] Section); the Women's Development Collective (WDC, a "progressive" women's group); and the Selangor Chinese Assembly Hall (Women [sic] Section). At the same time, there was an initiative to increase women's representation in Parliament, the Women's Candidacy Initiative (WCI), launched in September 1999.[21]

The history of these developments underlines the persisting themes of ethnicized division and strong subordination to the state, but it also points to the growing willingness to make more overt rights claims. The growth of the movement against violence from the mid-1980s raises some interesting questions: given the wariness about feminist agendas throughout the region, why did a number of women's advocacy organizations in Malaysia all move to campaign against violence against women at this point, mobilizing a specifically gender-based politics from within "civil society" reformism? One participant in the WCC in Penang recalls:

> I think it [WCC] was eclectic — comprising women who are both "feminists" like [academic] Rohana (Ariffin) and also elitish women who were in the earlier women's organizations in Malaysia — Pertubuhan Kaum Ibu, YWCA, etc... — who are largely very conservative and believe in the welfare mode. However, I have to say that the mood that saw to the setting up of the crisis centre was far from a benevolent [welfarist] nature — rather it was out of concern [for] what educated women saw as a neglect of women's rights and protection — children, rape,

violence, equal opportunities, etc. I see it really as an act to *assert a public space for women's issues* [my emphasis] which women saw as largely missing in Malaysia. Also remember the UN decade for women in 1985, etc, had in some ways led conservative women (the elitist group) to see some form of movement as vital. (Anonymous personal communication.)

I have suggested elsewhere that one might link the "success" of the campaigns against domestic violence to factors beyond the sheer hard work of the campaigners. It also seems likely that emerging fracture lines within the "private" sphere with massive social changes became dangerously exposed, in spite of the continuing powerful commitment to "family", not least within most of the women's movement itself (see Stivens 2002b).

Spaces

As argued below, the initiatives by the Women's Agenda for Change, and the WCI in particular, can clearly be read as overt moves to reconfigure ideas of rights within both the local and more global context of a (re)turn to rights claims within women's activism. One constituent group of the WAC, Sisters in Islam, formed in 1988, has had a large impact nationally and within feminist circles globally, with many overseas invitations and a successful workshop at the Beijing Women's Conference in 1995. A small group comprising tertiary-educated women (see SIS website), it has been part of an internationalist movement working to reclaim a social justice agenda within Islam (Wadud-Muhsin 1992). The SIS forum's stated mission is to promote the development of an Islam that recognizes equality between women and men and that adheres to the principles of justice and democracy.[22]

The group has operated through strategic submissions pressuring the government,[23] the organizing of important conferences on the Syariah law, *hudud* (Islamic criminal law) and Islam, reproductive health and women's rights, and other interventions all designed to contribute to a "more informed public debate on topical issues of concern". It is noteworthy that members have been given time and space as public intellectuals to debate important religious issues on television panel discussion shows; previously, Malaysian Muslim women were rarely given public speaking positions as religious "experts". These interventions have forcefully claimed a space within which to engage both an increasingly authoritarian state and religious authorities. The strategy of pursuing women's rights through a process of "cultural" dialogue stands in clear contrast to the "secular" approach of arguing for rights on the basis of universal claims to human rights (Norani Othman 1999). The careful positioning of the group's utterances about "rights" is especially significant. Their publications explicitly propose ideas of women's rights, citizenship and human rights, seeking to engage Malaysian society in a participatory process of "cultural" mediation. This involves finding sources for women's rights and internationally recognized human rights in the local Muslim "culture" and religious teachings, while also questioning the meanings and implications of dominant cultural norms.

Until recently, the language of "women's rights" and of the slogan "women's rights are human rights" has been far from central in the statements of aims and objectives of many NGOs, being confined to the more "radical" among them. The Sisters have been to some degree successful in reconfiguring "rights" in a complex dialogue with the state, religion, and everyday practices, even if some observers see dangers in the state co-opting their Islamic modernism. They have clearly provided a bridge across the longstanding divisions within the Malaysian women's movement between struggles for rights conceived of in more universalist terms and versions of a mediated womanism.

Aihwa Ong, herself an expatriate Malaysian anthropologist, has argued that women's activism in Malaysia and other "non-Western" countries should be based in a communitarian feminism that engages in local cultural dialogue, rather than imposing universalist claims for rights. She is highly approving of the Sisters in Islam, whom she sees as struggling for women's rights not by forming strategic partnerships with Western feminists, a strategy guaranteed to fail, but by engaging local men in (re)defining gender rights within the framework of Islamic morality, nation, and civilization (1996). As Othman herself notes, "defining [Malaysian] Muslim women's rights and freedom is a task that occurs not in isolation but on [a] complex cultural and political battleground, in the midst of acute polemical contests over Islamization, modernization and cultural relativism" (1998, p. 176).

Conclusion

The recent moves within global feminisms to pose women's rights as human rights have exposed the many definitional issues surrounding liberal ideas of rights in particular, signalling the instabilities surrounding the concept, and the inadequacies of formally juridical concepts of rights.[24] "Rights" within women's activism in Malaysia has been a slippery, elusive and highly contested term, deployed in a series of shifting meanings by a range of political actors. Goh Beng Lan has emphasized the particular interstitial location of women in Malaysia and elsewhere in the region at the borders of society, of East and West — as she notes, they are compelled to translate and reinscribe particular social imaginaries[25] of rights, citizenship, and equality from both the outside and the inside (personal communication). Constructing women as the subject of more communitarian, culturally particularist claims to rights may well resonate not only with an authoritarian anti-Western government but also with the larger populace, the "masses" of the more radical activists' perceived constituency. Activists themselves acknowledge that more modernist ideas of rights are often seen as problematic not only within the state, but beyond it as well. It is significant, nonetheless, that in spite of these concerns about the idea of rights as a "Western" import, and in spite of continuing problems with cultural particularisms, Malaysian women activists have felt increasingly willing and able to deploy "local" versions of frankly modern ideas of rights and gender equality within campaigns to advance feminist/womanist identities, including those within Islamic practices. This has been marked in the 1999 Women's Agenda for Change initiative, for example, which resonates with liberal and universalist discourses on human rights and democracy (cf. Martinez 2000), but is also apparent in the mediated interventions of the SIS. In the wake of the Anwar dismissal, Maznah Mohamad sees some willingness, too, among members of (more "conservative") Islamic women's organizations to attach themselves to ideas of democracy and justice in their opposition to the government (2002).

The class character of such NGOs may partly explain this. Most NGOs are dominated by middle-class educated women with close links to global feminist circuits, agendas, and funding. As I have argued elsewhere, Southeast Asian women's movement struggles have been increasingly linked to a "global feminist public" constructing itself around the international "women's rights are human rights" push (see Stivens 2000). One can also argue, however, that understandings of "rights" are very much a project-in-process, being constantly rescrutinized, reframed, and reworked. It is more useful, in my view, to understand such claims as locally produced and locally reinvented over a long period of time in highly particular dialogues, with a long and rich history of ideas about human rights, equality, justice, and democracy dating to the colonial period and longer. The recent campaigns by women's organizations have clearly drawn on that history. Such claims have too often been derided as "Western", but to sustain the idea that such agendas have been imposed from "outside" — a favourite argument especially of cynical authoritarian leaders — we have to ignore the long history of Malaysian women's organizations and their ongoing conversations with reformist and radical politics.

The specificities of local rights discourses and claims illustrate some of the slippages between apparently universalistic, ethical notions — which are by no means "Western" *per se*, but have long local histories — and their long-term historical reworkings in local contexts (see discussion in Stivens 2000). The strategy of mediated claims for rights also illustrates well the force of the argument that it is possible to transcend some of the polarities of the debates about universalism versus particularism and cultural relativism within global feminist politics by looking at how claims to rights are embedded in highly specific local contexts and struggles (cf. Stivens 2000).

These specificities also illustrate how processes of making rights claims have involved an ongoing reconfiguring of those ideas of rights within a fraught, delicate, and constantly shifting engagement with a repressive authoritarian state and religious authorities. The SIS project, for example, underlines the difficulties Malaysian women's groups have in finding spaces within which to lay claims effectively, and the difficulties in composing future strategies. Special problems are posed by the ways in which the ensemble of state relations manages opposition ideologies, activities, and identities. As the Penang informant who had been involved in the Women's Crisis Centre there emphasized, the tensions of working within institutions as well as trying to exert more space within the system are perpetually present: they are only too well recognized by activists, some of whom seem quite despondent in the post-*reformasi* period, in spite of the dramatic recasting of the Malaysian public that the reform movement has produced. However inadequate the implementation of actual policies about women and gender,[26] the Malaysian Government recently has paid particular lip service to modernist notions about women's rights, appointing a new minister of women's affairs, and promising women voters explicitly in public forums[27] to "look after women" (read "better than PAS"). Indeed, it would seem that the state is at present deploying gender relations as a key site for politicking, with uncertain outcomes for women's movement aims (cf. Stivens 1998a, 1998b, Maznah Mohamad 2002). The government, however, has attempted to define the "public" very much on its own terms: interventions into, contestations about, and representations of the relationships between modernity, the state, religion and women's place within them have necessarily operated within clearly delimited boundaries. The more pessimistic might feel that it is only possible, or at least strategic for Malay women at least, to contest women's place from within a very circumscribed discursive and political space, given the continuing power of neo-traditionalist versions of Islamic discourse and practice in the current political conjunctures. Within such spaces, however, the participatory processes of "cultural" mediation may on occasion be peculiarly effective in their refusal of the opposition between "universalism" and an essentialized concept of "culture".

The WAC and WCI initiatives have clearly contributed to an engendering of the democratization process surrounding *reformasi* — the outcome has been a complex dialogue between gendered rights and democracy. Many would emphasize the gains made in this process. The recent moves towards coalitions and alliances fit a common pattern in contemporary feminist practice, which is often a matter of alliances rather than of unified struggle around a universally shared interest or identity (Fraser and Nicholson 1990, p. 35). Indeed, although I have not seen the term used locally, recent developments fit very well into the emerging emphasis within global feminisms on *transversal politics* (cf. Yuval-Davis 1997) — the reconstitution of new versions of universalisms that transcend some of the old difficulties with a difference. As Yuval-Davis argues, transversal politics is based on dialogue and debate that take into account the different positioning of women (1997, p. 125).[28] "Concretely, this means that all feminist (and other democratic) politics should be viewed as a form of coalition politics in which the differences among women are recognized and given a voice" (1997, p. 126). While it is always problematic to prescribe solutions from outside, the idea of transversal politics has caused much excitement among feminists elsewhere and might well be equally appealing to the Malaysian women's movement.

Notes

1. The support of the Australian Research Council (ARC), which funded my project on "Work and Family in the New Malay Middle Classes" (1990–93) and "Public and Private: Gender and Southeast Asian Modernities" (1995–96), is gratefully acknowledged. From 1999 I have been working on a new ARC-funded project, "Inventing the Asian Family: Gender, Globalisation and Cultural Contest in Southeast Asia". I am also grateful to Lucy Healey, Goh Beng Lan, and Patricia Martinez for their advice and materials.
2. See Crouch (1996).
3. Rodan argues against the claim that the new middle classes of Southeast Asia are inherently opposed to authoritarianism (1996).
4. The powers of the executive have been incrementally increased at the expense of other centres of power, such as the legislature and judiciary; see Rahim (2000).
5. See discussion of definitional problems in Stivens (1998); and Kahn (1996).
6. Islam is the official religion of Malaysia, but the country is not an Islamic state. Article 11(1) of the Federal Constitution guarantees every Malaysian "the right to profess and practice his religion" (Nagata 1994). The Islamization process has worked at a number of levels: state funding of an Islamic think-tank in 1992, the Malaysian Institute for Islamic Understanding (IKIM) (see Nagata 1994; and Camroux 1996); growing support among some Malays for an Islamic state, Islamic banking, and Islamic industrialization (see Aidit 1993); campaigns by religious authorities against forms of entertainment and dress considered un-Islamic, including "traditional" Malay song and dance forms, and the adoption of proposals in the northeastern state of Kelantan to introduce Muslim criminal law (hudud) for Muslims and non-Muslims alike (see Norani Othman 1994, 1998).
7. A large feminist literature has provided useful deconstructions of these concepts. See Lister (1997).

8. See Rodan's discussion of the problems with "state" and "civil society" (1996).
9. Cited in Milner and Morris-Suzuki (1998).
10. This controversy was linked to a parallel one in Indonesia, where the language is very similar.
11. I am indebted to Ariel Heryanto (personal communication) for this observation.
12. See Ong (1995); Stivens (1998a, 1998b, 2002a, 2002b); cf. Kandiyoti (1991); Yuval Davis (1997); Mayer (2000); and Ranchod-Nilsson and Tétreault (2000).
13. See Milner (1998); and Kessler (1999).
14. See Tan Boon Kean and Bishan Singh's account of the role of NGOs *vis-á-vis* the state (1994).
15. See Manderson (1980); Dancz (1987); and accounts by scholar-activists Rohana Ariffin (1999) and Lai Suat Yan (1999).
16. See Omvedt (1990) for an account of the development of Indian feminist movements against violence towards women.
17. They formed a movement to combat "Violence-Against-Women" (VAW), called the Joint Action Group on Violence Against Women (JAG), setting up refuge and crisis centres. Led by mainly middle-class women, a number of new organizations to help victims of domestic violence and their children were set up: the Women's Aid Organization in Petaling Jaya (WAO, established in 1982) runs a refuge for battered women in Selangor; the Women's Crisis Centre in Penang (WCC, set up in 1985) serves as a centre for counselling, legal advice, emotional support, and temporary shelter for women and children facing crisis); and the All Women's Action Movement (AWAM) acts as a public forum on women's issues, provides education and training, and crisis counselling. In East Malaysia, parallel organizations working on violence against women include the Sabah Women Action Resource Group (established in 1987), and the Sarawak Women for Women Society (SWWS, established in 1985) (Lai 1999). Two of the most prominent organizations working on issues of violence are the Penang Women's Crisis Centre (WCC), established in 1985; and the Women's Aid Organization (WAO) in Petaling Jaya (established in 1982, when it opened Malaysia's first Women's Refuge; see http://www.wao.org.my/aboutus.htm). The WCC was developed from 1982 to 1985 by women from Universiti Sains Malaysia, the Family Planning Association of Penang, the Federation of Women Lawyers, and the Consumers Association of Penang, as well as some housewives. Today, the WCC serves as a centre for counselling, legal advice, emotional support, and

temporary shelter for women and children facing crisis. Like the WAO, the WCC serves as an advocate in terms of outreach, campaign, and lobbying to improve gender equality for women and children. Here, the staff "lend a listening ear", dispense legal advice, accompany the women to see welfare officers, make police reports, and go to court to get interim protection orders under the Domestic Violence Act (DVA) (see WCC http://www.wccpenang.org/). Besides counselling, the WCC had in May 1996 initiated the setting up of a one-stop centre for abused women and rape victims in the Penang General Hospital by training hospital staff, the police, and welfare officers to deal with traumatized women. Since then, the WCC Service team has been actively conducting gender sensitizing workshops for medical personnel in various states in Malaysia — in the northern region, east coast states, and also Johor. Marital problems and wife battery constitute the majority of the cases handled. Recently, it also campaigned on child sexual abuse. See the WCC website http://www.wccpenang.org.

18. See discussions at http://www.suaram.org/home.htm
http://www.suaram.orgttp://www.malaysia.net/aliran/hr/js6.html.

19. See discussion of problems in *Aliran Monthly*, "Women and Politics in Malaysia: An Interview with Cecilia Ng and Zaitun Kasim", at (http://www.malaysia.net/aliran/high9907.html, accessed on 16 October 2001). The UNIFEM website outlines some of the problems: (UNIFEM http://www.unifem.undp.org/trustfund/malaysia.html, accessed on 16 October 2001.).

20. In Malaysia, the Women's Manifesto was launched in 1990, prior to the general election, to secure commitments from all political parties to improve the status of women in the key concerns of work, the law, violence against women, development, health, corruption, and human rights. (Women's Development Co-operative, *As Malaysians and as Women: Questions for Our Politicians and a Manifesto for the '90s*). http://www.jim.org.my/wanita/wac/english.htm

21. This fielded a woman candidate in the tenth general election of 29 November 1999, with a platform which included issues outlined in the WAC (Martinez 2000).

22. The SIS' main objectives are:
   • to develop and promote a framework on [*sic*] women's rights in Islam which takes into consideration women's experiences and realities;
   • to eliminate injustice and discrimination against women by changing practices and values that regard women as inferior to men; and

- to create public awareness and reform laws and policies on issues of equality, justice and democracy in Islam. Advocacy for reform on issues of justice and equality is an important aspect of SIS activities (see SIS website at http:/www.muslimtents.com/ sistersinislam).

23. These relate to the Kelantan Syariah Criminal Bill (1993), the Domestic Violence Bill (1994), Islamic Family Law on Polygamy (1996), Reform of Islamic Family Law and Administration of Justice in the Syariah System (1997), and Reform of Syariah Criminal Laws (1997). The topics covered include: polygamy (1989), equality (1990), a dress code for Muslim women (1991), the Hudud Law (1993/94), domestic violence (1996), arbitrariness in implementation of Syariah criminal laws (1997), and decency in Islam: a Qur'anic view of modesty (1997). See the SIS website. The group has disseminated its views through press statements, newspaper articles, and letters in Bahasa Malaysia and English, academic writings, pamphlets on issues like dress codes and domestic violence, and also through television and other media appearances. See Norani Othman (1994, 1998, and 1999). Sisters in Islam publications include booklets in the Malay language and in English, entitled *Are Women and Men Equal Before Allah?*; *Islam and Family Planning*; *Are Muslim Men Allowed to Beat Their Wives?*; and larger publications such as Norani Othman (1994); *Islam, Gender and Women's Rights: An Alternative* (1994), and *Islam, Reproductive Health and Women's Rights*. See SIS website (http://www.muslimtents.com/sistersinislam/resources/index3.htm, accessed 1 January 2002).

24. See Ram (2000) for an Indian perspective, Jolly (2000) for a Pacific perspective, and Stivens (2000).

25. "Imaginaries" is a term denoting a complex of discourse, beliefs, ideologies, etc.

26. In 1995, Malaysia ratified the United Nations Convention on the Elimination of all Forms of Discrimination against Women (CEDAW), with a few reservations, particularly Articles 5(a) on eliminating prejudice in customs and culture, Article 7(b) on women in public life, Article 9(2) on nationality, and Article 16(a) on the minimum age for marriage. The Malaysian delegation stood with other Islamic states and the Vatican in their stand against abortion, reproductive rights, and the alleged breakdown of the nuclear family when it recorded a reservation on the resolution on reproductive rights and sexuality at the Fourth World Conference on Women (Ng and Chee 1996).

27. Statement by YB Dato' Shahrizat binte Abdul Jalil, Minister for Women and Family at the opening of the Conference on Malaysian Masculinities, Bangi, November 2001.
28. Differentiating between social identities and social values, transversal politics "assumes that... 'epistemological communities', which share common value systems, can exist across differential positionings and identities" (Yuval-Davis 1997, p. 131).

References

Aidit bin Haji Ghazali, ed. *Industrialization From an Islamic Perspective.* International Conference Proceedings, 21–22 January 1993. Kuala Lumpur: Institute of Islamic Understanding, 1993.

Amina Wadud-Muhsin. *Qur'an and Woman.* Kuala Lumpur: Penerbit Fajar Bakti, 1992.

Camroux, D. "State Responses to Islamic Resurgence in Malaysia: Accommodation, Cooption and Confrontation". *Asian Survey* 36, no. 9 (1996).

Corner, L. "Women's Participation in Decision-Making and Leadership: A Global Perspective". Paper delivered at a Conference on Women in Decision-Making in Cooperatives held by the Asian Women in Co-operative Development Forum (ACWF) and the International Co-operative Alliance Regional Office for Asia and the Pacific (ACAROAP) on 7–9 May 1997 at Tagatay City, Philippines. Also published in *"Women in Decision-Making Co-operatives: Report of a Regional Conference, 7–9 May 1997, Tagatay City, Philippines.* ACWF and ICAROAP, 1999. Bangkok: UNIFEM. Also on UNIFEM website. (http://unifem.undp.org.eseasia/TechPapers/wleaders.html, accessed on 6 October 2001).

Crouch, H. *Government and Society in Malaysia.* Sydney: Allen and Unwin, 1996.

Dancz, Virginia H. *Women and Party Politics in Peninsular Malaysia.* New York: Oxford University Press, 1987.

Fraser, Nancy, and Linda J. Nicholson. "Social Criticism without Philosophy: An Encounter between Feminism and Postmodernism". *Theory, Culture and Society* 5 (1988): 373–94. Reprinted in *Feminism/ Postmodernism,* edited by Linda J. Nicholson. New York: Routledge, 1990.

Jamilah Ariffin. *Reviewing Malaysian Women's Status: Country Report in Preparation for the Fourth UN World Conference on Women.* Population Studies Unit, University of Malaya. Kuala Lumpur, 1994.

Jesudason, J.V. "The Syncretic State and the Structure of Oppositional Politics in Malaysia". In *Political Oppositions in Industrializing Asia*, edited by G. Rodan, pp. 128–60. London and New York: Routledge, 1996.

Jolly, M. "Woman Ikat Raet Long Human Raet O No?: Women's Rights, Human Rights and Domestic Violence in Vanuatu". In *Human Rights and Gender Politics: Asia–Pacific Perspectives*, edited by A. Hilsdon, M. Macintyre, V. Mackie and M. Stivens, pp. 124–46. Routledge Advances in Asia Pacific Studies. London: Routledge, 2000.

Kahn, J. S. "Growth, Economic Transformation, Culture and the Middle Classes in Malaysia". In *The New Rich in Asia: Mobile Phones, McDonalds, and Middle Class Revolutions*, edited by R. Robison and D. S. G. Goodman, pp. 49–78. London and New York: Routledge, 1996.

Kandiyoti, D. "Identity and Its Discontents: Women and the Nation". *Millennium* 20, no. 3 (1991): 429–44.

Kessler, Clive. *Islam and Politics in a Malay State: Kelantan, 1838–1969*. Ithaca, New York: Cornell University Press, 1978.

———. "The Abdication of the Intellectuals: Sociology, Anthropology, and the Asian Values Debate — or, What Everybody Needed to Know about 'Asian Values' That Social Scientists Failed to Point Out". *Sojourn: Journal of Social Issues in Southeast Asia* 14, no. 2 (October 1999): 295–312.

———. "State and Civil Society: Global Context, Southeast Asian Prospect". *SOJOURN: Journal of Social Issues in Southeast Asia* 13, no. 1 (April 1998).

Lai Suat Yuan. "Winds of Change: The Women's Movement in Malaysia". Paper presented at the Second International Malaysian Studies Conference, 2–4 August 1999.

Lister, R. *Citizenship*. London: Sage, 1997.

Mahathir Mohamad and Shintaro Ishihara. *The Voice of Asia: Two Leaders Discuss the Coming Century*, translated by F. Baldwin. Tokyo: Kodansha International, 1995.

Manderson, Lenore. *Women, Politics, and Change: The Kaum Ibu UMNO, Malaysia 1945–1972*. Oxford: Oxford University Press, 1980.

Martinez, Patricia. "From Margin to Center: Theorizing Women's Political Participation From Activism on the Margins to Political Power at the Center". At http://www.philanthropy.org/GN/KEN/gntext/politicalrights_women_power_patricia.htm, 2000, accessed on 7 February n.d.

———. "Complex Configurations: The Women's Agenda for Change and the Women's Candidacy Initiative". Unpublished manuscript, 2001.

Mayer, T., ed., *Gender Ironies of Nationalism: Sexing the Nation*. London and New York: Routledge, 2000.

Maznah Mohamad. "Shifting Interests and Identities: The Politics of Gender, Ethnicity and Democratization in Malaysia". In *Gender Justice, Development and Rights*, edited by Maxine Molyneux and Shahra Razavi. Oxford Studies in Democratization. Oxford University Press, 2002.

Maznah Mohamad, and Wong Soak Koon, eds. "Feminism: Malaysian Critique and Experience". Special edition of *Kajian Malaysia: Journal of Malaysian Studies* 12, no. 1 and 2 (June/December 1994).

Means, G. P. *Malaysian Politics: The Second Generation*. Singapore/New York: Oxford University Press, 1991.

Milner, A. C. "What's Happened to Asian Values?" Faculty of Asian Studies, Australian National University, http://www.anu.edu.au/asianstudies/values.html, 1998 (accessed on 6 October 2001).

Milner, A. C., and T. Morris-Suzuki. "The Challenge of Asia". In *Knowing Ourselves and Others: The Humanities in Australia into the 21st Century*, Volume 3, pp. 113–28. Canberra: Australian Research Council, 1998.

Mohanty, Chandra Talpade, Ann Russo, Lourdes Torres, eds. *Third World Women and the Politics of Feminism*. Bloomington: Indiana University Press, 1991.

Nagata, J. *The Reflowering of Malaysian Islam: Modern Religious Radicals and their Roots*. Vancouver: University of British Columbia Press, 1984.

Nagata, J. A. "How to be Islamic Without Being an Islamic State". In *Islam, Globalisation and Post-modernity*, edited by Akbar Ahmed, and Hastings Donnan. London and New York: Routledge, 1994.

Netto, Anil. "Academics Speak Out At Their Own Risk". Institute of Policy Studies, 16 June 1999. Asia Times Online at http://www.atimes.com/se_asia/AF16Ae01.html (Alternative: http://www.hartford_hwp.com/archives/54/126.html, written 9: 03 p.m., 14 June 1999 by newsdesk in cdp:ips.english, accessed on 3 January 2002.

Ng, Cecilia, ed., *Positioning Women in Malaysia: Class and Gender in An Industrializing State*. Foreword by Swasti Mitter. Basingstoke: Macmillan, 1999.

Ng, Cecilia, and Chee Heng Leng. "Women in Malaysia: Present Struggles and Future Directions." *Asian Journal of Women's Studies* 2 (1996).

Norani Othman. "The Sociopolitical Dimensions of Islamization in Malaysia: A Cultural Accommodation or Social Change?" In *Shari'a Law and the Modern Nation-State: A Malaysian Symposium*, edited by Norani Othman. Kuala Lumpur: Sisters in Islam Forum, 1994.

————. "Islamization and Modernization in Malaysia: Competing Cultural Reassertions and Women's Identity in a Changing Society".

In *Women, Ethnicity and Nationalism*, edited by R. Wolford and R. L. Miller, pp. 170–92. London and New York: Routledge, 1998.

————— . "Grounding Human Rights Arguments in Non-Western Culture: Shari'a and the Censorship Rights of Women in a Modern Islamic State". In *The East Asian Challenge for Human Rights*, edited by J. R. Bauer and D. B. Bell, pp. 169–92. Cambridge: Cambridge University Press, 1999.

Omvedt, Gail. *Violence Against Women: New Movements and New Theories in India*. New Delhi: Kali for women, 1990.

Ong, Aihwa. "State Versus Islam: Malay Families, Women's Bodies and the Body Politic". In *Bewitching Women, Pious Men: Gender and Body Politics in Southeast Asia*, edited by Aihwa Ong and Michael Gates Peletz. Berkeley: University of California Press, 1995. (Updated version of "State Versus Islam: Malay Families, Women's Bodies and the Body Politic", *American Ethnologist* 17, no. 2 [May 1990]: 28–42).

————— . "'Strategic Sisterhood' or Sisters in Solidarity? Questions of Communitarianism and Citizenship in Asia". *Indiana Journal of Global Legal Studies* 4 (1997): 107–35.

Rahim, L."Economic Crisis and the Prospect for Democratization in Southeast Asia". *Journal of Southeast Asia* (March 2000).

Rai, Shirin. "Women and the State in the Third World". In *Women and Politics in the Third World*, edited by H. Afshar. Routledge, 1996.

Ram, K. "The State and the Women's Movement: Instabilities in the Discourse of 'Rights' in India." In *Human Rights and Gender Politics: Asia–Pacific Perspectives*, edited by A. Hilsdon, M. Macintyre, V. Mackie and M. Stivens, pp. 60–82. Routledge Advances in Asia Pacific Studies. London: Routledge, 2000.

Ranchod-Nilsson, S., and M.A. Tétreault, eds., *Women, States and Nationalism: At Home in the Nation*. London and New York: Routledge, 2000.

Robison, R., and D. S. G. Goodman, eds. *The New Rich in Asia: Mobile Phones, McDonalds and Middle Class Revolutions*. London and New York: Routledge, 1996.

Rodan, G., ed. *Political Oppositions in Industrializing Asia*. London: Routledge, 1996.

Rohana Ariffin. "Feminism in Malaysia: A Historical and Present Perspective of Women's Struggles in Malaysia". *Women's Studies International Forum*, July–August 1999.

Searle, P. *The Riddle of Malaysian Capitalism*. Sydney: Allen and Unwin/ Honolulu: University of Hawai'i, 1999.

Stivens, M. "Introduction: Theoretical Perspectives on Sex and Power in Affluent Asia". In *Gender and Power in Affluent Asia*, edited by K. Sen and M. Stivens. London: Routledge, 1998a.

———— . "Sex, Gender and the Making of the Malay Middle Class". In *Gender and Power in Affluent Asia*, edited by K. Sen and M. Stivens. London: Routledge, 1998b.

———— . "Introduction: Gender Politics and the Reimagining of Human Rights in the Asia Pacific". In *Human Rights and Gender Politics: Asia–Pacific Perspectives*, edited by A. Hilsdon, M. Macintyre, V. Mackie, and M. Stivens, pp. 1–36. Routledge Advances in Asia Pacific Studies. London: Routledge, 2000.

———— . "The Hope of the Nation: State, Religion and Modernity in the Construction of Teenagerhood in Contemporary Malaysia". In *Coming of Age in South and Southeast Asia: Youth, Courtship and Sexuality*, edited by L. Manderson and P. Liamputtong Rice, pp. 188–206. NIAS Studies in Asian Topics, 30. London: Curzon, 2002a.

———— . " 'Gendering Asian Exceptionalism: 'Public', 'Private' and Asian Modernities". In *East Asian Capitalism: Conflicts, Growth, and Crisis*, edited by Luigi Tomba. Milan: Annali della Fondazione, Giangiacomo Feltrinelli Editore, 2002b.

Tan Boon Kean and Bishan Singh. *The Role of NGOs in Development: Malaysian Case Study.* Kuala Lumpur: Gender and Development (GAD) Programme, Asian and Pacific Development Centre, 1994.

Weiss, M. L. "What Will Become of *Reformasi*? Ethnicity and Changing Political Norms in Malaysia". *Contemporary Southeast Asia* 21, no. 3 (December 1999).

Women's Agenda for Change website, 1995, http://wa4change.tripod.com/english.htm, accessed on 1 October 2001.

Yuval-Davis, N. *Gender and Nation.* London: Sage, 1997.

8

ISLAM, MODERNITY, AND THE POPULAR IN MALAYSIA

JOEL S. KAHN

Introduction: The Paradoxes of an Anthropology of the Malays

The anthropology of the Malays soon runs up against a paradox, even a contradiction, that seems irresolvable, at least within the parameters of the discipline. On the one hand, during the last thirty years at least, Malaysia has become more and more like the Western societies that gave birth to the discipline of anthropology in the first place. However we choose to characterize these changes — as industrialization, urbanization, bureaucratization, commodification, globalization, modernization, and so forth — Malaysia seems increasingly to have become "just like the West". The judgement of Claude Levi-Strauss, on first taking up his Chair at the College de France, seems especially pertinent to the case of the anthropology of Malaysia:

> The character of ethnographic investigation is undoubtedly changing as the small savage tribes we used to study disappear, merging into vaster groups in which problems tend to resemble

our own ... A sound scientific attitude would not seek to
develop ethnology where its method is mixed with other
methods, where its object is confused with other objects
(Levi-Strauss 1987, pp. 25–26)

To those who object that since Levi-Strauss uttered this critique
of "ethnology... in a diluted state", the discipline has acquired an
admirable record of coping with the study of modern society, one
can only point to a continuing impression among colleagues that
conducting anthropology in Malaysia is still somehow illegitimate,
if not downright boring, when compared to ethnographic research
in more exotic locales. In fact, it seems that the most successful
ethnographic accounts of Malays in recent years have been those
that have managed to demonstrate the "persistence" of a profound
otherness, even in the midst of a nation undergoing rapid
agricultural and industrial development. When such constructions
are absent, it seems that at least Western audiences, especially those
with a taste for anthropological writing, are simply not very
interested.

    Yet at the same time, as its social landscape has become
increasingly familiar, even mundane from the perspective of
Westerners in search of the exotic, the Malay community in Malaysia
has developed into a site of a self-exoticizing discourse that, while it
has its parallels elsewhere in the world, may be among the supreme
cases of "othering" discourses in the modern world. While most
non-Malaysians may come to know of this phenomenon primarily
through the widely-reported pronouncements of Malaysia's colourful
Prime Minister, Dr Mahathir Mohamad, any outsider who attempts
to carry out research on contemporary Malay culture and society will
soon find that, in this, Mahathir is otherwise entirely unexceptional,
particularly among those who choose to identify themselves as both
ethnic Malays and Muslims. A non-Malay, particularly a non-Muslim,
outsider will not have to spend very long in the company of
'ethnic' Malays before he or she is subjected to at least a gentle
reminder, and as frequently a diatribe, on the differences between
Muslim Malays and Westerners. The Malays are a community quite
literally obsessed with their own uniqueness with respect to a
godless, cultureless, but nonetheless imperialist "West". The self-

exoticizing tendency on the part of Malay Muslims with respect to Westerners sits very easily inside Malaysia as well, for Malaysia is a place where ethnic and religious identities are almost always the first thing anyone wants to know about someone else, whether that other is a fellow Malaysian of a different racial/ethnic/religious group, or a foreigner.

There have been, as might be expected, different ways of dealing with this paradox. Most frequently, observers of contemporary Malaysia downplay or even deny one side or the other of the contradiction. As implied above, there are those who have attempted to maintain the exoticism of Malaysia in spite of its recent modernization, sometimes arguing that the "otherness" of, particularly, Malay culture has "persisted" in spite of the "penetration" of capitalist agriculture and industrialism and the proletarianization of Malay workers (cf. Ong 1987; and Scott 1985). By contrast, a growing number of observers dismiss the self-exoticizing arguments about the uniqueness of Asian/Malay/Islamic values, seeing in all such talk a mere smokescreen thrown up by an authoritarian regime, eager to conceal its "real" instrumental projects of hegemony, surveillance, and exploitation (cf. Robison, 1996).

Yet to suppress the terms of the paradox in this way is, perhaps, inevitably to present a unidimensional and hence unsatisfactory account, particularly of everyday life in contemporary Malaysia. One cannot ignore the extent to which all of Malaysian culture and society are experiencing processes that are global and not purely local, even when they are couched in localizing and/or traditionalizing imagery. Yet, to take the opposite view, to dismiss peremptorily all claims to Malay uniqueness is also problematic. The solution is to produce analyses that retain both sides of the paradox. It is precisely because Clive Kessler — in his own writings, and importantly also in his personal and intellectual relations with Malays and other Malaysians over more than thirty years of researching Malay culture, society, and religion — has been more successful than any other anthropologist of the Malays in keeping this paradox constantly in frame as it were, that it becomes appropriate to place it at the centre of a piece written in his honour. I can only hope he appreciates the effort, if not the actual result, of such an exercise.

Exemplary and Popular Modernism

The so-called Asian economic crisis of 1997 gave added impetus to the argument advanced by liberals and left critics alike that Asian uniqueness was a mirage. Francis Fukuyama concluded, for example, that what "the current crisis will end up doing is to puncture the idea of Asian exceptionalism." Going further, Diane Coyle asserted that the crisis would "finally lay to rest this unquestioning worship of Asian values ... capitalism in its free-wheeling, Anglo-Saxon variety is coming into its own" (both cited in Milner 2000). I do not propose here to enter into this long-standing debate for and against Asian exceptionalism directly. Instead, the discussion that follows takes as its starting point a problem in all such accounts, that is, that they are presented and present themselves as philosophical debates, abstracted entirely from the contexts within which they are framed and uttered. What is being called for, in other words, is a shift in the focus of the so-called Asian values debate away from the existing concentration on abtract/analytic argument towards an examination of the context within which the argument takes place.

The argument that "Asian values" need to be embedded firmly in social and historical contexts amounts to somewhat more than the traditional anthropological plea for "emic" analysis. Instead, we need to go beyond the so-called "emic/etic" distinction altogether in the sense that all contributions to the debate on Asian exceptionalism must be considered to be "emic" and "etic" at the same time. This must be the case if one presumes, as I do, that analyses of meaningful social behaviour that does not place that meaning at the heart of the analysis is ultimately sterile, that is, that it fails even in its own terms. Put more crudely, the question of whether Asia is exceptional or not cannot be answered even analytically unless we engage with the meaning given by Asians to their own social behaviour. For the question of Malaysian exceptionalism is, at base, ultimately a cultural one — it asks whether social behaviour is, or is based on, the cultural orientations of liberalism, the sovereign consumer, or not.

This is, at least implicitly, accepted by Fukuyama and others when they argue against Asian exceptionalism from the standpoint, not of a set of liberal principles valid for all places and all times, but from the "fact" of a particular historical development (call it modernization) as a consequence of which such principles become valid. What makes Asia unexceptional for Fukuyama, in other words, is the fact that it has recently experienced an (unexceptional) trajectory of historical change that makes it so, a change marked in the final instance by the economic crisis of the late 1990s.

Recognizing the embeddedness of the debate over Malay exceptionalism can lead us in somewhat different directions. It might be, for example, that it leads us to examine the contextual dimensions of the positions of people such as Fukuyama and Mahathir. Within the debate itself, this is the tack most commonly taken: each side denouncing the other for its own, context-dependent motivations. A Mahathir is as likely to attack Fukuyama for his imperial designs as a Fukuyama is to point to Mahathir's underlying authoritarian impulses. However, what is at issue here is less the possibly instrumental motives of exemplary figures such as Fukuyama and Mahathir, but more the problem of whether Malay culture and society, more broadly, is or is not exceptional, a consequence perhaps of the questions posed above about the proper framing of the project on an anthropology of the Malays. Therefore, we would do well to investigate popular rather than exemplary narratives of modernity.

As I have discussed elsewhere, it might be argued that this is the proper task of an anthropology of modernity (Kahn 2001). In turn, such embedded/ethnographic accounts of modernization might allow us to pose the question of Malay uniqueness in a fresh way. For this reason, it is instructive to turn from the claims of political and intellectual élites towards more widely shared discourses on Malay exceptionalism. Mahathir, of course, in the tradition of both anthropology and exemplary modernist discourse more broadly, claims to speak for Malays as a group or nation. Yet those who deny his assertion of the uniqueness of the cultural identity of Malays, or of the trajectory of modernization in Malaysia, ignore the possibility that such pronouncements do in fact resonate more widely in contemporary Malaysian society. Ignoring the meanings that self-identifying Malays place on their experiences results only in empty and sterile analyses that ultimately tell us little about how Malaysians have reacted, and are likely to react in future, to changes in their circumstances (cf. Milner 2000).

I am not proposing to produce an inventory of the ways in which the economic, political, and social changes that have taken place during the last three decades of intensive modernization in Malaysia do, and do not, diverge from those anticipated within the modernizing metanarratives of a Fukuyama or a Coyle (or, for that matter, within the relativizing narratives of a Mahathir). The story of Malaysian modernization, particularly since the effects of state-led policies of industrialization and social reconstruction, classified under the heading of the New Economic Policy (NEP), began to make a mark in the early 1970s, does not need retelling here. It is enough to note that economic growth over a period of almost three decades, punctuated by brief downturns in the early 1980s, and more recently during the Asian financial crisis of 1997, has been consistently high and that this has been accompanied by changes in most of the social and cultural indicators that are typically associated with modernization and development. The economic developments and "restructuring" that followed from the early 1970s were to have a very significant impact especially on the Malay villages, which up to then had been considered, by ethnographers and Malay nationalists alike, to be the *locus classicus* of Malay society and culture.

These changes generated in turn significant upheavals in the lives of all Malaysians: the emergence of wage labour as the "quasi-universal form of distribution" for all "ethnic" groups, to borrow a term coined to describe the effects of late capitalism in Europe (see Sulkunen 1992); a substantial increase in the relative size of what sociologists are wont to call (problematically) the new middle class (cf. Kahn 1996); and a substantial growth in the size, functions and modernizing mission of the Malay-dominated state, as well as a transformation of all the predominantly communal political parties into organizations of full-time professional politicians. There have been parallel shifts in the cultural/religious landscape. Like Lisa Rofel in China, we found in doing research among a wide range of Malays — rural and urban, middle and working class — that modernity "was something that many people from all walks of life felt passionately moved to talk about and debate" (Rofel 1999, p. xi). However, such eagerness was tempered by a rising ambivalence towards "Western-style" modernization, a concern with the possible loss of cultural, moral, and spiritual values among most "ethnic" Malays. For this is the period of what is usually labelled "religious revivalism", in politics and in Malay society more widely, but which might be more accurately termed a new phase of modernist Islamization of both state and society (cf. Hussin Mutalib 1993, pp. x–xi) (with significant parallels in other Malaysian religions).

This simplified story of Malaysian modernization suggests the possibility of significant changes in the experiences of most Malaysians in the last few decades, but on its own in no way forecloses on the ways in which these experiences have been construed by those who identify themselves as Malays. Whether these experiences should be taken to mark the end of Malay exceptionalism, the triumph of "Anglo-Saxon capitalism", or the (continued) uniqueness of Malay life despite (or even because of) modernization is a question yet to be answered.

In attempting to answer the question of how Malays, or at least some Malays, have construed the implications of Malaysian patterns of change, an interesting point of departure can be found in contemporary changes in Malay popular culture, and in popular music and performance in particular.

Malay Muslims in the Popular Imagination

The popular success of *nasyid* musical groups in the late 1990s appears to mark a break with earlier popular musical forms that have their origins in the (late) colonial period. *Nasyid* describes a particular style of popular music, pioneered by the male singing group, Raihan (Arabic: heavenly scent). In key respects, consciously modelled on British and American boy and girl bands, typically consisting of four performers singing *a capella*-style songs and ballads, *nasyid* groups have been given a distinctive Islamic image — adopting a global form of Islamic dress and singing inspirational songs which, at least on the surface, avoid reference to sex and love in favour of positive Islamic sentiments. Lyrics such as "Let us find a way to know our God, feel the tortures of hell fire" are typical of Raihan songs.[1] Lisa Muhamad, a member of Huda, an all-female *nasyid* group, told a journalist: "Basically, the message is to love

Allah and instill good values in our children so they will be good citizens".[2]

In many ways, the emergence of *nasyid* music is typical of any other development in the contemporary popular music industry in Malaysia. New songs, groups, and styles emerge and disappear as rapidly as they do in the West. Consumers come across new songs on the radio and television, and buy compact discs (CDs) to be played at home, and the market for popular music is extremely dynamic. However, although there is space here only to examine the contention briefly, it can be argued that, for all that it can be seen to be just a case of the most recent fashion in popular music, and that it is likely to be as short-lived as any other. Nevertheless, there are certain senses in which *nasyid* testifies to a radical change in popular musical styles, and also in the self-perceptions of ordinary Malays.

It can be argued that modern "Malayness" was more or less invented, not so much by Muslim theologians and nationalist intellectuals during the colonial period, as is often argued (cf. Roff 1967; and Milner 1995), but more, at least as far as popular meanings are concerned, by the far less "exemplary" creators of the modern popular entertainment industry, which gradually but effectively replaced both more traditional forms of entertainment and localized ritual systems within which the popular meanings of Malayness had previously been constituted. A key development in the rise of modern notions of Malayness during the colonial period then becomes, not so much the development of "print capitalism" (cf. Anderson 1983), but that of the popular culture industries, and particularly the cinema.

The emergence of the Malay-language cinema, and its penetration into the Malay-dominated areas of the peninsula, was pioneered by Shaw Brothers in Singapore. Although others had attempted to make films for Malay audiences, Shaw Brothers came to dominate the market, both because it proved the most successful at tapping into the market for Malay themes in Malay-language films and, equally importantly, because it came to dominate the distribution of films through its control of movie houses throughout the peninsula. Without doubt, it was the musical films starring, and subsequently also directed by, the Penang-born musician P. Ramlee that came most closely to be identified with "Malay culture" in the minds of the Malay movie-going public.

This is not the place for a detailed look at the Ramlee phenomenon, nor at the discourses of Malayness constructed in and through his films.[3] However, Ramlee constitutes a useful baseline from which to explore more recent expressions of popular constructions of Malayness, such as those manifest in the *nasyid* phenomenon. Raihan, the first and still the best known *nasyid* group, enjoyed significant commercial success after being signed on and promoted by Warner Records in 1997. Their first album sold 600,000 copies in Malaysia, and over a million copies when overseas sales are taken into account.[4] According to some, the profits generated by Raihan and Huda rescued Warner Music in Malaysia, which had been hit badly by the 1997 financial crisis. The success of Raihan and Huda prompted most record labels in Malaysia to create their own *nasyid* groups in the late 1990s.

Like other popular musical forms, *nasyid* performances appear regularly on television. As a consequence, the visual dimensions of performance are equally, if not more, important than the audio, just as in the West. At a television spectacular in 1999, Raihan was awarded the music industry prize for best vocal group in Malaysia, as well as an award in the specially-created category of Islamic music, and their clips are regularly seen on television music programmes. In addition to seeing the televised video clips, fans of popular music in Malaysia will also consume performances visually at home because of the tremendous popularity of the video compact disc (VCD), which has almost completely replaced the cassette tape, and competes strongly with audio CDs in all CD outlets. Just as in the West, there is a wide array of fan magazines, as well as stories and photographs that appear widely in the popular press.

Because of the strongly "Islamic" nature of their image and message, *nasyid* groups appeal primarily, although not solely, to an ethnically-Malay audience, given the close association in Malaysia between Malayness and Islam. Their lyrics are mainly sung in Malay, with a liberal admixture of Arabic words and phrases, and the lyrics and the video clips that accompany them address Muslim themes explicitly. Like other manifestations of Malay popular culture, *nasyid* is completely silent on the diversity, particularly the religious diversity, of Malaysian society.[5] There are also musical similarities and parallels in instrumentation between *nasyid* music and broader currents of popular

Malay music. The influences on the most popular Malay singer and
musician of the modern period, P. Ramlee, were in no sense purely
indigenous to Malaya. Instead, Ramlee was heavily influenced by
Latin and American jazz. Nonetheless, the addition of elements from
Middle Eastern, Indian and Malay-Indonesian musical traditions makes
Ramlee's music recognizably Malaysian.[6] *Nasyid*, like other Malaysian
popular musical forms, draws on elements that have come to constitute
Malay pop, many of which were laid down by an earlier generation
of popular musicians in Malaysia.

    Nasyid obviously differs from early Malay pop too. For example,
while Ramlee's music, as opposed to his films, was probably mainly
designed to be listened to on the radio or the gramophone, Raihan
performances are clearly designed to be seen (on television, or in
popular VCDs and karaoke format).[7] Audiences in the late colonial
period would also have had ample opportunity to watch Ramlee's
musical performances because most of his films contained musical
interludes — the difference here lying in the collective nature of
audience behaviour for Ramlee music, as opposed to the more
privatized ways in which audiences nowadays consume television,
CDs, music videos, and video discs.

    There are also potentially significant differences between earlier
Malay pop and *nasyid* music, which testify to a hardening of the group
and genre boundaries established in earlier popular musical forms, and
thus a stronger adherence, at least in the Malay popular imagination,
to visions of Asian exceptionalism. The most striking of these is the
centrality of Islamic imagery in the whole *nasyid* phenomenon. It
would be wrong to suggest, for example, that Islam was not also a
significant part of the Ramlee image. Here religious ideas seem to be
inextricably bound up with symbols of Malayness, a good example
being dress. There is no mistaking the fact that Ramlee is, in most of
his films, a Malay, because he is wearing clothing that clearly signals
this fact. Raihan and Huda performers, on the other hand, wear
clothes that would never have been seen in Malay villages in Ramlee's
time. Their clothing styles are, at least read in contemporary Malaysia,
Islamic or even Middle Eastern, not Malay.

    Similarly, in late twentieth century Malaysia, most Muslims believe
that Islam encourages sexual segregation, and that it is this (rather
than the influence of all girl and boy bands in the West) that determines

that *nasyid* groups are always single sex. By contrast, most of Ramlee's musical performances involved males and females, as singers and dancers. Dancing, particularly women performing what Malay Muslims now think of as provocative dances, is completely absent from the *nasyid* clips.[8] Once again, the absence of dancing in Raihan videos may in part be due to the influence of the particular Western boy bands that inspired their creation. However, in Malaysia, this absence of "Western" dance forms is also seen to stem from Islam, whereas dancing in the clips of more recent groups is clearly intended to be viewed as if it were a classical Islamic dance form.

Another way in which *nasyid* performance parts company with mainstream Malay pop is in its landscaping. Ramlee, for example, almost always performed on film against the background of the Malay village, or *kampong*, its presence signalled by Malay houses, rice fields, tropical vegetation, and the like. Such an identifiably Malay landscape is rarely present in *nasyid* clips. Instead, when there is a landscape portrayed, it is more often intended to be a generic Islamic one, by which I mean that scenes of desert and barren hills, that most Malaysian viewers would identify as Middle Eastern, are projected behind the singers.

One might want also to argue that this Islamization of Malay popular cultural forms has served to accentuate existing divisions between Malays and the West, but also between Malays and other Malaysians. Although Malays are not the only Muslims in Malaysia, Islam has nonetheless always been a major factor distinguishing Malays from non-Malays. Indeed, adherence to the Islamic faith is part of the constitutional definition of Malayness. The perception, incidentally one that is shared by many Malaysians and outside observers of the Malaysian social landscape, that the nation has become more Islamic since the revivalist *dakwah* movements of the 1970s, signifies for some a hardening of the line between Malays and non-Malays. Given that this is a view expressed by some non-Malays who see, in the rise of Islamism, whether among government supporters or adherents of the most successful opposition party, an even greater threat to their rights as citizens in the future, then there is at least support at the phenomenological level for the argument that the system of antagonistic race relations forged in the late colonial period has continued to plague Malaysian society at the end of the twentieth century.

All this leads to the conclusion that the assertions of some Western observers that the historical processes of modernization, globalization, and commodification have resulted in the "triumph" of Western economic and political values, are misleading because, at least at the level of popular imagination, Malays are radically "exceptional". Indeed, that exceptionalism, at least in Malay-targetted popular culture, is, if anything, stronger than ever. One could certainly not argue that the *nasyid* phenomenon testifies to the rise in the popular imagination of liberal notions of civil society, or of the notion of a pan-Malaysian citizenry (*bangsa Malaysia*) so fondly hoped for by at least some members of Malaysia's own political élite. On the contrary, the Islamization of popular subjectivity, and of the political process in general, appears to violate principles basic to both Western liberal and republican traditions. The Malay–Muslim, constituted in local readings of *nasyid*, is no less "exceptional" than the Malay–Muslim represented in Ramlee's films. Indeed, they seem to be more so, given the degree of self-consciousness involved in the former. One might, as a consequence, argue that self-exoticization with respect to the West is stronger in the later period.

However, does the popularity of *nasyid* testify to a simple quantitative increase in Malay cultural exceptionalism? We have already had occasion to note the divergence between "Western" liberal and republican discourses of universal citizenship and of the separation between public and private, religious and secular life and those promoted through *nasyid* culture. This, however, does not mean that *nasyid* can be read as evidence of a rejection of non-Muslim, non-Malay Malaysians or of "the West" *tout court*. Indeed, in certain ways, *nasyid* allows a greater engagement with certain aspects of non-Malay and "Western culture" than did the Ramlee phenomenon.

This is manifest first in the relationships necessarily forged with youth culture in Malaysia and more broadly by the appearance of *nasyid* on the popular music scene. At the same time, as one can point to continuities in the exclusiveness of popular constructions of Malayness in the examples discussed here, it is also possible to see, through the example of *nasyid* music, evidence of a significant change in popular racial imaginaries in contemporary Malaysia. First, we could say that the Islamic subject, constructed in and through a cultural phenomenon such as *nasyid*, differs from Ramlee's Malay subject, not so much because one is more or less Islamic than the other, but because the former is primarily an urban and middle-class subject, while the latter is a member of a subaltern peasantry. In the Ramlee films, most of the individual heroes, and the kampong republic as a collective hero, is a salt of the earth peasant, a poor but honest man who battles against his physical urges, and also against untamed nature, aristocratic privilege and the like, to win through in the name of Malay virtue. The heroes and heroines of *nasyid*, epitomized in the images projected by the singers, are clean-cut, expensively dressed (if in Islamic rather than Western designer labels), educated, modern urbanites, members of the Malay middle classes resisting the (Western-style) temptations of urban life (sex, alcohol, drugs) through self-control and adherence to their religious faith, providing advice to a target audience composed of young people facing the classical dilemmas of the young urban middle classes. Indeed, although audience research is difficult to come by, it is likely that this describes the social profile of the large majority of consumers of *nasyid* music, just as it describes the main consumers of popular music more generally.

From this perspective, the culture of a *nasyid* performance is just as exclusive of Malaysian others as that of a Ramlee production. The two are completely silent about their others — non-Malay/non-Muslim Malaysians. However, it would be a mistake to treat *nasyid* as if it were an isolated musical style dominating the market for popular entertainment in the same way as Ramlee did in the late colonial period. *Nasyid* music is instead part of a much larger market for popular music that, by contrast with that for Malay films in the 1950s, is also characterized by significant diversity. It is diverse over time in the sense that popular musical styles change as fast in Malaysia as they do anywhere else. The rise of *nasyid* to the top of the pop charts followed a succession of other diverse musical styles — ethnic music, global music, heavy metal, Cantonese pop, Indian film music, local rap and hip-hop groups, dance music, and so forth, and its dominance of the market will doubtless be as short-lived as these others.[9] *Nasyid*, even at the height of its popularity, moreover, was merely one of a multitude of style niches in the popular music scene, each with its own dedicated band of followers. In one sense tribalistic, modern popular music also forces fans of particular genres into an acknowledgement that they are part of a wider if fragmented audience for popular music. Indeed, fans of each particular genre construct themselves precisely in opposition to others. There is, therefore, a shared sense among fans of popular music that in spite of the diversity of genres and associated styles — both over time, and at any point in time — they are also members of a more inclusive group of young urbanites with a taste for popular culture. There is evidence in contemporary Malaysia that the middle class urban youth especially identify themselves through popular music as a group distinct from others — older people, consumers of high culture, villagers, traditionalists (such as fans of Chinese opera or traditional Malay music and dance), and the like. In other words, although it may not always be expressly acknowledged, there is a growing sense of a generalized youth culture, particularly in Malaysian cities, that may be segmented according to the diverse and changing tastes in particular musical styles, but which as a whole differs in important ways from others who tend to be portrayed as rather old-fashioned, wedded to rural traditions, and the tastes of an older generation. There is a sense, therefore, that fans of *nasyid* music, provided they are members of this generation, will not be seen in exclusivist terms, since they are part of this more general category of young, urban Malaysians interested in contemporary popular music with all its diversity of styles, a sensibility nurtured by the popular culture industries through the sale of recordings, but also by youth fashion, magazines, television shows, and the like. The signs are that the formation of this intensely commercialized Malaysian youth culture draws on somewhat earlier traditions of youth alienation and protest.[10] This background still exists, to a certain extent, but it has been largely harnessed and repackaged by commercial publishers, record companies and so on, in ways entirely familiar to observers of the late twentieth century popular music scene in the West.

The nature of this youth market is, perhaps, thrown into relief by the growth of a nostalgic market for Ramlee films and music videos. These too are freely available in music shops throughout Malaysia, they have reached a fairly large audience, and Ramlee has been promoted by the government, eager to discover icons of Malay excellence. Yet young urbanites, including young Malays, are not particularly interested in the Ramlee revival, associating it with the interests of an older generation. A number of people have commented that Ramlee's appeal is limited to members of an older generation nostalgic for the old days, a time when, it is supposed, Malays led a simple village life, when the demands of religious leaders were less harsh, and when, one might surmize, the majority of Chinese Malaysians were forced to take a back seat in the political arena and in the creation of a national culture.

The growth in the generalized idea of a Malaysian urban youth culture, which includes the *nasyid* phenomenon, therefore implies a subtle but nonetheless significant shift in the patterns of racialization in popular Malaysian discourse. *Nasyid* music and performances, in other words, may manifest the same silences about the racial and cultural diversity found in Ramlee's work, but Malaysian youth culture, of which it forms a part, certainly does not. To hold a concept of youth culture is inevitably to acknowledge diversity within it, and hence explicitly to recognize that Malaysia is a multiracial society. This is more generally true of the Islamic, as opposed to the Malay, understanding of identity in contemporary Malaysia. As a number of observers have pointed out, adherence to Islam under current circumstances in fact implies a recognition of the existence of non-Muslims. It can even be argued that Islam provides a model for co-existence among peoples of different religious faiths (see Hussin Mutalib 1993). Certainly, part of the Islamic revival in Malaysia has involved attention to the terms under which non-Muslims should be accommodated within the political process: through the promotion by influential Islamist intellectuals of so-called civilizational dialogues; to attempts (so far not very successful) to forge alliances between Muslim and non-Muslim opposition parties; to the working through of the implications of the imposition of Islamic law in the northeastern states governed by the opposition Islamic party, Parti Islam SeMalaysia (PAS).

It is not possible to argue in all this that formulae satisfactory to Muslims and non-Muslims have been worked out yet. However, the problem of the racial diversity of Malaysia's citizens, and by extension also of the peoples of the world, is increasingly on the agenda, and the complete silence about non-Malays, manifest in expressions of Malay cultural nationalism from the late colonial period, is perhaps gone forever.

What might be said of the new relations established through the popular culture industry between Malays and non-Malays in

Malaysia also applies at a global level. As one might expect, there is a global dimension to *nasyid* music, and to middle-class Islamic culture in Malaysia more generally, that is absent in the Ramlee phenomenon. Recognition of the globality of particular musical genres further contributes to the opening up of popular tastes to the possibility of diversity. The ways in which the image of *nasyid* groups is constructed, and the ways in which that image is interpreted, as we have seen, implies identification with modern Muslims throughout the world. The contrast with Ramlee here is very striking. Ramlee films and songs are explicitly addressed to the nation, the audience being reminded of the importance of loyalty to God, country and nation (*Tuhan, negara, bangsa*). By contrast, reference to the nation is almost entirely absent in *nasyid*, the listening and viewing subject of *nasyid* performance always being first and foremost a member of a non-national, hence global, Muslim community.

The global dimensions go further, however, since at least the producers of *nasyid* music are seeking to go global, not just by marketing the music in other Islamic countries, but by producing musical collaborations between groups such as Raihan and what they see to be similar performers elsewhere. Tony Fernandes, vice-president of Warner Music Southeast Asia, for example, plans to combine Raihan with Take Six, Boyz 2 Men, or Stevie Wonder in the United States, while others have attempted to promote links between *nasyid* and American gospel groups (see Cheah 2000).

The important changes in ideas about cultural and racial diversity constructed in the Malaysian popular imagination become clearly manifest once *nasyid* is examined in the context of an emerging Malaysian, and global, youth culture. There is no doubt that the work of exposing the silences about racial diversity, manifest in the earlier work of someone like Ramlee, has been carried out mainly by multinational capital through the increasingly globalized culture industries. The effect has been the rise of a new generation of Malaysians who are at least far more predisposed than were their elders to engage with the racially and culturally diverse nature of their own society and of the new global order. Whether or not this also generates a predisposition among young Malaysians towards a greater tolerance of otherness remains to be seen, although there is much impressionistic evidence to suggest that common participation in this global youth culture is both increasing the levels of interracial interaction in Malaysian cities[11] and has facilitated interracial co-operation in the movement for reform that is currently focused on the conflict between the Prime Minister and his former deputy, Anwar Ibrahim, jailed on charges of sexual and financial misconduct. Many have commented on the fact that the rallies supporting Anwar, as well as the keADILan party headed by his wife, were composed overwhelmingly of young people from all of Malaysia's racial groups, raising the very real possibility for the first time in Malaysia's history of a serious challenge to a political system shaped entirely by considerations of race.

There is also evidence, however, of the opposite tendency — that is, of the continued salience of the exclusionary discourses of Malay nationalism. Most recently, partly as a result of splits in the Malay vote in the 1999 elections, Malay leaders including the Prime Minister seem to be appealing once again to the Malays not to forget their heritage and the goals of Malay nationalism. One observer has spoken of a re-communalization of Malaysian politics after a decade when it appeared that communal rhetoric seemed to have gone into decline.[12] It remains to be seen whether the strategy will be an effective one, or whether the new social and cultural circumstances manifest in the growth of an urban "youth culture" will mean that appeals based on the older vision of Malay nationalism will fall increasingly on deaf ears.

In sum, transformations within Malay popular culture suggest, on the one hand, that Malay exceptionalism has neither disappeared as a result of the historical experience of modernization, nor has it in any simple quantitative sense become stronger. Instead, we are dealing with something quite new, something anticipated neither by triumphalists like Fukuyama and Coyne, nor by "relativists" like Mahathir — namely, a vision of Malayness that is both exclusive and inclusive at the same time. This tension between "sameness" and "difference" in Malay popular culture is not easily resolved. It is a further example of the paradoxes of modernization that underlie the thinking and writing of that most acute of observers and analysts of contemporary Malaysia, Clive Kessler.

Notes

1. Lyrics for some Raihan songs can be found at http://pages.whowhere. lycos.com/internet/imnogman/Raihan.html

2. Quoted in Harrison (1999) from which the information on Huda was largely obtained.

3. I have explored certain aspects of this problem elsewhere (see Kahn 2001). Further discussions of the development of the modern Malay entertainment industry and of Ramlee's work and influence can be found in Lockard (1998); Tan (1993); Harper (1999); Kean Wong (1995); Zawawi Ibrahim (1995); and various websites devoted to Ramlee's life and films.

4. Some of the information on Raihan comes from an article in Malaysia's *New Straits Times* (see Cheah 2000). I am also indebted to Kean Wong in Kuala Lumpur, who was a wonderful source of information on Malaysian popular music.

5. I have described this aspect of modern Malay popular culture elsewhere (see Kahn 2001, Chapter 4)

6. I have been assured by some Malaysian musical experts that there is absolutely nothing distinctive about Malaysian popular music. They argue that the Western influence is so pervasive that only non-musical markers, such as the dress of performers, or the use of Malay lyrics, serve to give it a Malaysian feel. As a non-expert, I find it difficult to assess this judgement. Without wishing to disagree that at a purely musical level Malay pop music is almost entirely derivative, particularly of whatever is currently popular in the West, I would still argue that a style of popular singing and performance has been created that, however derivative, is nonetheless almost always recognizable as Malaysian for whatever reason.

7. Although there are now a number of Ramlee films, his musical performances have recently been released on video compact disc as well.

8. More recent versions of Islamic pop in Malaysia appear to contain scenes of dancing, however.

9. For summaries of changing tastes in popular music in Malaysia, written before the rising popularity of *nasyid*, see Lockard (1998); and Zawawi Ibrahim (1995).

10. In Malaysia, at least a subaltern youth culture of protest has been traced to the 1980s with the emergence of local metal bands, supported by an underground music press of crudely produced fanzines (see Kean Wong 1995).

11. Changes in the patterns of social interaction among, particularly, Chinese and Malays are treated in greater depth in a forthcoming book on Malaysian modernity that I am currently writing with Maila Stivens. Here, we also examine the ways in which patterns of urbanization and the formation of new middle classes, as well as changes in electoral patterns, are contributing to the possibility of a less racialized social order in contemporary Malaysia.

12. I first heard the term "recommunalization" used by the leader of the opposition Democratic Action Party, Lim Kit Siang, at a talk given at Monash University in May 2000.

References

Anderson, Benedict O'G. *Imagined Communities: Reflections on the Origins and Spread of Nationalism*. London: Verso, 1983.

Cheah, Julian. "Warner's Man with the Music Instincts". *New Straits Times*, Life Is… Section, 31 January 2000, pp. 6–7.

Harper, Timothy. *The End of Empire and the Making of Malaya*. Cambridge: Cambridge University Press, 1999.

Harrison, Francis. "Women's Band Sing Pop for Allah". *Guardian*, 27 May 1999, p. 14.

Hussin Mutalib. *Islam in Malaysia: From Revivalism to Islamic State*. Singapore: Singapore University Press, 1993.

Kahn, Joel S. "Growth, economic transformation, culture and the middle classes in Malaysia". In *The New Rich in Asia*, edited by Richard Robison and David S. G. Goodman. London: Routledge, 1996.

——— . *Modernity and Exclusion*. London: Sage Publications, 2001.

Levi-Strauss, Claude. "The Scope of Social Anthropology". In *Structural Anthropology* 2, edited by C. Levi-Strauss (Harmondsworth: Penguin, 1987).

Lockard, Craig A. *Dance of Life: Popular Music and Politics in Southeast Asia*. Honolulu: University of Hawaii Press, 1998.

Milner, Anthony. *The Invention of Politics in Colonial Malaya: Contesting Nationalism and the Expansion of the Public Sphere*. Cambridge University Press, 1995.

——— . "What happened to 'Asian Values'?" In *Toward Recovery in Pacific Asia*, edited by Gerald Segal and David S. G. Goodman, pp. 56–68. London and New York: Routledge, 2000.

Ong, Aihwa. *Spirits of Resistance and Capitalist Discipline: Factory Women in Malaysia*. Albany: SUNY Press, 1987.

Robison, Richard. "Introduction". Special issue of *Pacific Review* 9, no. 3 (1996): 305–08.

Rofel, Lisa. *Other Modernities: Gendered Yearnings in China after Socialism.* Berkeley, Los Angles and London: University of California Press, 1999.

Roff, W. *The Origins of Malay Nationalism.* New Haven: Yale University Press, 1967.

Scott, James. *Weapons of the Weak: Everyday Forms of Peasant Resistance.* New Haven and London: Yale University Press, 1985.

Sulkunen, Pekka. *The European New Middle Class.* Aldershot: Avebury, 1992.

Tan Sooi Beng. *Bangsawan: A Social and Stylistic History of Popular Malay Opera.* Singapore and New York : Oxford University Press, 1993.

Wong, Kean "Metallic Gleam". In *The Faber Book of Pop*, edited by Hanif Kureishi and Jon Savage. London: Faber and Faber, 1995.

Zawawi Ibrahim. *Popular Culture at the Crossroads: Malay Contemporary Music.* Kuala Lumpur: Akademi Pengajian Melayu, 1995.

PART III

Politics

9

HOW "TRADITIONAL" IS THE MALAYSIAN MONARCHY?

Anthony Milner

Just how does the pre-colonial culture of the Malay world influence political behaviour and political experience in Malaysia today? Some analysts seem to imply that little connection exists between the early monarchical forms of the region and modern societies. Harold Crouch (1996), for instance, seldom reaches back before the independence year of 1957 in his influential analysis of the Malaysian political system. Even some historians, although taking pains to examine the character of the pre-colonial social systems of Southeast Asia, make no connection between these and the particular structures of modern societies.[1] Against this view, certain specialists on Southeast Asian political cultures have insisted that ideas about power and government developed in pre-colonial systems have a direct relevance in the region today.[2] In the case of Malaysia, Syed Hussein Alatas (1972) has led a school of analysts who argue for the "historical continuity of attitudes and values from the feudal period to the present time" (p. 100), identifying in particular a stress on "unflinching loyalty" (p. 108). These analysts have noted the continued importance of royal titles and ceremony in modern Malaysia (Chandra Muzaffar 1979, p. 109) and the continuing stress on the heroic qualities of the Malay feudal model, Hang Tuah (Shaharuddin Maaruf 1984, p. 55). They have even suggested that the first Prime Minister of Malaysia, Tunku Abdul Rahman, provides an instance of the "feudal tradition re-asserting itself" (Shaharuddin Maaruf 1988, p. 127).

As he has done with respect to many other issues, Clive Kessler examines this relationship between past and present political cultures with subtlety and imagination. As he describes it, the relationship is real but deeply problematic. Drawing upon the work of Vivienne Wee, he suggests (in his 1992 essay "Archaism and Modernity in Malay Political Culture") that the past is like "the image that we see in a rear-vision mirror of a rapidly moving car. As we move forward, we see an image of what we have been through and experienced. But this view of the past is shaped by our direction into the future" (p. 134). Our image of the past, that is to say, is "formed on shifting ground in an ever-moving present" (p. 134).

In his own analysis of the impact of the past on modern Malay political culture, Kessler notes the observation that in the Malay *kerajaan* — the pre-colonial Malay polity — social existence is a "political condition, one of being involved in the reciprocal relationship between ruler and ruled" (p. 136). In this condition, leaders endowed their followers with "a full or completed Malay identity" (p. 136). In modern Malay political life, says Kessler, this stress on followership continues, but today it is focused on commoner rather than royal leaders. Even the seemingly anti-traditionalist Prime Minister, Mahathir Mohamad, for instance, endorsed a new "regime-stabilizing anthem — *Lagu Setia* (The Loyalty Song)" (p. 149). The semantic power of the song is conveyed through a set of concepts such as devotion, loyalty, service, sacrifice, and obedience. Much of this vocabulary, it should be said, is redolent of the *kerajaan* language of pre-modern times. It suggests the way elements of the *kerajaan* have been appropriated for present-day nationalist purposes of the Malaysian state — how they have been built into a broad Malay political structure; built "on the shifting ground" of the "ever-moving present".

What Kessler is less concerned about, however, is the influence of the *kerajaan* on the modern institution of kingship (or sultanship) itself — an institution that is today just one component of the modern Malaysian political system. When Kessler does refer to the sultanates, it should be noted, it is to remind us that they "enjoy powers that are not simply created by or based within but exist prior to and outside of constitutional authority and the constitution itself" (p. 144). They are powers not merely stipulated in a modern constitution but also "based in cultural and religious tradition" (p. 144) — but they are not powers which he goes on to analyse.

A new book on *Monarchy in South-East Asia* by Roger Kershaw (2001), however, does focus attention on the institution of the sultanate. Kershaw writes of the "importance of continuity of the monarchy itself" and insists that "such continuity of structures goes beyond the mere affinities between ancient South-East Asian structures and modern-era colonial structures..." (p. 18). This book is a timely reminder that with monarchs in Thailand, Cambodia, and Brunei, as well as Malaysia, kingship can certainly be viewed as a significant institution in the Southeast Asian region. In discussing the heritage of the past, however, it might have paid more attention to the "moving car" issues raised by Kessler. Kershaw is certainly aware of the presence of social change — indeed his book has the subtitle "The Faces of Tradition in Transition" — but the phrase "continuity of monarchy" is troubling. Just because we speak of sultans or kings today, as we might also use these words to describe rulers of the eighteenth century and earlier, we cannot assume that the monarchical institutions are largely the same. There is a case to be made, in fact, that in Malaysia and other parts of Southeast Asia, royal systems have been radically transformed over the years, and all the more successfully because the transformation has been partly self-generated.

When commentaries on the monarchy in the nineteenth- and twentieth-century Malay peninsula discuss change, they tend to focus on the loss of power that occurred during the colonial period. Thus, Rupert Emerson's magisterial study of colonial rule in Malaya (Emerson 1968) judged that, with the establishing of the British protectorate, the Malay monarchs were permitted to indulge only in "pomp and ceremony" (p. 140). The "actual substance of political power" now lay in British hands (p. 211). This view has been strongly supported by some historians (listed in Milner 1987), and opposed by others, the latter believing that the change in the sultan's influence was by no means dramatic (Gullick 1992; and Milner 1995). The analytical preoccupation with the issue of the sultan's power continues into the study of de-colonization and the development of the independent state of Malaya (and Malaysia) after independence in 1957. Ariffin Omar (1993) has argued that it was in 1946 — when the British tried to create a Malayan state (the "Malayan Union") in which the Malays and their rulers would no longer be dominant — that the Malay community moved decisively away from the sultans. In the midst of the passionate Malay opposition to the British initiative, says Ariffin, the monarchy was supplanted by race (*bangsa*) as the "focus of Malay identity" (p. 53). The leader of the nationalist movement (the United Malays National Organization or UMNO), Dato Onn, declared that "the *rakyat* have become the *raja*, the *raja* have become the *rakyat*" (Smith 1995, p. 172). It was at this point, according to the political analyst, Chandra Muzaffar, that the leadership of the UMNO became the "real or substantive protector of the community". The sultans, he said, were now "mere symbolic protectors" (Chandra Muzaffar 1979, p. 64).

Although the Malayan Union period was undoubtedly a turning point, a struggle for power is said to have continued in the years up to 1957, as sultans and nationalist leaders tussled over precisely what role the sultan would have in the new constitution of the Malayan, and later Malaysian, state (Smith 1995, p. 204). In this situation, the sultans were well aware of the need to promote their popularity with the people of their states. After independence, the rulers having been retained in the new national structure, the new Prime Minister hoped they would become "constitutional Rulers in that they will be more like figureheads" (Smith 1995, p. 204). In the following years, however, there were further instances of competition between them and the elected representatives of the states — in some cases involving virtually forced resignations of the chief ministers of state governments. In 1983–84 and 1991–92, major confrontations at the national level occurred between Prime Minister Mahathir and the rulers. Commentators observed that the Malay community was severely divided at that time (with competing rallies being held to support both Prime Minister and his royal opponents) — a clear indication of the continued authority of the rulers. In these struggles, nevertheless, the Prime Minister was eventually successful in making changes to the constitution that curtailed royal powers (Crouch 1996; Smith 1995; Stockwell 1988; and Milner 1996).

During both the colonial and post-colonial periods, this curtailing of royal power was indeed presented in terms of the creation of new "constitutional monarchies". As Simon Smith has put it, the British set about turning the sultans into "fully constitutional monarchs…" (Smith 1995, p. 126), and he suggests ways in which the British monarchy was used as a model in this process. A detailed analysis of what was involved in this remodelling of kingship would make an important contribution to the study of modern Malay history and political culture. Such a study would trace back the origins of change, at least to the early colonial period, but care would need to be taken not to attribute agency entirely to the British or other indigenous critics of the *ancien regime*. Kessler's observation that even today the powers of the sultanate lie partly outside the modern constitution is also critical and is supported by the comment in a recent study of "The Sultans and the Constitution", that in the Malay sultanates "the divine aspect of sovereignty" has "endured to the present day" (Muhammad Kamil Awang 1998, p. 314). However, the idea of cultural endurance, once again, requires caution. Remembering the link between current imperatives and "tradition" that is visualized in the "moving car" metaphor helps to draw attention to a deep-running fissure between the experience of rulership presented in pre-colonial Malay writing and forms of Malay political culture operating today. The transformation that occurred in the Malay monarchy cannot be comprehended merely in terms of a loss of one form of power and the retention of another, "divine" form.

To appreciate the extent to which the monarchy was reconstituted in the Malay States, it is necessary to recall certain features of the pre-colonial system. Writings from the nineteenth century and earlier, for instance, suggest that the *raja* himself was in that era the focus of allegiance, and this observation has profound implications. The polity was called the *kerajaan*, literally "the condition of having a *raja*". The word itself seems to have meant "kingship" and "kingdom", as well as "king", and the vagueness is revealing. Conceptually, there appeared to have been little to differentiate the institution of the monarchy or the person of the monarch from the monarchical community. European observers certainly noted the central role of the king, but it is especially helpful when these writings contain direct reportage of commoner Malay thinking. "I am the subject of the Raja of Lingga", was the reply of Malays questioned about their identity in 1836 during a British investigation into piracy (Milner 1982, p. 2).

Other categories of identification are also present in the documentation of the archipelago world of the sixteenth to nineteenth century, including identification by specific geographical location. People might be referred to as *orang Siak*, or people of Siak (which is a river in East Sumatra), or *orang Trengganu* (a river on the east coast of the peninsula). They might also be referred to as "Malay", but we must be careful not to read too much meaning into ethnic categories in those years. The Dutch and British certainly wrote of Malays, Moors (Indian Muslims), Makassarese, Menangkabau, and Butanese but, as Heather Sutherland has recently pointed out with respect to seventeenth and eighteenth-century Makassar, the "theoretical rigidity of ethnic classifications, especially those imposed by the bureaucratic V.O.C. [United Dutch East India Company], was at odds with the pragmatic opportunism and cultural flexibility" that was typical of Makassar (Sutherland 2001, p. 409). In fact, there were even porous boundaries between the "Malay" and "Chinese" communities (Sutherland 2001, p. 410).

In the case of the Malacca and Johor sultanates, the people referred to themselves as "Malays" and gradually (perhaps influenced by contemporary European usage) this self-definition was encountered more broadly among people from other areas of the peninsula as well as Borneo and Sumatra (Matheson 1979; and Shamsul 1996). Ethnicity crystallized in the British-governed territories in the mid-nineteenth century, however, and this development must have been influenced by the growing emphasis in Europe on "race" as a category for analysing humankind. In the 1830s and 1840s, the writer and translator, Munshi Abdullah, who had been much influenced by interaction with the European community, including such up-to-date thinkers as John Crawfurd and Thomas Stamford Raffles, wrote time and again not of the Malay kingdoms, or *kerajaan*, but of the Malays and the Malay race (*bangsa*). He persistently focused on the problems of the Malay race and urged its leaders to protect the Malays for the future (Milner 1995, Chapter 2).

It is in this colonial context, too, that we see a far greater stress on membership of the Muslim community — the *umat Islam*. This is not to deny that Malays in the pre-colonial *kerajaan* were Muslim, or that they identified themselves as Muslim. However, in the British- and Dutch-governed settlements, to some extent beyond the ideological and physical reach of the Malay royal courts, the fostering of a supremely religious allegiance was easier to achieve. In fact, the development of a powerful Islamic consciousness, including demands for specifically Islamic leadership for the Malay and other Muslim communities in the region, developed primarily in Singapore, Penang, and the other European-governed enclaves in the Malay world (Roff 1967; and Milner 1995).

The point to be stressed, therefore, is that in the *kerajaan* polities, up to the early nineteenth century, people possessed many forms of identity, from the specifically local to the proto-ethnic, and the religious. Nevertheless, the *kerajaan* ideologues made enormous claims — claims that require imagination to understand today — and we know that they exercised genuine influence over the population (Milner 1982).

It was during the colonial period, as already suggested, that the situation was transformed — partly due to initiatives coming from the sultanates themselves — and in examining this transformation we learn more about the old system as well as the new one. In this period, the Malay royal courts responded to a range of challenges, not only from the European powers but also from alternative élites in their own societies, including both proto-nationalist and Islamic élites. They confronted new idea systems, including new liberal concepts concerning the state, ethnicity, government, the individual, and the monarchy itself. A full account of the reconstituting of the Malay monarchy would move back and forth between the commoner critics (Malay and British) and the courtier ideologues, drawing attention to the dialogue of ideas that brought about change. The present purpose is merely to suggest some possibilities regarding the courtier contribution to that vital conversation, underlining the observation that the latter drew upon as well as resisted the new ideologies. The royal courts engaged in self-reform,[3] and Johor (situated closest to British Singapore, and able to resist incorporation into British Malaya until 1914) was the pioneer.

To begin with, there emerged in Johor a new territorial concept of the state which contrasted strongly with that of the *kerajaan*. At the end of the nineteenth century, a high-ranking courtier in Johor, Mohd. Salleh bin Perang, in an autobiographical document (Sweeney 1980), wrote of the work he had been carrying out to modernize the kingdom, giving it physical definition. He was mindful, he said, that Johor was a country adjacent to European territory, and he wrote of his concern for "surveying and determining boundaries" (p. 88), explaining that "after more than three years the map of Johor was complete". In fact, he said, the map was "pronounced correct by the head surveyor in London" (p. 89). The territorial defining of the state, of course, was consistent with what had been taking place in many other parts of the world, including the British-governed Malay States and contemporary Thailand (Thongchai Winichakul 1994). The mapped state also contrasted radically with the old *kerajaan* — a polity (if we can use the term for an entity that was as religious as political) that was understood in terms of relationships, specifically of the allegiance of the subject to the *raja*. The mapping of the state helped to make a distinction between ruler and state, a distinction that had been confused in former times — and it required an innovation in vocabulary. The word Mohd. Salleh used for state was *negeri*, a term once suggesting merely a settlement (Milner 1995, pp. 104–5). The way in which Mohd. Salleh, although a royal courtier, shifted the focus from *kerajaan* to *negeri* in his writing is expressed succinctly when he reflected in print on his own life and service. He employed the metaphor of a plant living on a giant tree, "spreading myself over and winding myself around every branch and fork" (Sweeney 1980, p. 79). The tree he referred to, however, was not the *raja*, as it would have been for an earlier generation of court writers, but the state (*negeri*) of Johor. That is to say, the official's allegiance was now to the state of Johor, defined at least partly in territorial terms, rather than to the person of the ruler.

Another turn-of-the-century courtier, Haji Mohd Said, added to this reformulating of the monarchy and pruning of the idea of *kerajaan*. He did so in writing the *Hikayat Johor*, first published in 1908 (Haji Mohd. Said 1919)[4] — a celebration of Johor and its monarchy that has been dismissed by some specialists on Malay literature as a "conventional eulogy" (Sweeney and Phillips 1975, p. xxxii). On the contrary, the text could be seen in certain ways as revolutionary. Like Haji Mohd. Salleh's writing, this *hikayat* presents Johor as a geographical entity, separating the state (*negeri*) from its *raja*, and the author also follows contemporary style in Malay writing in Singapore in separating out the terms *raja* and *kerajaan*. One Malay newspaper of the period, for instance, in using *kerajaan* to mean "government", had even gone so far as to define "republic" as *kerajaan ramai*, or the "government of the people" (*Utusan Melayu*, 12 March 1908). From the perspective of the royal court, the concept of *raja* was now distinguished both from the physical territory of the state, and from "government". Not only did these ideological moves diminish the *raja*'s role — a point to which we will return — but they also seem to have created a need to flesh out, or give substance to, the new concept of *kerajaan*. Thus, when Haji Mohd. Said at one point describes the Sultan of Johor as working vigorously to "make permanent" or "fix" the "*kerajaan* of Johor" (Haji Mohd. Said 1919, pp. 38, 64), he conveys a hint that the task was partly a conceptual one. It was also a task in which he himself engaged.

Haji Mohd. Said identified the written constitution — and Johor had proclaimed a written constitution in 1895 — as the means by which to ground the new understanding of *kerajaan*. One obvious reason that the constitution was proclaimed was to enhance the respectability of Johor in the eyes of the critics of Malay monarchy, including those in Singapore. However, the choice of the Malay phrase to describe the constitution is striking. It is called an *undang-undang tuboh kerajaan*. *Undang-undang* means "laws", and *tuboh* is defined as "body, in the anatomical sense". The constitution, it would seem, was conceptualized as giving "body" to the *kerajaan*. That is to say, the *kerajaan* (presumably intended to convey the new, narrower meaning) is now grounded in the constitution rather than the person of the *raja*. The constitution therefore helps to establish the *kerajaan* as an entity that is to some extent independent of the *raja*.

When we look at the 1895 constitution itself, the conceptual separation between *raja* and polity is apparent in a second way — and one that forms a dramatic break in the continuity of royal traditions. The constitution declares that the subjects of Johor "are not bound to any future sultan who cedes any part of the territory of Johor" to a foreign power (Fawzi Basri and Hasrom Harom 1978, p. 216) and, in making this concession, might be seen as putting Johor kingship on a contractual basis. It is true that some modern scholarship suggests that the fifteenth-century Malacca monarchy was contractual but this is a misunderstanding. In the *Malay Annals*, the classical text that is often quoted, the founder of the Malacca dynasty is said to have made a pledge never to "disgrace or revile" his subjects with "evil words". This pledge is, however, not a condition for allegiance because the subjects, on their part, agree that "until the end of time", even if they experience "tyrannical and evil" rule, they will "never be disloyal to their *raja*". This arrangement is at best a covenant, and not a contract.[5] The text gives the impression of not being able to conceive of the polity independently of the *raja*. Unlike the Johor constitution, it does not make the continued rule of the *raja* dependent on his carrying out, or not carrying out, specific acts. By contrast, in the Johor constitution the suggestion is clear that the ruler is an individual whose royal position and authority is dependent upon the capacity to serve his state, at the very least by ensuring its territorial integrity.

Another way in which the text of the *Hikayat Johor* distinguishes between the *raja* and his state and government — raising the significance of the latter two — is in being focused specifically not just on the ruling *raja* and his family but also on the state, or *negeri*, and the Malay race. This innovation is a surprise to any reader familiar with Malay royal texts (though not to the reader of Mohd. Salleh's autobiography). The title *Hikayat Johor* would suggest that, like other royal *hikayat*, even the contemporary *Hikayat Pahang* (from the neighbouring state of Pahang),[6] the text will be focused on the ruler and his genealogical line. In fact, the *Hikayat Johor* is actually described by its author as a short account of the "story of the affairs of the state (*negeri*) of Johor". The text certainly gives most attention to a specific *raja*, Sultan Abu Bakar — and in this sense has much in common with royal *hikayat* from other areas and other periods — but it is important that he is praised for creating "modern" institutions and for being clever at handling foreign governments. The frequent listing of his administrative talents, in fact, is also a reminder that the sultan's tenure is based on performance rather than mere inherited status — that the text recognizes the new contractual basis of government. Furthermore, the precise phraseology is important to note. Sultan Abu Bakar is described as "raising the reputation of the *negeri* and *kerajaan* of

Johor and also of its subjects who are of the Malay race". This is high praise, but it is certainly a modern, liberal formulation. It would have impressed the British and modern-thinking Malays but, from a *kerajaan* pre-modern point of view, it not only prunes back the scope of the sultanate but lowers its significance *vis-à-vis* the interests of the state and the Malay race. The individual sultan is being praised — and therefore could conceivably be condemned — for the way he carries out tasks on behalf of the state and the Malay ethnic group. Indeed, in mentioning his service to the Malay race — on the face of it, an important compliment — the text places the Johor ruler and his polity on a canvass that extends well beyond their own sphere in the south of the Malay Peninsula. It is a reminder that the sultan acts in a world defined in other than *kerajaan* terms — a Malay world that completely transcends the Johor sultanate.

A further delimiting of the monarchy is carried out in the epistemological sphere, when the *Hikayat Johor* explains that the information it contains is "gathered from various recollections and reports which have been proven to be true and also from printed books". This is a type of claim we would not normally find in a royal *hikayat*. In those texts, "knowledge" tends to be depicted as being dependent on or as descending via kingship — it is not presented as having been subject to "independent" tests. The *Hikayat Johor* implies the presence of a rational individual reader, keen to test the information transferred in the text against the criteria of "truth". (The mention of "printed books", we tend to observe today, is a reminder of the superstitious basis upon which "rational truth" is often based). To emphasize his point about the modern approach to the writing of the book, Haji Mohd. Said says that he aspires to write a history — and the word for "history", *tawarikh*, which had only been introduced into Malay in recent times (Milner 1995, pp. 86, 173–74, 191), suggests the empirical history encountered in contemporary European writing.

As the *Hikayat Johor* continues, the author proceeds to examine other Malay texts, gravestones, and so forth in a manner that suggests the earnest verification of sources promised in his opening pages. In fact, the whole presentation of what today might be called the methodology of the text suggests the presence of a new, rational audience. As author, Haji Mohd. Said explicitly addresses his audience. The text, unlike most royal *hikayat*, commences with a preface in which the author (whose name is given) communicates the aim of the book, describes his approach, anticipates some of the themes to be introduced (including the creation of *modern* institutions), thanks a number of people who helped him in the writing, and states the place and date of publication (according to both the Western and Arabic calendars). All royal *hikayat* had audiences, of course, but the audience was not usually addressed explicitly in this manner, bringing it into view, so to speak, in the text itself.

Addressed in this way, there is no pretence that the *Hikayat Johor* audience's horizon is limited to the *kerajaan*. The impression given in many *hikayat* is that the Malay subject was embedded in monarchy, a portion rather than a mere subject of the *kerajaan*, possessing no independent perspective and no status other than that assigned in the rigid hierarchical structure focused on the monarch. Malay subjects tended to be portrayed in such texts as mere statuses rather than individual persons. Far from possessing a status or title, they are presented as if they were their titles. In the *Hikayat Johor*, on the other hand, the implication is that the Johor reader has a range of priorities — good government, the protection of the territorial state and the welfare of the Malay race — and that he, or she, is capable of assessing the effectiveness with which a particular ruler may serve these objectives. Just as the physical "state" and "government" are made conceptually independent of the *raja* in this text, so are the subjects themselves. Once again the *raja*, or the sultanate, is diminished — and yet, it must be stressed, this reformulation is being implemented in a text that is produced in a royal court, a text that is, in fact, a celebration of the sultanate and of individual sultans.

The implication of a community of individuals is especially significant with respect to court titles and ritual — and it will be remembered that the continued presence of the royal ceremonial structure in modern Malaysia has been described as a demonstration of the persistence of feudal traditions. In the *kerajaan* ideology of the past, ceremony was central — it articulated the community — and that is not to imply that the *kerajaan* was concerned about frivolous, superficial matters. To speak of the *kerajaan* as a "theatre state" (Geertz 1980) is valuable in alerting present-day readers to the distance between the "modern" and "traditional" state, but as a phrase it inevitably carries an implication of superficiality. From an outsider's perspective, it is true that the Malay passion for titles and court ceremonies and the obedience towards sumptuary laws — for example, the use of yellow by non-royals was punishable by death — suggest a powerful preoccupation with what we would today consider to be externals. Nevertheless, the "ceremonial polity" needs to be understood in the context of the Malay concern for *nama* (reputation in this world and the next). Titles, ceremonies and sumptuary laws were the ways in which *nama* was exhibited. The title one held, the position one was allocated in the royal court, the type of house one lived in — all expressed a person's status. In the *kerajaan* ideology, there was no other independent criteria for establishing personal worth. It is in this sense that the member of a *kerajaan* seems to have been a status rather than an individual — a status defined only in relation to the *raja*. Without a *raja*, as one royal text after another explains, there was utter confusion — a confusion that reached beyond the sphere of government and society into what we would call the personal psychology of the Malay subject (Milner 1982).

Understanding the ceremonial centrality of the *raja* in this way makes it possible to appreciate the vehemence and abhorrence with which Malay texts condemn treason. The horror with which treason is treated suggests something more than the production of propaganda to protect a patron. So pivotal is the *raja* in the polity, so inseparable from the personal worth of his subject (in this life and the next) that in that culture the act of treason is perhaps best understood as a form of psychological, social, and spiritual suicide. It is the destruction of one's *nama*. A contract, holding open the possibility that the *raja* who failed his subjects could be overthrown, would have been unthinkable. Rather (just as the *Malay Annals* state), the *raja* could merely be asked not to "disgrace and revile" his subjects with "evil words" — a request that makes good sense in a polity in which "words" were a critical contribution which the *raja* made to the ceremonial (*nama*) system, and in which a good sultan was conventionally praised for his sweet manner and fine performance of ceremony.

By contrast, moving back again to the perspective of the *Hikayat Johor*, the new Sultan — though praised as a fine administrator, and a modernizer, as well as someone with a "sweet" voice — does not possess this type of profound intimacy of involvement with his subjects. Royal ceremony cannot have had the same meaning in this new sultanate of Johor. The ruler's subjects are citizens of a state and members of a race — not mere fragments or particles of kingship, dependent on the royal court to give meaning and purpose to their lives. In the case of Haji Mohd. Said's Johor, where it is possible to conceive of a contract between ruler and subject, the community of individuals had the advantage of this new critical distance in the understanding of ceremony. In fact, in the *Hikayat Johor*, although the sultan continues to engage in rituals, bestowing titles on people who "do service to the Raja or to the *kerajaan*" (Haji Mohd. Said 1919, p. 47), the treatment of ceremony tends to convey a degree of ambivalence. The sultan is said to hold celebratory feasts in the "European style", and attention is given to British ceremonies in which he engaged, not only with the Queen's representative in Singapore but also in England itself. In one instance, a state dinner, Sultan Abu Bakar is described as sitting on the right side of the "Queen of the United of Kingdom of Great Britain and Ireland and the Empire of India". What is important here is the fact that, although the sultan holds a position of honour at the British royal dining table, it is the Queen not the sultan who is the focal point. Moreover, the text seems almost to boast of the different honours the sultan receives from England, such as the GCMG (Knight Grand Cross of the Order of St Michael and St George) and the KCSI (Knight Commander of the Order of the Star of India), and here again the sultan is being portrayed on a wider canvas — a British imperial canvas that extends vastly beyond the small Johor Sultanate on the Malay Peninsula. There is no doubt about the emphasis on ceremony in this early twentieth-century text. It has been suggested, in fact, that in a number of Malay states there was an elaboration of ceremony in the royal courts during the colonial period (Gullick 1987, p. 33). However, the ceremony in the *Hikayat Johor* is no longer focused specifically on the structuring of a specific *kerajaan*, and, as we have seen, in any case can no longer claim an exclusive role in defining the person.

The suggestion in the Johor text of a reduction in the potency of royal ritual happens to be consistent with several other types of commentary on the early twentieth-century sultanates. Reports from Selangor and Pahang in that period suggest that it was becoming less frequent for commoners to squat on the ground as a ruler passed (Gullick 1987, p. 92; and Heussler 1981, p. 101). An influential Malay author of that time also observed that "nowadays the royal customary ceremonial and sumptuary regulations are fading" (Abdul Hadi 1925, p. 215). This is a period in the twentieth century, of course, when the literary novel — a genre that inevitably promotes and sometimes celebrates the concept of the individual — was emerging in society, and when commoner Malays began to assert their independence and empowerment by expressing their views as correspondents to newspapers. It was the era of the rise of citizenship as a concept and a mode of behaviour (Milner 1995).

Reviewing the *Hikayat Johor*, it is striking how innovative this text really is, defending the Johor sultan at a time when British power and British ideas were extending across the Malay Peninsula. The book is a reformulation of royal ideology for a new era, written in a state under threat from British expansionism. It seeks to present a modern territorial state governed by an effective administration. It assures those who see themselves first and foremost as "Malays" that the sultan will look after their interests and, in addition, assures the British that they are fortunate in having a friendly, well-governed state on their borders. The text is a response to the British — people who had been critical of what they saw as the chaotic, ill-managed sultanates located on the Peninsula — and political systems that they could barely understand. However, the text also answers the claims of a new commoner élite emerging in Malay society, particularly in the Straits Settlements. Haji Mohd. Said, we know, was educated in Singapore with members of that élite (Milner 1995, p. 199), and he would have been well aware of the claims they were making to lead the Malay community. It was with this threat in mind that the *Hikayat Johor* had to do more than establish the genealogical credentials of the man Haji Mohd. Said served. The author had to present his patron as an effective modern administrator.

To defend the monarchy in this novel way, transforming the concept in doing so, made good sense in the short term. It assisted the sultan in his attempt to hold off his enemies and rivals. In the longer term, however, surely as an unintended consequence, it entailed co-operation in a process of dismantling the *ancien régime* — a process that is disguised by the fact that an institution still called the sultanate or *raja* continues to survive today, together with a certain amount of royal ritual and status hierarchy. The ideological task which the *Hikayat*

Johor carries out is encapsulated in the new vocabulary which the text
invokes. Apart from conceptually separating the ruler from the "state",
"government" and individual subject or citizen, key terms such as
"truth", "modernity", and administrative "diligence and energy" are
emphasized more than such old key terms as *kerajaan* (in its earlier,
broader meaning), *nama* and *adat istiadat* (ceremonial and custom).
Using this new language, as we have seen, was critical to the redefining
(including the pruning) of the idea of the *raja* or sultanate.

The reformulating of the Malay monarchy continued in other
Malay writings into the twentieth century. A coronation text from
Perak in 1939[7] — that is, a booklet issued at the time of the installation
of Sultan Abdul Aziz, and describing the ceremonies, the sultan's
career, and the history of his state — is a good example. Written in
the spirit of Haji Mohd. Said's account of the Johor sultans, the text
could be read almost as a political manifesto for Sultan Abdul Aziz.
Again, the defence is written in a modern idiom — the territorial
state and the progress of Perak are described, for instance, and it is
striking how little attention the text gives to detailing the royal
ceremony, even that of the coronation itself. In the ceremonial detail
that is provided, it is noteworthy that in some situations the ceremonies
are presented as being bolstered by the incorporation of such modern
institutions as a state ball, sporting events, and electric lighting. In
discussing the ruler himself, as in the case of the Johor text, the stress
is placed on him being an exemplary modern administrator. His former
career in the state administrative service is recorded, and he is said to
enjoy working to "modernize education" in his state and "to improve
the lives" of his people. He is said to be "careful and conscientious".
The reader is also reminded of the new epistemology introduced by
such texts as the *Hikayat Johor* when the coronation album explains
that these qualities "are not merely presented as praise" but "are true
statements and can be proven".

The sultan's specific concern for the Malay community in his
state is given particular emphasis. He had "busily sought ways to
encourage" the Malays and, in addition, had been concerned about
the way debates over religion could divide the Malay community. The
sultan is said to have asked "how can we possibly unite our race
(*bangsa*)?" In this quotation, he is presented as actually assisting in
promoting the unity of the Malays — that is, his subjects are not

merely conceptualized as being members of the Malay race, an entity that is separate from and transcends the sultanate, but the ruler is also praised for contributing to the development of (for serving the purposes of) the Malay *bangsa*. Once again, the purpose of the text appears to have been to reply to the challenge of the potential commoner leadership of the Malays — to demonstrate that the sultan himself had particular qualifications to promote Malay unity. However, in promoting Sultan Abdul Aziz's credentials in this way, the text is also forcing the monarchy to cede ideological ground, confirming the impression of a performance-based monarchy able to be tested and expected to serve the purposes of other institutions and interests.

Further areas in which the sultan's particular capacities are mentioned include his handling of the Chinese and other races in the state (by the late 1930s the Malays were less than half the population of Perak), and the British authorities. In these areas, the sultan's "careful and conscientious" administration is conveyed. As in the Johor text, the argument for the sultan is couched in terms that would be accepted by the liberal critics of the *kerajaan*, whether they be Malay or English. Once again, in stressing good government (and particularly the ruler's administrative skills), the territorial state and its people, the Malay race, and the maintenance of social unity, the text employs the language and the priorities of the modern commoner élite of the Malay community. As with the Johor text, it also makes less use of *kerajaan* vocabulary — for example, words such as *nama* and *adat istiadat*. Certain older features of the monarchy, it is true, remain in the text. The book itself is described as a "memento of loyalty to the Raja" and the "Preface" does stress the importance of recording the ritual for future generations. Such an account of ritual, even in the abbreviated form presented in this text, would continue to have had meaning for many conservative Malays. However, it is the innovations on the old *kerajaan* ideology which are most important in the long term — innovations designed perhaps for a liberal readership, and which were to appear again and again in later royal texts.

In the post-independence (1957) period, a number of royal publications show the extent to which the Malay *rajas* had come to be presented in terms of this new royal discourse. One text of 1957, honouring the twenty-fifth anniversary of the accession to the Pahang throne of another Sultan Abu Bakar, takes pains to outline the career of the ruler. His education is stressed (including his education in English) and his experience in government (including the administration of the neighbouring state of Perak) is described. Much emphasis is placed on his commitment to bringing progress (*memajukan*) to the State of Pahang (Mohamed Mokhtar 1957, p. 44). If we examine a souvenir book to celebrate the birthday of the Sultan of Selangor in 1970, again the brief biography of the ruler draws attention to his education (including a period at the School of Oriental and African Studies in London). After his return to Malaya, the book explains, he gained administrative and military experience, and also travelled to the United States and Europe to further his education (Anon 1970). A later text from Pahang is also of interest. This work was issued in 1975, at the time of the coronation of Sultan Ahmad Shah, which again outlines his education in Malaya and England, his experience of working in government in Pahang (where he gained an understanding of "the intricacies of administration and government") and his commitment to development (*kemajuan*) in his *negeri* (Anon 1975). Finally, the Perak Sultan's coronation volume of 1985 presents a particularly convincing track record for an incoming ruler. Sultan Azlan, after study in England, had returned to Malaysia to a distinguished record in the legal profession, reaching the position of Chief Justice in 1982–84 (Anon 1985).

In praising the experience and achievements of individual sultans, therefore, the post-independence courtier-authors continued to develop the idea of a performance-based monarchy — and this claim, it can be argued, suggests a continuing expectation that the monarch might still conceivably play a practical role in the administration of his state. The courtier-authors have also continued to foreground royal service to the individual states (in the last case, the nation-state of Malaysia), and this is not the only way in which these modern royal texts focus on the state rather than merely the royal personage and royal family. The 1957 work from Pahang, marking twenty-five years of Sultan Abu Bakar's reign, commences with a brief description of that state, noting its relatively large territorial size, relating briefly the early history of that part of the peninsula, and then giving the contemporary population figures and their ethnic proportions. The text also includes a reminder of the perspective of the ordinary Malay people of Pahang, and spells out their aspirations to gain a living by opening up the land, and securing their rights to the land. For all its stated concern to honour Sultan Abu Bakar, therefore, the text nevertheless grounds his reign in the state of Pahang, and the expectations or perspectives of its Malay subjects.

Turning to the golden coronation book issued at the time the Pahang ruler was succeeded by his son, Sultan Ahmad, once again the state itself is in the foreground. The souvenir book not only contains biographies of the new sultan, his consort, and his late father, and an account of the titles awarded in the state. It also includes a section on the "development of the economy of Pahang" (Anon 1975). A further royal volume — one celebrating the Sultan of Selangor's birthday in 1970 — again includes not only an account of the ruler and his family but also material on the "progress and development of the state under the government of the Sultan". There are sections in the book on plantations, mining, education, and specific measures to assist the economic development of the Malay community (Anon 1970). Finally, in the coronation volume for Sultan Azlan of Perak (in 1985), the state and its inhabitants once more receive focus — this time with the assertion that this new sultan will bring a bright future to his state, and a high standard of living (*taraf kehidupan yang berkualiti*) to all his subjects (Anon 1985).

The Malays, it is clear, are given privileged attention in these royal documents, written as they are in a period when Malay nationalism had won much broader support than it had ever secured during the colonial period. The 1957 Pahang text, in fact, speaks proudly of the royal family's role in assisting the early nationalist movement, including its part in establishing a Malay Association in Pahang (Mohamed Mokhtar 1957). A royal "Album" from Kedah (Anon 1988) praises the sultan of that state for helping the "struggle of the Malay people led by Datuk Onn Jaafar" — that is, the struggle against the British-proposed "Malayan Union" of the immediate post-war period. The text goes on to recall that the Sultan of Kedah opened the third supreme council of the nationalist party (the UMNO) in Penang in 1946.

Although often presented in handsome gold albums, frequently adorned with photographs of the sultan and his family going about their royal duties, these modern court writings nevertheless tend to read as contestatory statements designed to convince an audience possessing non-*kerajaan* horizons. The defensiveness in the presentation of the Malay *raja* — noted first in the Johor text at the beginning of the twentieth century — is all the more apparent in these later royal writings. The sultanate's position continues to be justified not in its own terms, as it had been in the old *kerajaan* texts, but in terms of its usefulness to other causes, such as that of the state or the Malay community. In addition, the stress on the administrative track record of the ruler conveys the admission that leadership is no longer to be justified in genealogical and ceremonial terms — an admission that also acknowledges the new contractual nature of royal authority.

As noted above, stressing the ruler's administrative talent is, in one sense, provocative in a political situation in which, since the 1940s, administrative power had supposedly passed from the royal courts to the UMNO élite. Foregrounding royal administrative talent in court publications could be seen to sustain royal political ambitions. With this in mind, it is not surprising that the current Sultan of Pahang, in a rare casual interview, at one stage half admitted that he would enjoy becoming a politician (Rosnah Majid 1985, pp. 242–43) and it deserves noting that some speeches on "politik" are included in a recent volume of speeches by the Sultan of Kelantan, published by the Kelantan museum. Although the latter ruler — Tuanku Ismail Petra — recognizes he is a "constitutional monarch", he cannot, he says, "as a *raja* responsible before God" ignore his obligation to "guard, watch over, foster, issue warnings about, give advice on, and continue to provide protection for the carrying out of justice in my state" (Mohd Sayuti Omar 1995, p. 80).

Political aspirations, however, are bound to bring rulers into a head-on collision with the commoner politicians of the UMNO, and the constitutional confrontations with the monarchy in the early 1980s and early 1990s certainly demonstrated the determination of one nationalist leader, Prime Minister Mahathir, to resist such aspirations. The way most court formulations have in recent times conceptualized the role of the monarchy is in terms of metaphor, symbol, and cultural source. As was so clearly anticipated in the Johor and Perak texts of the first half of the twentieth century, the monarchy is now defended in terms of its capacity to serve other interests or institutions. Once presented as the anchor institution of the community, the sultanate began to be described as a "symbol of the unity of the people" of the state (Shariff

Ahmad 1983, pp. xvii, 32), or (in the words of a lavish 1987 book on the Kelantan royal family) as "umbrella sheltering" the people (Mohd. Zain 1987, p. 14; and Mohd Sayuti Omar 1995, pp. ii–iii). According to a statement by a senior member of the royal family of Pahang, the customs and ceremonial of the Pahang monarchy — which would once have been of central importance merely because of their *kerajaan* functions — are now to be considered important as a "branch of Malay culture" and a reflection of the "national characteristics of the Malay people (*bangsa Melayu*)".[8] According to the 1987 Kelantan text, the *establishmen Raja* is also a "fertile source from which flows the arts and culture of the Malay people".

At a glance, these statements are powerful claims for the monarchy (many would say too powerful), reminiscent of the claims made in early royal *hikayat* for the centrality of the *raja* in what we might today term the psychological and spiritual lives of his subjects. However, those early monarchs were not merely sheltering and symbolizing; they were pivotal in themselves and not just branches of (or sources for) a transcending Malay ethnic culture, and a Malay ethnic unity. Those pre-colonial rulers, furthermore, were not there to serve a territorially-defined state, or even "the people". The role and responsibilities of the sultan in that period — in that epistemic era — were defined in a radically different manner. The sultanate existed, as it were, for itself.

At this point, let us return to Kessler's comment that the sultanate during the constitutional crisis of 1983 possessed a power that inevitably reached beyond constitutional monarchy. This statement is undoubtedly true. There are traces of the pre-colonial *kerajaan* system in the ideological armoury of the modern sultans, and these would certainly enhance the position of the ruler in the minds of some sections of the Malay community.[9] However, it is equally important to point out that even in their royal publicity — recall that all the twentieth-century texts discussed above are in some sense products of royal courts, or royal propaganda — a far-reaching transformation is outlined. The change went beyond the loss of power, as we have seen. It certainly involved alterations in the sultan's relationship to the religious establishment of the polity — alterations which have not been discussed here.[10]

The transformation that has been analysed in this chapter entails a reformulation of the monarchy, a process that cannot yet be said to

have been completed. To take one area of royal activity frequently
cited as demonstrating the persistence of feudal tradition, the change
is apparent in the new way in which titles and ritual are understood.
In the last few decades, as court publications themselves reveal, titles
and the rest of the ceremonial system began to be seen not so much
as key structural features of the polity but as a "branch of Malay
culture". The 1985 coronation text from Perak also points out that
the titles bestowed by the sultan of that state could now be given for
service either to "the *negeri Perak*" (the state of Perak) — note it is
service to the state not the sultan — or to the "*negara Malaysia*" (the
nation-state of Malaysia). The mere mention of "Malaysia" suggests
the broader context in which both the sultan and the recipient of
such an award now operated. When we remember also that royal
sumptuary regulations were said to be "fading" even in the early
twentieth century — just as individualism was emerging in society,
tending to make the former royal subject into an independent citizen
— it is easier to understand how diluted the ceremonial system has
become as a feature of Malay experience. To be more precise, just
because we continue to encounter royal rituals and titles in Malay
society, it does not mean they continue to be vital, life structuring
institutions as they were in the old *kerajaan* — essential components
in a system of social and spiritual allegiance focused on a *raja*. Like
the sultan himself, they are a residue from the past and operate in new
contexts. For many Malays, the sultanate, with its ceremonial structure,
is no longer vital for its own sake but important primarily as a
"symbol", "umbrella", or "branch" of something that is held even
more deeply — of Malayness, a Malay state, or a Malay construction
of the Malaysian nation-state.

   To conclude, it is true that both the sultanates and the nationalist
leadership appropriate elements from the *kerajaan* tradition, building
them into a new understanding of political and social life. Malay
politics, like other aspects of Malay society, certainly need to be analysed
in a historical context. I have suggested elsewhere, for instance, how
kerajaan elements might have helped to shape modern self-perceptions
of Malay ethnicity — the Malay *bangsa*.[11] However, here and elsewhere,
the use of "tradition" takes place on the "shifting ground" of a new
present. The relationship with the past is always problematic. The
survival of the sultanate itself, it should be stressed, ought not to be

understood in terms of institutional or feudal continuity. In fact, it would probably be difficult for most Malays today — even those connected to the royal courts — to imagine the experience of living in the *kerajaan* system. The Malay Peninsula, of course, was not the only place in Southeast Asia where the monarchy was transformed during the colonial period (Lockhart 1993; and Thongchai Winichakul 1994). Nor was the *kerajaan* the only longstanding institution in Malay society that in the process of reform (including self-reform) lost its essential character. In the present volume, M. B. Hooker suggests that in the Syariah (Islamic law) we meet another institution that continues in name, but has been reformulated beyond recognition in its substance.[12] The past, to employ a valuable cliché, is indeed another country.

Notes

1. See Kershaw's (2001, p. 14) discussion of the latest edition of D. G. E. Hall, *A History of South-East Asia* (London: Macmillan, 1981).
2. See, for instance, Anderson (1972); and Pye (1985).
3. On Johor in this period, see Thio (1969); and Fawzi Basri and Hasrom Haron (1978).
4. I discussed this text in detail in Milner (1995), chapter 8. The 1908 edition is mentioned in Anon (1984), p. 23.
5. See De Josselin De Jong (1964); and Cheah (1998), pp. 112–14. I prefer the analysis of Chandra Muzaffar (1979) who uses the term "covenant".
6. Muhammad Yusoff Hashim and Aruna Gopinath (1992); and Milner (1982).
7. Raja Lob Ahmad (1940). I discussed this text in some detail in Milner (1995), chapter 9.
8. Tungku Ibrahim Ibni Al-Sultan Abu Bakar, Tungku Arif Bendahara Pahang, in Anon (1971).
9. But see Muhammad Yusoff Hashim (1991), p. 281, noting that the "element of spirituality (in Malay royal sovereignty) only exists in the form of heredity tradition and as a belief amongst a small section of the indigenous population who wish to believe in it".
10. See Milner (1995) on this issue.
11. Milner (1998); and Milner (1995).
12. See also Maier (1998) and Sweeney (1987) for an analysis of the transforming change that has taken place in the reception of *kerajaan* literature in Malay society.

References

Abdul Hadi bin Haji Hasan. *Sejarah Alam Malayu.* Vol 2. Singapore: Malaya Publishing House, 1925.

Anderson, B. R. O'G. "The Idea of Power in Javanese Culture". In *Culture and Politics in Indonesia,* edited by Claire Holt. Ithaca: Cornell University Press, 1972.

Anon. *Hari Keputeraan Duli Yang Maha Mulia Sultan Selangor yang ke-44. 10 haribulan Mach, 1970.* Kuala Lumpur: Government Printer, 1970.

————. *Peraturan Adat Istiadat Raja Negeri Pahang.* Pekan: Pejabat Adat Istiadat Pahang, 1971.

————. *Hari Pertabalan Kebawah Duli Yang Maha Mulia Sultan Pahang.* Kuantan: Pahang Properties, 1975.

————. *Pertabalan Kebaurah Duli Yang Maha Mulia Sultan Haji Ahmad Shah.* Kuantan: Nordin Abd. Ghari, 1975.

————. *Major Dato' Haji Mohd. Said bin Haji Sulaiman Dalam Kenangan.* Kuala Lumpur: Perpustakaan Universiti Malaya, 1984.

————. *Pertabulan Duli Yang Maha Mulia Paduka Seri Sultan Azlan,* 9 December 1985.

————. *Album Di Raja Kedah Darulaman.* Petaling Jaya: Penerbitan Kerabat, 1988.

Ariffin Omar. *Bangsa Melayu. Malay Concepts of Democracy and Community 1945–1950.* Kuala Lumpur: Oxford University Press, 1993.

Chandra Muzaffar. *Protector? An Analysis of the Concept and Practice of Loyalty in Leader-led Relationships within Malay Society.* Pinang: Aliran 1979.

Cheah Boon Kheng. "The Rise and Fall of the Great Melakan Empire". *Journal of the Malayan Branch of the Royal Asiatic Society* (JMBRAS) LXXI, no. 2 (1998): 104–21.

Crouch, Harold. *Government and Society in Malaysia.* St Leonards: Allen & Unwin, 1996.

De Josselen De Jong, P. E. "The Character of the Malay Annals". In *Malayan and Indonesian Studies,* edited by J. Bastin and R. Roolvink. Oxford: Clarendon Press, 1964.

Emerson, Rupert. *Malaysia: A Study in Direct and Indirect Rule.* Kuala Lumpur: University of Malaya Press, 1968 (originally published in 1937).

Fawzi Basri and Hasrom Harom. *Sejarah Johor Moden 1855–1940.* Kuala Lumpur: Jabatan Muzium, 1978.

Geertz, Clifford. *Negara: The Theatre State in Nineteenth-Century Bali.* Princeton: Princeton University Press, 1980.

Gullick, J. M. *Malay Society in the Late Nineteenth Century: The Beginnings of Change.* Singapore: Oxford University Press, 1987.

————. *Rulers and Residents*. Singapore: Oxford University Press, 1992.

Hall, D. G. E. *A History of South-East Asia*. London: Macmillan, 1981.

Heussler, R. *British Rule in Malaya: The Malayan Civil Service and Its Predecessors 1867–1942*. Oxford: Clio, 1981.

Kahn, Joel S. "Constructing Malaysian Ethnicity: A View from Australia". In *Ilmu Masyarakat* 14 (1988–89): 6–8.

Kershaw, Roger. *Monarchy in South-East Asia*. London: Routledge, 2001.

Kessler, Clive S. "Archaism and Modernity: Contemporary Malay Political Culture". In *Fragmented Vision: Culture and Politics in Contemporary Malaysia*, edited by Joel S. Kahn and Francis Loh Kok Wah, pp. 133–57. North Sydney: Allen & Unwin, 1992.

Lockhart, Bruce McFarland. *The End of the Vietnamese Monarchy*. New Haven: Yale Centre for International and Area Studies, 1993.

Maier, H. M. J. *In the Centre of Authority. The Malay Hikayat Merong Mahawangsa*. Ithaca: Cornell University Southeast Asia Programme, 1998.

Matheson, Virginia. "Concepts of Malay Ethos in Indigenous Malay Writings". *Journal of Southeast Asian Studies* 10, no. 2 (1979): 351–71.

Milner, Anthony. *Kerajaan: Malay Political Culture on the Eve of Colonial Rule*. Tucson: University of Arizona Press, 1982.

————. "Colonial Records History: British Malaya". *Modern Asian Studies* 21, no. 4 (1987): 773–92.

————. *The Invention of Politics in Colonial Malaya*. Cambridge: Cambridge University Press, 1995.

————. "Malaysia". In *Communities of Thought*, edited by Anthony Milner and Mary Quilty, pp. 157–83. Melbourne: Oxford University Press, 1996.

————. "Constructing Malayness". In *Making Majorities: Composing the Nation in Japan, China, Korea, Malaysia, Fiji, Turkey and the United States*, edited by Dru C. Gladney, pp. 150–69. Stanford: Stanford University Press, 1998.

Mohamed Mokhtar bin Haji Mohd. Daud. *Singgahsana Negeri Pahang*. Pekan, 1957.

————. *Singgahsana Negeri Pahang Darul Makmur*. Kuantan: Syarikat Percitakan Ihsan, 1987.

Haji Mohd. Said. *Hikayat Johor dan Tawarikh al-Marhum Sultan Abu Bakar*. Kept at Dewan Bahasa dan Pustaka, Kuala Lumpur, 1919.

Mohd Sayuti Omar, ed. *Tuanku Ismail Petra: Idealisme & Keprihatinan Kepada Agama Bangsa dan Negara*. Kota Bharu: Perdanan Muzium Negeri Kelantan, 1995.

Mohd. Zain Saleh. *Keluarga Diraja Kelantan Darulnaim*. Kota Bharu: Perbadanan Muzium Negeri Kelantan Istana Johor, 1987.

Muhammad Kamil Awang. *The Sultan and the Constitution*. Kuala Lumpur: Dewan Bahasa dan Pustake, 1998.

Muhammad Yusoff Hashim. *The Malay Sultanate of Malacca*. Kuala Lumpur: Dewan Bahasa dan Pustaka, 1992.

Muhammad Yusoff Hashim and Aruna Gopinath. *Tradisi Persejarahan Pahang Darul Makmur 1800–1930*. Petaling Jaya: Tempo, 1992.

Pye, Lucien W. *Asian Power and Politics: The Cultural Dimensions of Authority*. Cambridge MA: Harvard University Press, 1985.

Raja Lob Ahmad bin Raja Mohamad Ali. *Riwayat Pertabalan Yang Maha Mulia Sultan Sir Abdul Aziz*. Penang: Persama Press, 1940.

Roff, W. R. *The Origins of Malay Nationalism*. Kuala Lumpur: University of Malaya Press, 1967.

Rosnah Majid, ed. *Koleksi Temuramah Khas Tokoh-Tokoh*. Kuala Lumpur: Utusan Publications, 1985.

Shaharuddin Maaruf. *Concept of a Hero in Malay Society*. Singapore: Times Eastern Universities, 1984.

————. *Malay Ideas on Development*. Singapore: Times, 1988.

Shamsul A. B, "Construction and Trajectory of a Social Identity". *Journal of Asian and Pacific Studies* 52 (1996): 15–33.

Shariff Ahmad. *Menjunjung Kasih*. Kuala Lumpur: Berita, 1983.

Smith, Simon C. *British Relations with Malay Rulers from Decentralization to Malayan Independence, 1930–1957*. Kuala Lumpur: Oxford University Press, 1995.

Stockwell, A. J. "Princes and Politicians: The Constitutional Crisis in Malaysia, 1983–4". In *Constitutional Heads and Political Crisis 1945–1985*, edited by D. A. Low, pp. 182–97. Basingstoke: Macmillan, 1988.

Sutherland, Heather. "The Makassar Malays' Adaptation and Identity, c. 1660–1790". *Journal of Southeast Asian Studies* 32, no. 3 (October 2001): 397–422.

Sweeney, Amin. *A Full Hearing: Orality and Literacy in the Malay World*. Berkeley: University of California Press, 1987.

Sweeney, Amin, ed. *Reputations Live On: An Early Malay Autobiography*. Berkeley: University of California Press, 1980.

Sweeney, Amin, and Nigel Phillips, ed. *The Voyages of Mohamad Ibrahim Munshi*. Kuala Lumpur: Oxford University Press, 1975.

Syed Hussein Alatas. *Modernization and Social Change*. Sydney: Angus and Robertson, 1972.

Thio, Eunice. *British Policy on the Malay Peninsula 1880–1910: The Southern and Central States*. Singapore: University of Malaya, 1969.

Thongchai Winichakul. *Siam Mapped. A History of the Geo-body of a Nation*. Chiang Mai: Silkworm, 1994.

10

THE LOCALIZATION OF ISLAMIST DISCOURSE IN THE *TAFSIR* OF TUAN GURU NIK AZIZ NIK MAT, *MURSHID'UL AM* OF PAS

FARISH A. NOOR

Power and Politics do not pre-exist Culture. On the contrary, they are culturally constructed. ... It is in culture that people fashion power and the acceptance of it. If power and its transmutation through a process of legitimization into authority is intrinsically a cultural phenomenon, then Culture itself is inherently political. The fundamental question therefore is not the mechanics but the *symbolics* of power.[1]

— Clive S. Kessler

"Hei Tuhan! Ajarlah aku perkara yang aku masih jahil"
(Tuan Guru Nik Aziz Nik Mat)[2]

This chapter focuses mainly on the *tafsir* (Quranic exegesis) by the *Murshid'ul Am* (Spiritual Leader) of the Pan-Malaysian Islamic Party (PAS), Tuan Guru Nik Aziz Nik Mat. It attempts to analyse the various ways and means through which the Quran has been interpreted, recontextualised and communicated by the spiritual leader of PAS to his own domestic audience and political constituency, the Malay-Muslims of Kelantan.

195

By using the tools of discourse analysis, the chapter will show just how and why the *tafsir* by Nik Aziz has the appeal that it does to his local constituency and how it manages to communicate both religious and political meanings that are relevant and understandable to the local audience. It is also important to note that Nik Aziz's use of the vernacular and localized idiom is unique in Malaysia: no other recognized *ulama* has ever attempted a localized reading of the Quran in this way. Furthermore, the political slant that is clearly apparent in these *tafsir* is also another factor that accounts for their appeal and continued relevance to the intended audience. It is this dimension of religio-political culture, and the cultural mediation of religion and politics, that will be the main concern of the chapter.

Change and Continuity in the Evolution of *Ulama* Discourse

> Ceramah yang kita adakan bukan hanya bermula sekitar tahun empat puluhan atau lima puluhan, iaitu sebelum merdeka, malah ianya sebagai kesinambungan ceramah-ceramah yang dilakukan oleh para Nabi dan para Rasul sejak dulu lagi.[3]
>
> — Tuan Guru Nik Aziz Nik Mat.

There are *ulama*, and there are *ulama*.

The historical development of *living* Islam in its myriad forms has given birth to successive generations of *alim ulama* (literally, men of learning and/or knowledge) whose knowledge and expertise in the fields of Islamic law, theology, philosophy, and mysticism have given them immense power and influence among their devoted followers. Some of these *ulama* have given their lives for the defence of Islam against the onslaught of external and internal dangers and threats. Others have paid lip service to authority and ended up being reduced to rubber-stamps of the state. Yet one thing unites them all, and it is the fact that the *ulama* as a whole represent a conservative constituency whose task it was (and is) to conserve and protect the dogma and praxis of Islam through good and bad times.

The spread of Islam from the Arab lands to other parts of the world — Europe, the Mediterranean, Africa, Central Asia, the Indian subcontinent, the Far East, and Southeast Asia — owes a significant debt to the labours of the *ulama* and generations of Muslim mystics (*sufis*) who brought Islam to new audiences and new communities. In the process, they helped to alter the socio-cultural and political terrain of the countries they visited, and in many cases their intervention helped in turn to create new political-cultural constituencies.

The coming of Islam to the Malay archipelago was such a case of a *penetration pacifique* where Islam slowly managed to find its way in an already overcrowded cosmos populated by the gods and demigods of Hinduism, Buddhism, and a host of local belief and value systems. Yet, Islam managed to gain a foothold in this tumultuous universe of competing divinities and epistemologies, and eventually gained the upper hand by the thirteenth to fifteenth centuries.

Much has already been said and written about the role played by the early *sufis* and *ulama* who brought Islam to the Malay world. Scholars such as Hurgronje, Kern, Drewes, Fatimi, al-Attas, and Alatas have written at length about the various ways and means through which Islam slipped through the net of Hindu-Buddhist mysticism and found its own place in the Malay order of things.[4] Many of these writings have focused on developments in the past, and have tended to look at the process of adaptation and acculturation that took place during the initial stages after Islam's arrival in the Malay isles. Few contemporary scholars have been concerned with examining the constant process of adaptation and localization, which continues still, perpetuated by later generations of *ulama* in the present age.

Any attempt to analyse and understand the role played by the *ulama* in the present age must take into account a number of relevant factors. For a start, such an analysis needs to be couched in terms of modernity and its elements. The *ulama* of today live in an age of nation-states and they inhabit a thoroughly modern political universe where concepts and values such as citizenship, rights, law and communitarianism/individualism come into play. Though it would be impossible to deny that the *ulama* have played a political role all along, the *ulama* of today have themselves evolved to become political animals inhabiting a political wilderness of their own. The *ulama* now belong to political parties and movements and have themselves played an important role as agents of social and political change in their societies.

Furthermore, political considerations are also close at hand in the work of the *ulama* today: they speak of their constituencies and parties;

guard their discursive territory jealously; utilize the tools of politics and political mobilization in expanding and strengthening their respective followings; and many of them talk openly of the need for political power, authority, and control. For many *ulama*, the discourse of Islam has long since developed to become a religio-political project, with the Islamic state as its final goal.

In this political struggle, language and discursive practice play a major role in the battle for hearts and minds. This was the crucial point raised by Clive Kessler (1992) in his observation of Malay-Muslim politics nearly a decade ago when he wrote that:

> Power and Politics do not pre-exist Culture. On the contrary, they are culturally constructed. ... It is in culture that people fashion power and the acceptance of it. If power and its transmutation through a process of legitimization into authority is intrinsically a cultural phenomenon, then Culture itself is inherently political. The fundamental question therefore is not the mechanics but the *symbolics* of power.

This chapter follows on from Kessler's observation to examine the contestation over the symbols of power and authority. The focus is mainly on the discourse of the *ulama*, in the field where their dominance has remained so far unchallenged: the *tafsir* (exegesis and interpretation) of the Quran. The main works of *tafsir* analysed in the chapter are the *tafsir* by the *Murshid'ul Am* of PAS, Tuan Guru Nik Aziz Nik Mat. The chapter explores the various ways and means through which the Quran has been interpreted, recontextualized and communicated by the spiritual leader of PAS to his own domestic audience and political constituency, the Malay-Muslims of the state of Kelantan, in northeast Malaysia.

The Poverty of Riches and the Riches of Poverty: Explaining the Popularity and Influence of Tuan Guru Nik Aziz Nik Mat

> The option elected by any religious community will be determined — not by the timeless truths of scripture but by the struggle for the influence among rival bearers of the Word.[5]
>
> — Robert Hefner

Any attempt to explain the popularity and influence of Tuan Guru Nik Aziz Nik Mat must begin with a cursory examination of the development of PAS[6] in the course of Malaysian politics.

Though it would be impossible to cover here the development of PAS and its arch nemesis, the UMNO[7] (the United Malays National Organization) party, it suffices to note that both parties have regarded the Malay-Muslims of Malaysia as their natural constituency. Since their emergence in the late 1940s and early 1950s, both the UMNO and PAS have vied for the support of the Malay-Muslims throughout the country, and both parties have tailored their policies and political discourse accordingly. PAS and the UMNO have both played the anti-colonial, anti-communist, ethno-nationalist, communitarian and Islamist cards at different times and, from the late 1950s onwards, Malaysia has experienced the cumulative effects of an Islamization contest brought about by the intense (and at times violent) rivalry between these two Malay-Muslim parties.

It was, however, only from the 1980s onwards that the influence of the *ulama* in PAS really grew. After the fall of the Islamist party's fourth president, Muhammad Asri Muda (who was overthrown after an internal party coup), the entry into PAS of the "Young Turks" faction (led by defectors from the Malaysian Islamic Youth Movement, or ABIM)[8] and the rise of the *ulama* faction, led by men such as Ustaz Yusof Rawa and Tuan Guru Nik Aziz, PAS was set on a course of conflict with its arch rival, the UMNO.

From 1982 onwards, PAS came under the leadership of *ulama* who turned to the Iranian revolution as their model for the future (though they firmly rejected the *Shia* teachings of the Iranian *mullah* themselves). The language and rhetoric of PAS was radically altered to suit its new mood and temper, and the "Arabization" of PAS politics was clearly evident in the sartorial changes that occurred among PAS leaders: suits, ties, and leather shoes were abandoned in favour of *jubah* (robes), *janggut* (beards), *kepiah* (skull-caps), and *serban* (turbans). For the *ulama* of the party — which included men like Nik Aziz — these changes seemed to come with little difficulty.

The Islamization race between PAS and the UMNO-led Barisan Nasional (National Front) government that took place in the 1980s and 1990s led to an obvious attempt by all parties concerned to out-Islamize each other. Apart from PAS, the other Islamist movements in the country, like ABIM and the neo-*sufi* Darul Arqam[9] movement, also joined in the fray. The key objective during this struggle was control over the content, definition, and meaning of Islam and Islamist discourse itself. The leader of the Darul Arqam movement, Ustaz Ashaari Mohammad, claimed that his interpretation of Islam was the correct one — a boast that was bolstered by the additional assertion that he enjoyed direct contact with God and the Prophet Muhammad on a personal basis.

Not to be outdone, the UMNO-led government also had a few tricks up its sleeve. In response to the growing tide of Islamist activism on the campuses and in the Malay heartland, the government of Dr Mahathir Mohamad initiated its own state Islamization programme, which culminated in the formation of numerous Islamist think-tanks and research centres. Among these were the Malaysian Institute for Islamic Research (IKIM), and the International Institute of Islamic Thought and Civilization[10] (ISTAC), which came under the leadership of the influential Islamist thinker, Professor Syed Naquib al-Attas.[11]

Nevertheless, despite the enormous advantages that both Syed Naquib al-Attas and Ustaz Ashaari Mohammad enjoyed — the former closely linked to the government, the latter closely linked to God — neither had managed to develop the same following as the *ulama* of PAS, both quantitatively and qualitatively. In time, a number of internal and external problems helped to diminish the popularity and influence of both these Islamist leaders.

From its beginning in 1991, ISTAC was associated with its founder-director, Syed Naquib al-Attas. Himself the product of Eton, Sandhurst, and the School of Oriental and African Studies (SOAS) in London, Naquib al-Attas happened to be the mentor to the ex-ABIM leader Anwar Ibrahim[12] (who was by then Minister of Finance in Dr Mahathir's government). Al-Attas' influence was also spread far and wide among a whole generation of Malaysian university graduates, and ABIM members in particular.[13] Al-Attas's most influential book was *Islam and Secularism*, first published by ABIM in 1978 (the same year that Edward Said's *Orientalism* was published). It became the standard reference for an entire generation of middle-class professionals, politicians, students, and teachers in the country.

In Malaysian academic circles, Naquib al-Attas was known as the Malaysian proponent of the "Islamization of knowledge" project, now a major international effort, for which he claimed credit. In high-level social and political circles, he was well received, thanks to his mixed Malay-Arab ancestry, his aristocratic background, and his intimate links to the early founders of the dominant conservative UMNO party. By co-opting Naquib al-Attas into its expansive network of Islamic institutions and research centres, the government of Dr Mahathir had hoped to gain an upper hand against the Islamist opposition in the country.

However, Syed Naquib al-Attas' dominant stature and image were precisely the factors that made ISTAC an impenetrable and inaccessible institution whose relevance to daily life diminished day by day. Set as it was in one of the most exclusive (and expensive) parts of the capital, ISTAC was allowed to carry on with its academic work in blissful isolation. The highly complex writings of al-Attas — dutifully published in luxuriously bound (and prohibitively expensive) volumes by ISTAC — were well beyond the reach of the ordinary masses, who had neither the opportunity to buy them nor the time to read them. While the research and academic staff of the Institute busied themselves with questions about the need for a radical paradigm shift that would bring about an essentially Islamic epistemology that Muslims could call their own, ordinary Malay-Muslims in the country went about their lives as they had always done.

ISTAC was not the only institution whose star was set to wane: Ustaz Ashaari and the neo-*sufi* Darul Arqam movement, which he led, also would ultimately fall victim to their own success.[14] By the mid-1990s, the movement had managed to spread its wings not only across the entire country but also abroad. From its headquarters in the Madinah Al Arqam Saiyyidina Abu Bakar As-Siddiq, Sungai Pencala (near Kuala Lumpur), the neo-*sufi* revivalist movement established and expanded its own network of *dakwah* (missionary) and training camps, shops, and business premises, agricultural production centres (that produced organic vegetables for their own use and sale), and transport and logistics services all over West and East Malaysia, Indonesia, Thailand, Singapore, and even up to Central Asia. Darul Arqam members travelled as far as Uzbekistan in order to spread their teachings and to form working relationships with various *sufi tariqas* there, such as the Naqshbandiyyah. The movement had its own bureaus, which mirrored the departments of the federal government, and senior leaders of the movement were put in charge of "ministries" and "departments", such as foreign affairs, media and communications, *dakwah* and education, and so on. In terms of its structure, goals and tactics, Muhammad Khalid Masud (2000) has referred to Darul Arqam as a prime example of a transnational movement for faith renewal, in line with the Tablighi Jama'at of the Indian subcontinent.[15]

By the late 1980s, however, Ustaz Ashaari's pronouncements became more and more forceful and provocative. Owing to his growing popularity, he was invited to appear on television and radio several times, but his ideas on Islamic governance and an Islamic state did not win him the approval of the state, which did not share his inclination towards *sufism* and mystical practices. Ustaz Ashaari's discourteous comments on the Islamic credentials of senior UMNO leaders did not earn him the support of men like Dr Mahathir and Anwar Ibrahim either. During the Gulf conflict of 1990–91, he wrote and published a book entitled *Perjuangan Teluk: Islam Akan Kembali Gemilang* (The Gulf War: Islam Shall Re-emerge Triumphant), in which he predicted that the American-led international force against Saddam Hussein would be defeated and that the conflict would result in victory for Saddam Hussein and Islam.[16] In the book, he condemned "craven and hypocritical" Muslim leaders who supported the multinational effort against Iraq, on the grounds that they had a higher moral obligation to support other Muslim leaders in distress. It was clear that the real target of Ustaz Ashaari's book was Dr Mahathir, Anwar Ibrahim, and the other Malay-Muslim leaders of the UMNO.

Ustaz Ashaari got himself into further trouble when he began to speculate publicly about the internal conflicts within the UMNO between 1993 and 1994. Rumours about plots and counter-plots by UMNO leaders against each other were soon traced back to Ustaz Ashaari, who was then seen as a maverick mystic whose other-worldly aura and charisma had clearly gone beyond the bounds of acceptability. Ustaz Ashaari may have believed that he enjoyed good personal relations with God but, by meddling in the internal affairs of the UMNO and the disputes between its leaders, he was courting disaster for himself and his own organization. Soon enough, the hand of the UMNO-led government was roused and the first to feel its blow were the leaders of Arqam themselves.

The crackdown on Darul Arqam began in earnest in September 1994. Co-ordinating their activities with their counterparts in Indonesia, Thailand, and Singapore, the Malaysian security forces and the Special Branch (SB) began a wave of arrests that managed to catch practically every senior leader of the movement.[17] Ustaz Ashaari and the other senior leaders of the movement were detained and interrogated at the government's Islamic rehabilitation centre. In the end, they were made to admit their mistakes: Ashaari and the other leaders of the movement appeared on television and confessed that their beliefs were wrong and against the principles of Islam. They then repented their errors and declared that the teachings of the Arqam movement had led others astray. Finally, in November 1994, the movement was formally disbanded by the leaders themselves.

The appeal and influence of both Syed Naquib al-Attas and Ustaz Ashaari Mohammad were limited, because they were seen as élitists and their respective institutions and movements were open only to a limited following. While the Islamist institutions of the state, such as IKIM and ISTAC, were engaged in their project of re-presenting Islam as a modern system of values and way of life, they overlooked the fact that their message was not being delivered to all quarters of Malay-Muslim society. Despite all its efforts, IKIM and ISTAC were seen as institutions that had been set up under the patronage of the Mahathir administration and as part of the government's own Islamization campaign (described as a cosmetic gesture at best by the *ulama* of PAS). The efforts of the state's Islamist institutions were also being negated by the other economic policies being pursued by the government at the same time.

Like ISTAC, the Darul Arqam movement was also hampered by its own success. Ustaz Ashaari had strengthened the profile of the organization by winning over influential and important members of the establishment, like Tamrin Ghaffar (son of the Deputy Prime Minister, Ghaffar Baba). The movement also boasted that it enjoyed the support of members of royalty, the Malay aristocracy, and large sections of the urban Malay intelligentsia and middle class. However, the fact that a large number of Darul Arqam's followers were university-trained professionals added to the élite image of the movement as a whole and eventually isolated it from the mainstream of Malay-Muslim society.

One of the factors that account for the failure of the state's own Islamist institutions, such as ISTAC and IKIM, and non-governmental Islamist movements like Darul Arqam, is the fact that they were all seen to be élitist in their orientation and practice. Neither ISTAC nor Darul Arqam was truly populist in the sense of being able to transcend the cleavages of class, wealth, and power that remained all too real in the lives of millions of ordinary Malay-Muslims in the country. What was needed was a "third force" that could speak the language of the man in the street, the farmer in the field, and the corporate manager in the high-rise apartment block. By the 1990s, such a voice was on the scene: that of the *ulama* Tuan Guru Nik Aziz Nik Mat. If the story of ISTAC and Darul Arqam spoke of the poverty of riches, Tuan Guru Nik Aziz at least understood and appreciated the riches of poverty.

Deoband's Own: Tuan Guru Nik Aziz Nik Mat and the Return of the Vernacular

> The political structure of Islam begins to take shape after the leader is in place. The leader is the 'plug', the essential link, the conduit or the intermediary link who draws power and legitimacy from the ultimate source. Power can only flow along channels that are compatible with the leader's own source of power, which is of course Allah.[18]
>
> — Kalim Sidiqqui

Throughout the 1970s and 1980s, PAS had been in a state of limbo and was searching for a sense of direction. Under the leadership of its fourth president, Dato' Asri Muda, the Pan-Malaysian Islamist Party had performed a radical U-turn by adopting the ideology of ethno-nationalism as its political platform. This had cost the party dearly and its brief entry into the ruling Barisan Nasional coalition (between 1974 and 1978) led to a massive erosion of support from its traditional supporters.

All that was set to change after Asri Muda was ejected from the party in 1982, and PAS finally managed to regain control of its home state of Kelantan at the elections of 1990. Following PAS's victory in Kelantan, the party had to decide on a suitable candidate for the position of Chief Minister. The honour was bestowed upon Tuan

Guru Nik Aziz Nik Mat, who became the first *ulama* in Malaysia to hold such a high position in government. The president of PAS, Ustaz Fadzil Noor, supported the decision to select the Tuan Guru as the Chief Minister on the grounds that this move would bring PAS one step closer to realizing its ultimate political goal: to create an Islamic State under the rule of the *ulama*.

In the eyes of Nik Aziz — inspired by the great *Alim Ulama* of the past and the architect of the new PAS of the 1990s — the purpose of the Islamic party was nothing short of winning over the control of the State and, having done that, winning the battle for the heart and soul of the people. This was the sacred duty and covenant carried by the *ulama* in particular, as the inheritors of the Prophet's mission on earth.[20] In order to understand how and why the party has developed into what it is today, it is necessary to understand more about the personal background and beliefs of the *ulama* who was singularly responsible for turning PAS into the most important Islamist opposition party in the history of Malaysia: Tuan Guru Nik Aziz Nik Mat.

The second *Murshid'ul Am* of PAS, Tuan Guru Nik Aziz Nik Mat, was born in Kampung Pulau Melaka in 1931. His lineage (*salasilah*) can be traced all the way back to the rulers of Kelantan, Patani, and Langkasuka, including Maharaja Srimat Trailokyaraja Maulibhushana Warma Dewa, Raja Surendra, Raja Bharubhasa (Sultan Mahmud of Langkasuka), Sultan Iskandar Shah (the first Sultan of Kelantan), Sultan Mansur Shah, Raja Abdul Rahman, Raja Abdullah, Raja Mohammad, and Raja Banjar.[20] His father was Raja Mohammad II, also known as Ustaz Nik Mat Alim Raja Banjar, one of the most prominent *ulama* in Kelantan during his lifetime. Ustaz Nik Mat had studied the Quran, *Hadith, fiqh, tasawwuf, tafsir* and *tajwid* under the famous Kelantanese *ulama*, Tuan Guru Mohd Yusuf bin Muhamad, who was also known as Tok Kenali.[21] His mother, Raja Tijah, was herself of noble stock, from one of the aristocratic families of Kelantan.

Nik Aziz was brought up in a prestigious and conservative religious household. His father Ustaz Nik Mat Alim had his own religious school, the Sekolah Agama Darul Anwar, and he was well known for his curious habits and daily rituals. Nik Mat Alim objected to the fact that his son was forced to wear short trousers to school when he was undergoing his primary (state) education. After Nik Aziz had spent

only three months in the state government school, his father decided
to send him to a traditional *pondok* school instead, which had been
set up by the famous *ulama* and religious leader, Tok Kenali, at Kubang
Kerian. Nik Aziz later studied at another traditional *pondok* school in
Trengganu, run by Tuan Guru Haji Abbas of Besut.[22] This makes Nik
Aziz the first PAS leader whose education occurred almost entirely
within the traditional *pondok* and *madrasah* system.

In 1952, Nik Aziz travelled to India to study at the Dar'ul
Ulum Deoband seminary, otherwise known as the Deobandi College
of Islam.[23] It was at Deobandi that Nik Aziz first underwent formal
religious education at the hands of the Deobandi *ulama* and *Shaikh al-
Hadith*, such as Maulana Husain Ahmad al-Madani, who taught him
that Islam was in need of purification and that the task of safeguarding
the interests of Muslims fell on the *ulama*. The Deobandi school was
known for its emphasis on the role of the *ulama* class. It had created
a reputation for itself, thanks to its intensive mode of teaching and its
closed academic atmosphere, which helped to bring the students (*murid*)
closer together, thereby creating strong *ulama-murid* networks.

After completing his studies at Deobandi in 1957, Nik Aziz
travelled to Lahore, Pakistan, to study *tafsir* (exegesis) of the Quran.
He then went to Egypt where he was impressed by the progress and
development that he saw around him.[24] He studied at the University
of al-Azhar in Cairo, where he first read Arabic and then Islamic law
and jurisprudence (*fiqh*). In Cairo, he also became acquainted with
the writing and work of other famous Islamist thinkers, such as Hassan
al-Banna and Sayyid Qutb, and movements such as the Ikhwan'ul
Muslimun.[25] Nik Aziz finally graduated with a degree in Law in 1962,
after having studied abroad for a total of twelve years. When Nik Aziz
returned to Malaysia, his family and friends could not recognize him
at first. His appearance had changed radically, as he had grown
accustomed to wearing Western dress, including black leather shoes,
coat, and tie, but Nik Aziz soon altered his sartorial style to suit the
needs and norms of the local environment.[26]

The ideas and beliefs of Nik Aziz were very much shaped by his
educational experiences abroad. The Deobandi school, for instance,
taught the values of self-reliance and independence to its students.
The lessons drawn from his experience at Deobandi and al-Azhar,
however, also convinced Nik Aziz that the salvation of the Muslims

depended on the source of the guidance they received. The Deobandi school, shaped as it was by its *Ashraf* culture, argued that Muslims should be guided only by the *ulama*, and that society would be best governed when it is led by the spiritually inclined.[27] Nik Aziz reflected these values in both his personal beliefs as well as his activities. In 1964, he took up a teaching post at the Ma'ahad Muhammadi religious school in Kota Bahru, and later at the Sekolah Menengah Agama Tarbiah Mardiah, Panchor. In 1967, inspired by the example set by the activists of the Ikhwan'ul Muslimun, Nik Aziz took his first steps into the world of politics by joining the Islamic party, PAS, which he regarded as the only party that tried to uphold the *iqamah ad-Din*, uplift the *khair al-ummah* and pave the way for *daulah islamiyyah*. He then stood as a PAS candidate for elections in the constituency of Kelantan Hilir (Pengkalan Chepa).[28] By taking these steps, Nik Aziz became part of the *harakah islamiyyah*.

From this period, Nik Aziz began to lecture his followers and constituents about their religious as well as socio-political obligations. In the curriculum and co-curriculum programme he developed for his fellow teachers and students, he stressed the importance of the role of the *Alim Ulama* as the "spiritual guides" to the community, who would care for both the material and spiritual well-being of the *awamm* (community).[29] He reminded his students in the religious school that they were not a group that was separate from society and that they had a moral and spiritual obligation to return to society as leaders and teachers.[30] For Nik Aziz, religious education was a means to create a class of spiritually-inclined and knowledgeable leaders, who would safeguard the welfare and concerns of Muslims and ensure that the law of the Syariah would reign supreme in the land.[31]

The other aspect of Deobandi thinking that was clearly evident in Nik Aziz's style of leadership was the desire to purify Islam and Muslim culture from elements regarded as un-Islamic (*khurafat*), heretical (*shirk*), innovative (*bid'ah*), and deviationist (*ajaran sesat*). As soon as he returned to Malaysia, Nik Aziz announced his arrival in no uncertain terms by declaring that many of the traditional practices sanctioned by the older generation of traditional *ulama* were in fact un-Islamic. The traditional *ulama*, he argued, were wrong because their scriptural knowledge rested on old books (*kitab kuning*[32]) that were faulty or incompletely understood.

Within PAS itself, Nik Aziz's reputation as the Tuan Guru (respected teacher) grew rapidly. After he took command of the Dewan Ulama (Council of *Ulama*), Nik Aziz sought to build up its importance as the party's "inner chamber" of consultation and arbitration.[33] Together with the president, Ustaz Yusof Rawa, he sought to strengthen the position of the *ulama* leadership within the party through the Dewan, which continued to issue judgements that sanctioned the policies held by the political leadership of the party. His position within the party was strengthened even more in 1986 when he became the only PAS candidate to win a seat in the Parliament. Following the party's worst performance at the polls ever, the Tuan Guru was given the authority to make whatever changes he felt were necessary in order to bring the party back into line, and to broaden its appeal to the masses. This Nik Aziz did in his own unique way: by bringing Islam back down to earth, right up to the doorstep of the humble peasant, living in his wooden house by the padi field.

God Amidst the Padi Fields: Localizing the Message of Islam

> Dari Raja dalam istana, sampai kepada Pat Mat yang duduk dalam kampung, semua sekali kena diberitahu perkara ini: Kamu ini hamba Tuhan![34]
>
> — Tuan Guru Nik Aziz Nik Mat

From 1986 to 1990, PAS's efforts were directed towards one simple objective: regaining control of its home state of Kelantan and reclaiming the political constituency it had lost to the UMNO-led Barisan Nasional government. Towards this end, Nik Aziz and the *ulama* of PAS redoubled their efforts in the area of both religious and political education, the party utilizing whatever avenues were left open to it. Religious classes, lectures, study groups and consultations in the mosques, *surau*, *madrasah*, and religious schools became the centres of PAS's political activity as PAS *ulama* and activists sought to win over support from the uninitiated.

During the election campaign in 1990, the use of religious discourse, rites, and rituals was widespread among PAS leaders and activists, in Kelantan in particular. PAS (which was then in an instrumental alliance with the now non-existent Semangat 46 party led by Tengku Razaleigh Hamzah) had as its election slogan "*Membangun Bersama Islam*" (Developing With Islam). Nik Aziz himself had urged the people to go out and vote in the elections and to use their votes as part of the *jihad* to topple the UMNO-led government, which they claimed had gone beyond the pale of Islam.[35] The *ulama* had also urged the people to perform special prayers (*sembahyang hajat*) and to read the *do'a qunut nazilah* prayer during their rallies, in order to guarantee their success.[36] Together with its coalition partners, PAS managed to sweep the state of Kelantan *in toto*, wiping out all traces of the UMNO. Altogether they won all thirty-nine state assembly seats and all twelve parliamentary seats for Kelantan.

From the moment that it took over the government of the state of Kelantan in 1990, PAS geared its activities towards rebuilding and strengthening its power base and expanding its constituency.[37] Following the pattern set by many other Islamist movements, the party focused its attention on the sponsorship of religious colleges, *madrasah* and traditional religious *pondok* schools. In the 1991 Kelantan State budget, the PAS-led state government allocated RM15 million to the Yayasan Islam (Islamic Foundation) of Kelantan, in order to uplift the standard of religious (Islamic) education. State funds were also allocated to *pondok* schools in the state.[38] Nik Aziz even arranged for the Sultan of Kelantan to tour the *pondok* schools of the state on the occasion of his birthday celebrations in 1991.[39] Such investments paid off very quickly: in 1990, there were 34,721 students enrolled in religious schools that were sponsored by the Yayasan Islam of Kelantan. By 1991, the figure had risen to 37,726; by 1992, to 39,633; and by 1993, to 41,864.[40]

It was through the renewed patronage and support of the *pondok* and *madrasah* of Kelantan that PAS hoped to create a second generation of Islamist students, scholars, and activists who would later take up the struggle of the party as well. It was envisaged that, in time, this extensive network would expand even further and link itself with the wider network of Islamist *madrasah* in countries like Indonesia, India, and Pakistan.

The local network of mosques, *surau*, *pondok*, and *madrasah* also became the centres for the propagation of PAS's reading of Islam. As indicated above, the use of religious, educational, and research centres for the dissemination of religio-political ideas is not new to Malaysia. For example, the Malaysian Government had attempted to create a number of Islamist research institutes and academic centres (the most prestigious of which was the International Islamic University [IIU], based in Kuala Lumpur). However, these institutions had failed to penetrate the grass-roots level of society. In Kelantan, the new PAS state government under Nik Aziz was attempting to do the same thing — albeit on a more modest budget but with greater success. The *ceramah* (lectures) of PAS leaders continued to attract large audiences, much to the frustration of the government. While PAS's opponents understandably dismissed reports of large gatherings at PAS rallies and *ceramah* as party-political propaganda or bad journalism, questions remained about how and why these *ceramah* were so popular. One factor that was left out of the discussion was the cultural mediation of religio-political discourse.

God Comes to *Kelante'*: Nik Aziz's Use of the Vernacular *Tafsir*

From the mid-1990s onwards, the *kuliah* (classes) and *ceramah* (lectures) of Tuan Guru Nik Aziz have been compiled by the staff and students of the Ma'ahad ad-Dakwah wal-Imamah (MDI). The first set of lectures, given during the fasting month of Ramadhan, was compiled and published as a book, *Islam Boleh* (Islam Can Succeed), which appeared just in time for the election campaign of that year (1995). This book was immediately followed by a second compilation, issued under the title, *Kelantan: Universiti Politik Terbuka* (Kelantan: Open University of Politics).[41]

Most of these lectures were delivered by Nik Aziz at the MDI, or Dewan Zulkiflee in Kota Bahru. The format of the lectures was simple and they followed the same procedures that the Tuan Guru had set himself since he began lecturing to the public in the 1980s. They began on each Friday morning at about 9:30 am, with the audience ready to take notes and record the speeches, to be listened to again. Nik Aziz would begin the lectures with a *doa* (prayer) and then read out a few lines from a *Surah* of his choice from the Quran. The lines would follow the order of the *Surah*, and the process would continue until the entire

Surah was completed. After reading a few lines, the Tuan Guru would then offer his own interpretation of the lines, this making up a large part of the lecture itself. Each lecture lasted between one and two hours.

What is interesting to note is the way in which Nik Aziz always tailored his speeches to suit the needs and interests of his local audience. Himself of Kelantanese origin, the Tuan Guru speaks Malay but with a strong Kelantanese *loghat* (dialect) that is immediately recognizable to all Malay speakers, even if it remains incomprehensible to some. He uses phrases and terms like "*aku*", "*kamu*", "*tuan ambo*" and "*ambo*" in his speeches — terms of reference that are so familiar that they may border on rudeness for many non-Kelantanese speakers. The lectures were also given in an easy-going, informal and even humorous style, filled with jokes and puns that made sense to the local (and largely rural) audience whom he referred to as "*orang Kelante*".

One point that the Tuan Guru has never tired of repeating to his audience is the specificity of their own local situation and condition in Kelantan. It is clear that what he has really been trying to do is to localize what is a universal religious discourse and tailor it to the local socio-cultural, economic, and political conditions of his own people. Rather than write and speak at length about abstract theological and epistemological concerns, Nik Aziz's real expertise lies in his ability to localize the universal and universalize the local. By so doing, he has made Islam a living reality and a solid presence in the daily lives of ordinary Kelantanese people.

To illustrate this point, it is worth looking at one *tafsir* in particular — Nik Aziz's *tafsir* of the *Surah Hud*. The *Surah Hud* (Chapter of Hud, a Prophet in Islam) is the eleventh *Surah* of the Quran. It was revealed during the last year of the Prophet Muhammad's stay in Mecca, shortly after the *Surah Yunus*.[42] Both *Surahs* share similar themes and concerns and there is some continuity in terms of the subjects and personalities featured. As Asad (1980) has shown, the main theme of the *Surah Hud* is the revelation and proof of the existence of God, and God's will through his Prophets, lessons that Nik Aziz tries to bring home to his fellow Kelantanese listeners. The Tuan Guru begins his exegesis of the *Surah* thus:

Walaupun Surah ini dipanggil Surah Hud tetapi bila Allah bercerita Dia punggut habis cerita-cerita orang seperjuangan

dengan Hud — cerita Nabi Nuh, dan dua tiga Nabi lain —
yang dikira tokoh yang ada banyak cerita. Orang yang tidak ada
cerita dalam hidup diatas mukabumi ini laksana orang lesu,
orang kaku; bangun pagi bawa lembu ke padang, sebelah petang
sabit rumput, balik ke rumah tidur. Kalau kita hidup macam ini
saja orang kata kita hidup tak ada cerita, hidup tak ada bernama.
Bila dia hidup tak bernama, semasa hidup orang tak berasa dia
ada dikampung; kalau mati orang tak berasa kosong. Tidak merasa
sangkut dihati dia tidak ada benda yang dibuatnya di muka
dunia ini.[43]

In these opening lines, the cosmic drama of the Quran and the
tales of the Prophets are brought down to the level of the local
Kelantanese audience. As if to remind them of their own present
state of affairs, Nik Aziz tells his listeners that those who spend their
days just tending to their buffaloes and rice in the fields (and go back
to sleep afterwards) do not really merit much discussion — be it in
religious texts or profane ones. No-one in the *kampung* (village) will
remember them. The stories (*cerita*) in the Quran are therefore about
those who have led important and eventful lives, unlike them, the
little village folk (*orang kampung*) of Kelantan.

From the outset, a great deal of stage-setting has gone into the
tafsir of Nik Aziz. The stories he tells and the lessons he teaches come
from a higher plane, occupied by God's Prophets and "men with
stories to tell". At the peak of this hermeneutic universe is, of course,
God, the author and prime mover of all things. They, the audience, are
located right at the bottom of the order of things, at the foot of the
stage of life, so to speak. Here, the world of Nik Aziz is already being
divided along vertical and horizontal planes that separate the worthy
from the ordinary.

It is also interesting to see where Nik Aziz locates himself and
the *ulama* of PAS within this grand universal schema. In his *tafsir*,
Nik Aziz spells out the role and duties of the *"guru yang benar-benar
murshid"* like himself: they are the ones who will lead the Muslim
ummah both here in the world and onwards and upwards to the life
hereafter:

Guru yang murshid maknanya guru yang boleh memimpin
manusia ke akhirat, bukan hanya memimpin manusia ke pejabat
sahaja. Inilah guru yang dikehendaki oleh Islam.[44]

It thus falls to the *ulama* to lead the Muslim *ummah* both in this world and onwards to the hereafter (*dunia akhirat*). If a vertical cleavage between God and Man has been drawn in the *tafsir* of Nik Aziz, the ones who are meant to straddle the divide between the sacred and profane are none other than the *ulama* themselves. They are, in a sense, the ones who stand between the life in the present and the one to come.

Among the ordinary masses, there are also differences and divisions. Elsewhere in the *tafsir* of Nik Aziz, there are references to Muslims and non-Muslims, and the latter are further divided into groups and subgroups ranging from *kafirs* (non-believers) to *munafikin* (hypocrites), *mushrikin* (idolaters/deviants), and *fasiq* (evil ones). At times, these distinctions coincide with racial and ethnic ones, and it is not unusual for Nik Aziz to refer to non-Malays in his lessons as well, be they Hindus who "worship" the cow "as their God"[45] [*sic*] or unscrupulous "*Cina Apek*"[46] (a derogatory term for the Chinese) who exploit and swindle the Malays of Kelantan. Nik Aziz's condemnation of all these non-Malay and non-Muslim groups is final and applied with a broad brush which tars all and sundry:

> Semua orang kafir di muka dunia ini jahat belaka — tidak ada seorang kafir yang baik… Maksiat yang berlaku di dunia ini sama ada oleh orang kafir ataupun fasik.[47]

It is clear that the audience that Nik Aziz wishes to address is a local Malay-Muslim one. After setting to one side all other sections of the public (Westerners, non-Malays, and non-Muslims), his target audience has been narrowed to his Malay-Muslim students and followers.

However, the stage that is set in the *tafsir* of Nik Aziz is also all-embracing and all-encompassing. No single individual or group is ever located radically outside the parameters of God's orderly universe. God is forever present and even the *kampungs* and padi fields of Kelantan remain within the panoptic scope of the omniscient God, who surveys all that there is to see and knows all that there is to know. The vertical axis connects even the lowliest of Kelantanese to God above, but the peasant in the audience is also reminded of his status and station in life, which is on par with the other nonentities and nobodies sitting next to him or her.

Having reminded his listeners that God's vision is greater than
theirs, Nik Aziz goes on to point out that God's wisdom and
intelligence are also infinitely greater than that of the padi farmers of
Kelantan. He does this by trying to answer the questions that continue
to trouble the ordinary farmer in the field:

> Cuba ambo semua tanya: Mengapa Tuhan buat rumput, buat
> lalang? Takkanlah Allah Ta'ala yang begitu cerdik sanggup membuat
> benda-benda yang tidak berfaedah. Kita yang bodoh ini ini pun
> tak dapat buat benda-benda yang tidak terpakai kerja, inikan pula
> Tuhan yang maha cerdik, Tuhan yang maha bijak. Sudah tentulah
> tiap-tiap perkara yang dibuatnya ada faedah, ada hikmah belaka,
> cuma terletak diatas kita rajin atau tidak didalam mengcungkil
> rahsia masalah ini.[48]

Here again, we see how the *tafsir* of Nik Aziz emphasizes the
hierarchical nature of the Islamic cosmos. By emphasizing the
insurmountable gulf of knowledge and wisdom between God and
ordinary men, he underscores the fact that the universe is fundamentally
an uneven and unequal one. Having convinced his rural audience that
the weeds and *lalang* (a type of long grass regarded as a nuisance by
farmers) that threaten their fields and crops are actually part of God's
divine plan for the cosmos (if only they knew), Nik Aziz then turns
to their stomachs. This he does when he attempts to explain to them
the complex mystery surrounding God's existence and the limits of
mankind's finite knowledge of the world:

> Kamu hendak tahu kebijaksanaan Tuhan, ukurlah apa yang ada
> pada diri manusia kerana manusia sendiri tak tahu keadaan
> dirinya… Sampai sekarang ini manusia tidak boleh jelaskan lagi
> apa yang dia berasa… Begitu juga masalah nasi dalam pinggan.
> Sedang kita asyik berbual, bila masuk kedalam dapur terbau
> masakan. "Bau apa ini? Bau bawang goreng, bau sup. Aloo!!
> Sudahlah bersembang, hei berhenti, mari makan nasi." Cuba
> jelaskan bagaimana kamu rasa terasa lapar. Macam mana kamu
> buat? Tidak ada siapa yang boleh kata, yang lapar ini begini,
> kerana saya buat begini. Buat macam mana? Molek-molek kamu
> sedang berbual, apabila terbau sup serta-merta kamu lapar. Jadi
> usahlah kamu hendak tahu hal langit dan bumi, hal dalam tubuh
> badan kamu pun kamu tak tahu.[49]

Obviously not persuaded by the theories of a certain Professor Pavlov, Nik Aziz, in his elaboration of the "*masalah nasi dalam pinggan*" (problem of the rice in the plate), aims at the gut instincts and intuitions of his audience instead. For die-hard sceptics who remain unmoved by the ironclad logic of Nik Aziz, the Tuan Guru goes one step further and aims below the belt when he introduces another parable of sorts, involving bodily functions usually kept private:

> Kalau ada juga orang yang mengaku dia tahu belaka, kata begini saja: "Bila kamu bangun pagi dan selak kain, memancut keluar air kencing. Sebelum kamu duduk di jamban, kenapa air kencing tak keluar? Kamu buat macam mana?" Kalau paip, bila kita pulas air terbit memancut. Kamu pulas apa? Pulas pun tidak, mulut pun tak berbunyi, tangan pun tak bergerak, tahu-tahu air kencing memancut keluar. Kenapa air kencing tidak keluar lepas kamu sudah masuk dalam jamban? …Sampai sekarang ini manusia tak dapat jelaskan lagi apa yang dia berasa.[50]

Putting aside the fact that some of Nik Aziz's parables and metaphors obviously hail from the store of *kampung* jokes and toilet humour, the fact remains that the discourse of the *tafsir* work because they operate within the well-established and time-honoured parameters of a localized discursive economy. Employing the symbols, tropes, and metaphors of a rural agrarian discourse, replete with its host of bawdy jokes, risque puns, and sexual innuendoes, Nik Aziz's *tafsir* is a classic example of local genius and sensitivity at work. It is this ability to transpose an alien message into a local context that allows Nik Aziz to do something else with his *tafsir*, namely, to use them as a convenient and highly effective vehicle for the communication of political and moral messages in order to reach the ears of his local constituency.

God is with the *Kampung*: Nik Aziz's *Tafsir* as Political Critique

> … Apa perbezaan antara kerajaan dengan gengster? Perbezaan pertama ialah gengster tidak ada bendera[51]
>
> — Tuan Guru Nik Aziz Nik Mat

The *tafsir* of Nik Aziz consists fundamentally of multifunctional discourses that are aimed at securing a number of objectives. On the surface, they function as tools for teaching and *dakwah* (missionary activity), a means to communicate the message and morals of Islam to a local audience — albeit via the use of some rather unorthodox case studies. However, it is clear that for Nik Aziz, the message of the Quran is not confined to the kitchen or the bathroom only. For in the *tafsir*, we also see an obvious and sustained attempt to bring to the foreground a political critique couched in religio-cultural terms that borrow extensively from the cultural repertoire and discursive economies of the Kelantanese themselves.

One of the recurrent religio-political themes that occur time and again in the *tafsir* of Nik Aziz is the idea of the fundamental equality of all before God and that God alone deserves the love, worship, and total obedience of men. For no one — be it the Sultan of Kelantan or *Pak Mat* (Uncle Mat) in the *kampung* — should think that his life of splendid isolation shields him from the sight of God. As Nik Aziz himself points out:

> Dari Raja dalam istana, sampai kepada Pat Mat yang duduk dalam kampung, semua sekali kena diberitahu perkara ini: Kamu ini hamba Tuhan![52]

Furthermore, for Nik Aziz, God is clearly on the side of the peasantry and the labourers. God's mercy flows in abundance to the poor and the pious, and it tends to run short for the very wealthy:

> Tuhan kata: "Bahawa laknat sentiasa mengekori dibelakang penderhaka-penderhaka dalam sepanjang hidup mereka di dunia ini dan di akhirat kelak." Tuhan berkata di atas dunia mereka dilaknatkan dengan diturun azab sepanjang hayat. Laknat ini maknanya disumpah, kena murka. Kepada orang-orang tua yang hati dan jiwanya masih bersih, mereka akan merasa sangat gerun kalau disumpah orang-orang kampung, apalah lagi bila mendengar orang yang disumpah Tuhan. Tapi bagi orang yang hidup dalam suasana kebendaan, hidup yang suasana materialis — orang yang bergaji besar, rumah besar, kebun besar, berduit banyak — mereka ini tak mengerti apanya kena sumpah. "Takut apa kena sumpah? Pitis aku banyak, pandailah aku hidup."[53]

Here the Tuan Guru's neat chain of equivalences strings together a host of adversaries of the just and righteous — those with huge salaries, grand houses, large estates, plentiful riches (*orang yang bergaji besar, rumah besar, kebun besar, berduit banyak*) — while the poor and the pious remain as the beloved of God. The moral economy of the peasant has been elevated and re-inscribed by the moral economy of the *ulama*, turning the class struggle in the town and countryside into a grander cosmic struggle between Good and Evil, Right and Wrong.

At no point, however, does Nik Aziz, the grand *ulama* and supreme spiritual leader of the Islamist party, forget that his adversaries are also political ones. He makes clear his opposition to the UMNO-led federal government based in Kuala Lumpur on a number of occasions. In another *tafsir* (*Tafsir Surah Yunus*), he goes as far as stating that:

> Saya ketua parti politik, bukan ketua guerrilla. Kalau saya ketua guerrilla, saya beli SCUD — yang Iraq tidak habis kirim ke Tel Aviv dan Riyadh — untuk bidas Kuala Lumpur.[54]

Because he is the spiritual leader of a political party, however, Nik Aziz explains to his audience that he is forced to limit himself to less explosive tactics, such as writing proposals and papers, engaging in seminars and debates. However, political engagement for Nik Aziz can, and does, take place on a number of levels, and his *tafsir* provides him with yet another avenue to criticize his opponents. This awareness is clearly shown in his *tafsir* when he describes the nefarious tactics of his political foes. Consider, for example, the way in which he explains the concept of the *munafikin* (hypocrites) with reference to the Special Branch (secret police) of the Malaysian state:

> Tuhan kata: "Ingat-ingat bahawa mereka itu gulung dada mereka, dengan tujuan hendak melindung diri atau menyusut daripada Allah, daripada Nabi Muhammad." Iktibar Quran ini benar-benar menyayat hati, melukakan hati orang-orang tertentu. Serupa kita kata beginilah, didalam majlis ini tentulah ada polis SB (Special Branch) yang datang bukan hendak mengaji, tetapi hendak mencari rahsia. Walaupun dia SB tetapi orang kenal dia sebab dia juga keluar masuk pejabat. Kalau ambo renung adik kakak dan kebetulan ambo kena sungguh pada dia, dia tentulah

perkecil sedikit badan dia. "Aloo! Ustaz nampak aku! Ustaz nampak aku!"[55]

References to the police, special branch, state security forces, Malay capitalists, the urban élite and, of course, PAS's foremost rival, the UMNO, appear in the *tafsir* of Nik Aziz with such regularity that they underscore the fact that the narratives themselves are clearly a political exercise. By presenting the enemies of PAS via the medium of a religious discourse as he does, Nik Aziz has also managed to heighten the conflict between PAS and the UMNO, where the boundary line between the two parties is no longer simply an ideological one but also a moral and religious one.

To hammer the point home, Nik Aziz reminds his followers that, not only is God on the side of the poor and oppressed, he is also on the side of PAS. In a controversial and problematic paragraph from his *Tafsir Surah Yunus*, Nik Aziz goes as far as to say that PAS and God are practically one and the same thing:

> Dalam kubur pula (malaikat) Munkar Nakir tidak tanya banyak mana kamu bawa pitis, banyak mana kamu ada senjata. Dia tanya siapa Tuhanmu? Apa Agamamu? Siapa Nabimu? Apa Kiblatmu? Jawab dengan hujah. Dia tidak tanya: Kamu anak siapa? Kamu jadi wakil rakyatkah? Kamu rajakah? Kamu Tok Gukukah? Di padang Mahsyar begitu juga... Apabila menjawab, hendaklah jawapan itu serupa dengan ajaran Nabi kerana tidak ada hujah yang paling gagah selain dari ajaran Nabi. Ketika itu jiwa kita akan berasa puas seperti Saidina Bilal apabila dia yakin dengan ajaran Nabi dia sanggup melawan bosnya, ketuanya. Walaupun dipukul dia tetap mengatakan Ahad: maknanya, Tuhan Esa. Dijemur panas dia mengatakan: Ahad. Diletak batu diatas dada, dia katakana Ahad, Ahad, Tuhan Esa. Kalau guna istilah politik sekarang ini kita kata: PAS, PAS, PAS. Hendak kata Ahad, Ahad, Ahad atau hendak kata PAS, PAS, PAS — kedua-duanya benda sama — sebab kita kata agama dan politik mesti disatukan. (emphasis added)[56]

The perennial struggle between God and the Devil has thus been recontextualized in the local conflict between PAS and the UMNO, Kelantan and the federal government in Kuala Lumpur. Kelantan is no longer a locality stuck in the northeastern corner of the Malaysian map; it is now relocated at the centre of a cosmic struggle where God Himself is at hand to help the oppressed and downtrodden.

Conclusion: Local Genius in the *Tafsir* of Tuan Guru Nik Aziz Nik Mat

This chapter argues that the *tafsir* of Tuan Guru Nik Aziz deserve greater scrutiny and analysis than they have received so far, despite the numerous jokes and parables that could be said to be wide of the mark. Critics and opponents of PAS have, over the years, bemoaned the fact that the *ulama* of the Islamist party have instrumentally used the discourse of Islam for what are obviously political ends. This is clearly evident in some of the more politically slanted comments and readings that appear in the various *tafsir* that have come from Tuan Guru Nik Aziz and Tuan Guru Hadi Awang.[57] Putting aside the overt political uses of such Quranic exegesis, it is nonetheless the case that scholars of political religion still have to address the dimension of culture and the cultural mediation of politics so evident in the writings and speeches of Islamist leaders like Nik Aziz.

Though it cannot be claimed that the success of PAS at the polls and at the grass-roots level is due solely to the popularity of the religious lectures, classes, and *tafsir* of its *ulama*, it is clear that these activities have played a major part in the *renaissance* of the Islamist party from the early 1980s onwards, a fact that the Islamists themselves do not deny. What is more, the Islamists themselves often readily admit that the religious lectures and classes given by the leading *ulama* of the party have served a number of other political ends: they have helped to undercut the claims and gains made by the UMNO-led government (which had embarked on an Islamization programme of its own from the 1980s), helped to consolidate PAS's own local constituencies, and to bridge the gap between the ideologues of PAS and the electorate.

Delivered as they are in a local idiom and a style that is familiar to the local audience, the *tafsir* of Tuan Guru Nik Aziz has proven invaluable in consolidating the aims of PAS. As far as the aims of *dakwah* (missionary activity) are concerned, the *tafsir* has helped the Deobandi-educated Tuan Guru to preach to a local audience ideas and values that have changed the way of life of so many Kelantanese.

This change has added to the further erosion of many aspects of traditional Kelantanese culture, now regarded as un-Islamic and bordering on *shirk*. The local rendition of the Quran has helped to localize a discourse which would otherwise have remained alien in origin for a vast number of Kelantanese, who have obviously not taken to the technocratic and academic approach to Islam favoured by the state-sponsored Islamist think-tanks and research centres such as IKIM and ISTAC.

The reverse, however, holds equally true. While localizing the universal, the *tafsir* of Tuan Guru Nik Aziz has also helped to universalize or globalize what was once seen as a local affair, namely, Malaysian politics and, more specifically, the intra-Malay politics of Kelantan. By bringing God and the Prophets of the Abrahamic faith to the theatre of Kelantan, the political arena of this Malay state has also been expanded well beyond its territorial boundaries. The conflict between the PAS state government and the UMNO-led federal government has now taken on universal, cosmic dimensions, making it a clash between the faithful and the sinners. What was once a local drama has been transformed into a celestial pageant.

If there is a lesson to be gained from this, it is that both scholars and politicians should never underestimate the capacity of subaltern discourses to disrupt the discursive field of politics on a wider (national, regional or even international) level. The "metaphysics of rice" from the likes of Tuan Guru Nik Aziz may strike the intellectual and political élite of Kuala Lumpur as a sad instance of the "dumbing down" of politics. It nevertheless remains one of the most powerful and effective tools in the arsenal of the Pan-Malaysian Islamic Party that has helped its star to rise, from the moment that its leaders began talking to the farmer in the field.

Notes

1. Clive Kessler, "Archaism and Modernity in Contemporary Malay Political Culture", *Fragmented Vision: Culture and Politics in Contemporary Malaysia*, edited by Joel S. Kahn and Francis Loh Kok Wah, ASAA Southeast Asia Publication Series (Sydney: Allen and Unwin, 1992), p. 135.
2. Translation: "Hey God! Teach me what I still do not know"— the first line of a *doa* (prayer) by Tuan Guru Nik Aziz Nik Mat, which comes

before each *kuliah tafsir* (exegesis class) session. It is interesting to note that Nik Aziz adopts a highly informal tone in his prayer to God. The opening phrase *"Hei Tuhan!"* (Hey God!) would seem almost provocative to many Malay-Muslims and the use of the term *"aku"* (a very familiar form of "I" or "Me") is regarded as bordering on rudeness in everyday Malay conversation. Yet, the use of such terms in the local Kelantanese dialect makes sense, as these are the terms commonly used in everyday conversation by Kelantanese and the Malays of the north (including other northern states like Kedah).

3. Translation: "Our lectures are not something that began in the 1940s or 1950s, that is, the years before independence. They are really a continuation of the lectures that were given by the Prophets of God that began long ago". Tuan Guru Nik Aziz Nik Mat, *Berceramah: Kesinambungan Tugas Nabi dan Rasul*, in *Kelantan: Agenda Baru Untuk Umat Islam*, edited by Tuan Guru Nik Aziz Nik Mat (Segambut, Kuala Lumpur: Rangkaian Minda Publishing, 1995), p. 62.

4. It is not the aim of this chapter to discuss the arrival and early development of Islam in the Malay world. Suffice it to say there has already been much written on this vast topic. For further elucidation and analysis on the subject, one could turn to the following sources: on Islam's early arrival in the Malay world, see S. Q. Fatimi, *Islam Comes to Malaysia* (Singapore: Malaysian Sociological Research Institute [MSRI], 1963); S. Hussein Alatas, "On the Need for a Historical Study of Malaysian Islamisation", *Journal of Southeast Asian Studies* 4, no. 3 (March 1963); S. Naguib Al-Attas, *Preliminary Statement on a General Theory of the Islamization of the Malay-Indonesian Archipelago* (Kuala Lumpur: Dewan Bahasa dan Pustaka, 1963); and Russell Jones, "Ten Conversion Myths from Indonesia", in *Conversion to Islam*, edited by Nehemia Levtzion (London: Holmes and Meier, 1979). On the topic of contemporary developments in the Malay-Muslim world, see Chandra Muzaffar, *Islamic Resurgence in Malaysia* (Petaling Jaya: Fajar Bakti Press, 1987); Sharon Siddique, "Conceptualizing Contemporary Islam: Religion or Ideology?" in *Readings on Islam and Society in Southeast Asia*, edited by Ahmad Ibrahim, Yasmin Hussain and Sharon Siddique (Singapore: Institute for Southeast Asian Studies [ISEAS], 1985); and Judith Nagata, *The Reflowering of Malaysian Islam* (Vancouver: University of British Columbia Press, 1984). For a comparative approach which situates Islamic resurgence in Malaysia within a global context, see Chandra Muzaffar, "Islamic Resurgence: A Global View", in *Islam and Society in Southeast Asia*, edited by Taufik Abdullah and Sharon Siddique (Singapore: Institute for Southeast Asian Studies [ISEAS], 1986). For an insight into the ideas and philosophy

of one of the foremost Islamists and defenders of Islamization in Malaysia, see Syed Naquib al-Attas, *Islam and Secularism* (Kuala Lumpur: Angkatan Belia Islam Malaysia [ABIM], 1978).

5. Robert Hefner, *Civil Islam: Muslims and Democratization in Indonesia* (Princeton: Princeton University Press, 2000), p. 220.

6. The nucleus of the Pan-Malaysian Islamic Party was actually located in the Bureau of Religious Affairs of the conservative-nationalist Malay party, the United Malays National Organization (UMNO). In 1951, PAS was formed under the leadership of Haji Fuad Hassan, who was the head of the UMNO Bureau of Religious Affairs. The radical nationalist and Islamist thinker, Dr Burhanuddin al-Helmy, was later invited to take over as president of PAS in December 1956. Between 1956 to 1969, the combined leadership of Dr Burhanuddin and Dr Zulkiflee Muhammad (the party's vice-president) managed to broaden the political base of PAS and open it up to the rest of the Muslim world. In 1969 Dr Burhanuddin died after his detention without trial by the Malaysian Government. PAS then came under the leadership of Mohamad Asri Muda, who was a staunch defender of Malay rights and privileges. Asri Muda later brought PAS into the ruling Barisan Nasional coalition, and then out again (1973–78). The period of Asri Muda's leadership was highly controversial. After a leadership crisis, the federal government declared a state of emergency in Kelantan in 1978. In 1982, Asri Muda was forced to step down by a new generation of Islamist *ulama* who had infiltrated the party from ABIM, and taken over. The 1980s and 1990s witnessed the radicalization of PAS as its new leaders began to confront the UMNO-led coalition government and the state apparatus on the grounds that the latter was "secular", "unIslamic" and working in league with Western and Zionist interests. In 1990, PAS regained control of the state of Kelantan, and in 1999 it won control of Trengganu as well.

7. The conservative-nationalist UMNO party's roots lie in the First Malay Congress that was held in Kuala Lumpur on 1–4 March 1946. The Congress discussed the plan to form PEKEMBAR (Persatuan Kebangsaan Melayu Bersatu), but later opted for the title UMNO instead. On 11 May 1946, the UMNO party was officially launched at the Istana Besar (Grand Palace) of Johor Bahru. The first President of the UMNO was Dato' Onn Jaafar. When the party was first established, it was a broad and all-encompassing organization that included Malay political movements from across the entire political spectrum. In time, however, the conservative character of the UMNO came to the surface as the Leftists and Islamists began to leave the organization to form

parties of their own. In the 1950s and 1960s, the UMNO was under the leadership of the royalist-aristocrat Tunku Abdul Rahman, who was also the country's first Prime Minister (1957–69). The Tunku placed Malaysia on the initial path towards rapid development and during this period the country's foreign policy was clearly aligned to the West. The Tunku's era was also one where religion and politics were kept separate, and the state did not attempt to play the religious card against its opponents. Between 1970 and 1981, the UMNO was under the leadership of Tun Abdul Razak (1970–76) and Hussein Onn (1976–81), both of whom kept the country on the same trajectory. A major shift in orientation occurred when UMNO came under the leadership of Dr Mahathir Mohamad (1981–), who took the country down the road of state-sponsored Islamization. However, Dr Mahathir's Islamization policy was also an attempt to outflank the growing Islamist opposition in the country as well as a calculated attempt to redefine the meaning, content, and expression of Islam and Muslim religiosity in terms that were compatible with modernity, progress, and economic prosperity. This happened when the Muslim world as a whole was experiencing a major resurgence of Islam, and the opposition Islamist movements in Malaysia were rapidly gaining ground among the populace.

8. The Angkatan Belia Islam Malaysia (ABIM — Malaysian Islamic Youth Movement) was formed by a number of Malay-Muslim university student activists from the National Association of Muslim Students led by Razali Nawawi, Anwar Ibrahim, and Siddiq Fadhil on 6 August 1971. ABIM's first president was Razali Nawawi. At the beginning, the small organization had only forty members. However, as it developed, the movement became centred on the charismatic and dominant personality of Anwar Ibrahim, who took over as the movement's second president in 1974. In their intellectual formation, Anwar Ibrahim and the leaders of ABIM were very much influenced by the ideas of the Malaysian Islamist scholar, Prof. Seyyed Naguib al-Attas. Chandra (1987) has noted that Anwar's thinking was also shaped by the teachings of the founder of the Jama'ati Islami of Pakistan, Ab'ul Al'a Maudoodi, the founder-leader of the Ikhwan'ul Muslimun of Egypt, Hassan al-Banna, Malek Ben Nabi of Algeria, and the Islamist intellectual, Ismail Raj Faruqi of the United States. The movement's leaders were made up of Malay-Muslim students from the liberal arts faculties of the local universities, such as Universiti Malaya (UM) and Universiti Kebangsaan Malaysia (UKM). On the campuses of the country, ABIM's impact was clear for all to see: the members of the organization were among the few who did not smoke and who dressed according to Islamic standards of decency

and modesty. The young men who joined ABIM were also reminded not to be in close contact with women and to avoid shaking hands with them. They also encouraged their parents and the elders around them to follow their example. In time, the policing of sartorial and behavioural norms became one of the defining features of the ABIM movement. ABIM's aim was to spearhead the struggle for Islamic reform and revival in the country, and to work towards "Islamization from within". The movement sponsored a number of religious *pondok* and *madrasah* schools all over the country, such as the Madrasah Sri ABIM at Kuala Ketil, Kedah, and the Ma'ahad Tarbiah Islamiah at Pokok Sena. It also established its own private school, called Yayasan Anda. ABIM's leaders condemned secularism and other Western ideologies that they regarded as antithetical to Islam, and called for the control and purification of Muslim culture in the interests of creating a healthy Islamic society.

9. The Darul Arqam movement was formed by Ustaz Ashaari Muhammad in 1968. It began as a study group among Muslim scholars and reformers, many of whom were university lecturers and academics. In time, it evolved into a *sufi*-inspired alternative lifestyle movement that was very much centred on the personality of its founder. Its activities were based at the Madinah Al Arqam Saiyyidina Abu Bakar As-Siddiq, Sungai Pencala, near Kuala Lumpur. The movement's aim was to create an alternative model of an ideal Islamic society that was organized and managed according to the standards and norms set by the Prophet Muhammad himself and his companions. The Darul Arqam movement grew in size until its membership expanded to tens of thousands. Its followers dressed and lived according to Ustaz Ashaari's interpretation of the *Sunnah*. The men wore green robes and turbans while the women wore black *hijab*. The movement practised *purdah* and its female members were kept out of public view as much as possible. They set up co-operative movements, self-help groups, and links with other Islamic movements in the country and beyond. At one stage in its development, Darul Arqam was even accused of being an organization secretly funded by the Saudi government in its effort to eradicate Shia influence in the Malay archipelago. Such controversies helped to boost the group's image and appeal even more. The Arqam movement was always under the control of its charismatic leader, who built a personality and leadership cult around him. Other leaders of the movement, like Ustaz Mokhtar Yaakub and Ustaz Akhbar Anang who dared to challenge the dominant role and status of Ustaz Ashaari, soon found themselves expelled from the movement for good. By the 1970s, Ustaz Ashaari was widely regarded as one of the most powerful and influential (if not controversial) *ulama* in the country.

10. The International Institute for Islamic Thought and Civilization (ISTAC) was officially opened in 1991. It was, from the very beginning, the brainchild of its founder-director, Syed Naquib al-Attas. Anwar Ibrahim, the ex-president of ABIM, was the first Chairman of ISTAC. In its early years, ISTAC received a great deal of support and patronage from the Malaysian Government, in terms of financial assistance, as well as publicity and endorsement of its activities by the government. In the preface of the second edition of his book, *Islam and Secularism* (1993), al-Attas outlines the mandate and agenda of his institute: "Among its most important aims and objectives are to conceptualise, clarify, elaborate scientific and epistemological problems encountered by Muslims in this modern age; to provide an Islamic response to the intellectual and cultural challenges of the modern world and various schools of thought, religion and ideology; to formulate an Islamic philosophy of education; including the definitions, aims and objectives of Islamic education, to formulate an Islamic philosophy of science" (p. xiii). In short, the aim of ISTAC was to spearhead al-Attas's own project of the Islamization of knowledge, which, in turn, was intimately linked to his political project of the revival of the spirit of Islam through the creation of a new class of intellectually competent and knowledgeable Islamic leaders who conform to the rules of *adab* and the social and political hierarchies which al-Attas regards as essentially Islamic. Al-Attas was given much freedom in designing ISTAC, down to its architectural details. The main building which houses the library, conference hall, and research units, was designed by him and reflect strong Hispano-Moorish styles and features.

11. Syed Naquib al-Attas is perhaps one of the most influential (if not controversial) Islamist thinkers in Malaysia today. His influence extends well beyond the confines of academia, and he has played an important role in the cultivation of the Islamic élite in the country. He comes from one of the most renowned aristocratic families in the south and is of mixed Malay-Arab stock. In his youth, he studied in England, first at Eton and then at Sandhurst Military Academy, and later at the School of Oriental and African Studies (SOAS), University of London. His early academic research work was in the fields of Malay *sufism* and literature. His fame was established through the publication of his two-volume dissertation, *The Mysticism of Hamzah Fansuri* (1965, published 1970). He later developed much of his educational philosophy, with this *sufi* influence clearly apparent in his work. He also prides himself as a designer, calligrapher, and artist. He was given the opportunity to create the International Institute for Islamic Thought and Civilization (ISTAC) in

1991, and in 1993, he was awarded the Al-Ghazali Chair of Islamic Philosophy by the Malaysian Government. (The award was presented by none other than his own student-turned-politician, Anwar Ibrahim, who was then a Minister in the Cabinet). He was awarded the membership of the Royal Jordanian Academy in 1994, and honoured with an honorary doctorate from the University of Khartoum in 1995.

12. Chandra Muzaffar has noted that "within the country the person who had the greatest influence on Anwar Ibrahim in his ABIM years was Syed Naquib al-Attas, then professor of Malay Studies at the National University of Malaysia" (Chandra 1987, p. 54, n. 23).

13. The anti-secular rhetoric of al-Attas was taken up by the leaders of ABIM with gusto. Chandra noted that "ABIM criticized secularism and other Western ideologies as antithetical to the ideal of an Islamic state. Secularism, for ABIM, is an ideology that restricts the concept of existence to 'this world' and the 'here and now'". A consequence of this secularism, as an ABIM leader once argued, has been a modern society "inflicted by such diseases as hedonism, materialism, individualism, utilitarianism, permissiveness, relativistic values and anomie". This view of secularism is found in the works of al-Attas as well. See, for example, his *Islam and Secularism* (Chandra 1987, p. 48).

14. By 1994, the Darul Arqam movement had developed into one of the richest and best organized Islamist organizations in the country. It boasted 10,000 members and at least 100,000 other sympathizers in Malaysia alone. Arqam's business assets were estimated to be worth around RM300 million (US$116 million) and it had 417 companies and businesses officially listed as part of its concern. The movement also had 257 schools under its care in Malaysia, and its own university in Indonesia. Its network of *madrasah*, schools and *dakwah* centres stretched across the ASEAN region and went as far as Uzbekistan and the Central Asian states. With such an extensive network of businesses and educational centres under its control, Arqam was more than a match for both the UMNO and PAS.

15. For a comparative account of the similarities and differences between the Darul Arqam movement and the Tablighi Jama'at, see Muhammad Khalid Masud, ed., *Travellers in Faith: Studies of the Tablighi Jama'at as a Transnational Islamic Movement for Faith Renewal* (Leiden: Brill, 2000), p. lvii.

16. See Ustaz Haji Ashaari Muhammad, *Perjuangan Teluk: Islam Akan Kembali Gemilang* (Kuala Lumpur: Jabatan Sheikhul Arqam, 1991).

17. The federal government justified its actions against the movement on the grounds that Darul Arqam was linked to a clandestine militant

grouping called Asykar Badr, which consisted of more than 300 militia troops based somewhere in Southern Thailand (though, in the end, the state prosecutors could not prove any direct link between the two.) Arqam members had also been accused of being involved in militant activities abroad. In 1994, the government of Egypt arrested 19 Arqam members — all of them female students — for their association with Islamist militant cells in the country. The State's Council of *muftis* and *ulama* also issued a *fatwa* against the teachings of Ustaz Ashaari, which they claimed was a danger to Islam and Muslims in general, and argued that he had deliberately misled his followers with false and deviationist teachings (*ajaran sesat*) that were contrary to the basic principles of the religion.

18. Kalim Sidiqqui, *Stages of the Islamic Revolution* (London: The Open Press, 1996), p. 94.

19. The *ulama* leadership of PAS has, since the 1980s, relied on the slogan, "*Ulama pewaris Nabi*" [The *Ulama* are the heirs of the Prophet].

20. For the complete genealogy of Nik Aziz Nik Mat, see Jamal Mohd Lokman Sulaiman, *Biografi Tuan Guru Dato' Haji Nik Abdul Aziz: Seorang Ulama serta Ahli Politik Malaysia di Abad ke-20'* (Kuala Lumpur: Sulfa Press, 1999).

21. Sulaiman notes that while Nik Aziz came from a long line of royalty and nobles, the family's fortunes had declined over the years. His grandfather, Raja Banjar, was a modest agriculturalist who owned farming land in Kelantan and opened up several plantations there. Nik Mat Alim was a student of Tok Kenali (Tuan Guru Mohd Yusuf bin Muhamad) and the religious teacher Tuan Guru Haji Musa bin Abdul Samad (p. 9).

22. Ibid. p. 15.

23. The Dar'ul Ulum Deoband (sometimes referred to as the Deoband College), was founded in the town of Deoband to the northeast of Delhi. It was formed in the late nineteenth century, after the failed Indian Mutiny of 1857. The two major figures behind the founding of the Deoband College, Muhammad Qasim Nanautawi and Rashid Ahmad Gangohi, both came from prominent *ulama* families and had experienced traditional conservative as well as *sufi*-inspired forms of education. In 1867, they chose to settle in the town of Doad and opened a *madrasah* at the Chattah Masjid. This was the nucleus of the Deobandi School. Both Muhammad Qasim and Rashid Ahmad had new ideas about improving the standards of Islamic education. Their *madrasah* was cut off from the mosque complex itself. The school was finally established in 1879 and it was funded by contributions from the public rather than depending on *waqf* (trusts for religious purposes).

The college borrowed the techniques and methods of the government colleges, with a rector, principal, and salaried teachers but it also had a *mufti* who supervised the issuing of *fatwa*. The Deobandis accepted Sufism in principle as a legitimate branch of Islam, but rejected many *sufi* practices and customs on the grounds that they were contaminated by Hindu and pre-Islamic elements. Thus, the Deobandi school became famous for its strict adherence to the Quran, *Hadith* and *Sunnah*, and its zeal to purify Islam of Hindu, Hellenic, Persian, and pre-Islamic elements. The students were kept at the *madrasah* and the teaching periods ranged from six to ten years. During this time, the students developed close bonds, and ultimately the school produced a network of Deobandi *ulama* who shared a similar outlook and approach to Islam. The Deobandi *ulama* were known for their uncompromising and confrontational approach towards outsiders. The school issued 269,215 *fatwa* in its first hundred years, and its *ulama* engaged in many polemics against Hindus and Christian missionary movements. See Kenneth W. Jones, "Socio-Religious Reform Movements in British India", in *The New Cambridge History of India* III, no. 1 (Cambridge: Cambridge University Press, 1989), pp. 48–60.

24. Sulaiman, op. cit., p. 16.
25. Ibid., p. 55.
26. Ibid., p. 17.
27. Jones, op. cit., pp. 58, 61–62.
28. Nik Aziz took over the constituency from the previous PAS candidate, Tuan Haji Ahmad Abdullah. Sulaiman (1999) notes that even then Nik Aziz's popularity was very much due to his "scriptural authority" and image as an Islamic leader among the people (Sulaiman, op. cit., pp. 73–74).
29. Sulaiman, op. cit., p. 32. Nik Aziz's earliest writings were mainly focused on the topics of religion and spirituality. His books touched on the subjects of religious obligations (*fardu 'ain*), life after death, and *Qiamat* (the Day of Judgement) (p. 61).
30. Ibid., p. 33.
31. Ibid., pp. 36–37.
32. *Kitab Kuning*: literally "yellow books" — the "classic" texts of Islam, used for teaching and so called because of their yellow covers.
33. Sulaiman, op. cit., p. 97.
34. Translation: "From the Raja in his Istana (Palace) to Pak Mat who lives in the village, you all need to be told this one thing: You are all servants

of God!". Tuan Guru Nik Aziz Nik Mat, *Tafsir Surah Hud*, Ma'ahad ad-Dakwah wal-Imamah, Nilam Puri, Kelantan, 1996. p. 11.

35. Sulaiman, op. cit., p. 109.
36. Ibid., p. 110.
37. As soon as he came to power as Chief Minister of Kelantan, the *Tuan Guru* introduced a package of radical reforms to the administration of the state. He announced that the legal system and procedures in the state would be changed in line with Islam, based on the Syariah. The new Chief Minister then stopped the issuing of gambling licences, prevented companies from using advertisements that displayed women in public, banned both modern and traditional cultural practices (like rock concerts, *wayang kulit, Mak Yong* and *Manora* dances) that were regarded as un-Islamic, forbade public events (including religious ones, like *nashid* performances where men and women mixed freely together), promoted a campaign for women to wear the veil (*hijab*), and radically reduced the expenditure and privileges of politicians and administrators in the state's civil service. Henceforth, all state events and assemblies were to begin with the recitation of the *Surah al-Fatihah* and conclude with the *Surah al-Asr* and the *Tasbih Kafarah*. Along the streets of the capital and the countryside were erected banners that read "*Allahu Akbar*", "*Alhamdullillah*", and "*Subhan'allah*". Islam had arrived in no uncertain terms to the quiet state of Kelantan Darul Naim. Working on the basis of the Quran and Sunnah, Nik Aziz radically transformed the socio-cultural, political, and economic milieu of the state of Kelantan. From the moment he took over the office of the Chief Minister, the Tuan Guru informed the members of the state government and assembly that he would be introducing a new form of *ulama* leadership and state-management. Thus, from the outset, the space for debate and consultation on issues was circumscribed by the provisions that only those matters not touched upon in the Quran and Hadith were open to discussion. Moreover, if any discussion were to take place, then only the learned Alim Ulama was in a position to participate. By forcing through these controversial changes, the rejuvenated PAS of the 1990s showed that it was now a party that was prepared to go all the way in its promise to radically reinvent the political terrain and political culture of the country.
38. Sulaiman, op. cit., p. 141.
39. Ibid., p. 160.
40. Nik Aziz, *Kelantan: Universiti Politik Terbuka* (Ma'ahad ad-Dakwah wal-Imamah, Nilam Puri, Kelantan, 1995), p. 236, n. 18.

41. See Tuan Guru Nik Aziz Nik Mat, *Islam Boleh* (Ma'ahad ad-Dakwah wal-Imamah, Nilam Puri, Kelantan, 1995); and *Kelantan: Universiti Politik Terbuka*.

42. See Muhammad Asad, *The Message of the Quran* (Gibraltar: Dar al-Andalus Press, 1980), pp. 310–35.

43. Translation: "Although this particular *Surah* is called *Surah Hud*, when Allah was telling us this story, he picked up all the stories he could find from those who were Hud's companions — the story of Noah, and two or three other prophets — who were regarded as having stories of their own to tell. The one who lives his life on this earth without a story to tell is like one who is worn and mute; he gets up in the morning and takes his buffalo to the field, in the afternoon he cuts the grass and then in the evening he goes back home to sleep. Throughout his life no-one knows him; in the *kampung* (village) no-one has heard of him, when he's dead no-one misses him. No-one remembers him because he never did anything worth remembering" (p. 2).

44. Translation: "The spiritual *guru* is the one who can lead the people to Heaven, not only lead them to their offices and places of work. These are the sort of *guru* that Islam wants" (Nik Aziz, *Tafsir Surah Hud,* p. 68).

45. See Nik Aziz Nik Mat, *Tafsir Surah Yunus* (1998), p. 61.

46. Ibid., p. 83.

47. Translation: "All the *kafirs* in this world are evil — there is no such thing as a good *kafir*… And all the vice that is committed in the world is due to them, the *kafirs* or the *fasiq*". It is important to note that Nik Aziz's own definition of what constitutes a *kafir* or *fasiq* is broad enough to include "bad" Muslims as well. For he goes on to argue that even Muslims who commit acts of vice should be regarded as *kafir* or *fasiq* too (Nik Aziz Nik Mat, *Tafsir Surah Yunus* [1998], p. 217).

48. Translation: "Why don't you all ask yourselves: Why did God make weeds, and *lalang* (a type of long grass regarded as a nuisance by farmers)? Sure God who is so clever would not waste his time making things that are useless. We who are so stupid can't even make things like that which are of no use to anyone, what more God, who is so wise and clever. Surely all the things God has created have their uses, surely there must be a wisdom behind it all. It is just up to us, whether we are curious enough to try and learn the secret behind these mysteries" (pp. 4–5).

49. Translation: "You who wish to know the extent of God's wisdom, try first to measure the ignorance of human beings who still know nothing about themselves. Till today people still can't explain how and what they feel… It's like when you come across a plate of rice. There you are,

sitting nicely having a good laugh with your friends, when suddenly you smell something cooking in the kitchen. What's that, you ask? You can smell fried onions, you can smell the soup on the boil. Suddenly, 'Aloo!! That's enough talking, let's eat instead!' Try to explain how this hunger comes to you. How did you do it? Who can say 'I'm hungry now because I did this or that?' How did it happen? There you were chatting away nicely and suddenly you feel hungry, you smell the soup and then you feel the hunger pangs. So don't waste your time thinking about heaven and earth, you don't even know what's going on in your belly" (p. 9).

50. Translation: "If there are still those know-it-alls who think they know everything, just say to them: 'When you get up in the morning and lift your *sarong*, out shoots your pee. How come you weren't peeing before you sat on the toilet? How did you do it?' If it was a pipe, all you have to do is turn the tap. So what did you turn this time? You didn't turn anything, didn't say anything, didn't touch anything — but the next thing you know your pee is spraying everywhere. How come you don't pee yourself after you've left the toilet? ...Till today people still can't understand how they feel what they do" (p. 9).

51. Tuan Guru Nik Aziz Nik Mat. Translation: "What is the difference between the government and gangsters? For a start, gangsters don't have a flag". *Tafsir Surah Hud* (p. 187).

52. Translation: "From the Raja in his Istana (palace) to Pak Mat who lives in the village, you all need to be told this one thing: You are all servants of God!" (p. 11).

53. Translation: "God has said: 'My curses shall fall on those who have turned against Me and shall follow them throughout their lives and in the hereafter'. God has said that his wrath shall fall on them and they will suffer throughout their lives. This wrath is a curse, eternal damnation. The old folks whose hearts are still clean and pure are afraid of being cursed by their fellows in the *kampung* (village), what more being cursed by God. But those who live in the midst of wealth and riches, amidst materialism — those with their huge salaries, grand houses, large estates, plentiful riches — they do not know what it means to be cursed. "Why should I fear the wrath of God? My wealth is aplenty, I can take care of myself" they say" (p. 148).

54. Translation: "I am the leader of a political party, not a guerrilla force. If I was a leader of guerrillas, I would buy SCUD missiles — that Iraq had not sent to Tel Aviv and Riyadh — and I would send them to Kuala Lumpur". Nik Aziz Nik Mat, *Tafsir Surah Yunus* (1998), p. 16.

55. Translation: "God has said: 'Remember that they (the hypocrites) will conceal their hearts, in order to protect themselves and to shy away from God, from his Prophet Muhammad'. This passage from the Quran really touches the hearts of some, and hurts the feelings of some. For example, in this *majlis* (meeting), there are bound to be members of the SB (Special Branch), who have come not to learn but to acquire information. Even if he is meant to be an undercover SB, he is still known to others as they have seen him coming in and out of his office. If I were to look around at the brothers and sisters in the audience, my eyes might just fall on him, and he will surely shy away. 'Aloo! The *Ustaz* has seen me! The *Ustaz* has seen me!' he will think" (p. 24).

56. Translation: "While in our graves the angels Munkar Nakir will not ask us how much money we have brought with us, or how many weapons. They will ask: Who is your God? What is your religion? Who is your Prophet? In which direction do you pray? Answer with confidence. They will not ask: whose child are you? Are you a people's representative? Are you a King? Are you a *Tok Guru*? On the field of Mashyar (on Judgement Day) it will be the same... When you answer you have to answer as our Prophet has taught you, for there is nothing as strong as the argument of the Prophet. Then our soul will be as contented as that of Saidinna Bilal, who, when convinced of the Prophet's teachings, was prepared to confront his boss, his leaders. Even though he was beaten he kept saying *Ahad*: God almighty. When exposed to the desert heat he kept saying *Ahad*. When they covered his chest with heavy rocks, he kept saying *Ahad, Ahad*, God almighty. *If we were to use the political terminology of today, we can say PAS, PAS, PAS. Whether we want to say Ahad, Ahad, Ahad or PAS, PAS, PAS — the two are the same —* because for us religion and politics must be made one" (emphasis added.) (Nik Aziz Nik Mat, *Tafsir Surah Yunus* [1998], p. 186).

57. Tuan Guru Abdul Hadi Awang was born on 20 October 1947 in the village of Rusila in Marang, Trengganu. His father, Ustaz Haji Awang Mohamad Abdul Rahman, was the *Tok Guru* of the village of Rusila and the *Imam* of the local mosque. In his early childhood, Hadi Awang was taught by his own father. He then studied at the Arabic school in Marang for five years. Between 1965 and 1968, he studied at the Sultan Zainal Abidin Islamic Secondary School in Marang. Having completed his secondary studies in Malaysia, Hadi Awang was sent abroad to study at the University of Medinah (1969–73) under the

sponsorship of the Saudi government. There he gained his first degree in Syariah law. While studying at Medinah, he was the President of the Malaysian Muslim Students Association of Madinah and the Secretary-General of the Association of Southeast Asian Students there. Hadi Awang entered the world of politics and joined PAS in 1964. In 1969, he was appointed Secretary of the PAS branch in Rusila but, soon after, he left for further studies abroad again. Between 1974 and 1976 he studied *Siasah Shariyyah* at the University of Al-Azhar in Cairo, Egypt. While in Egypt he became involved in the activities of the Ikhwan'ul Muslimin together with Dr Said Hawa, Professor Muhamad al-Wakeel and Dr Abdul Satar al-Khudsi. He also served as the Secretary to the Syariah and Regulations Bureau of the Malaysian Association in Egypt. He returned to Malaysia in 1976 and took up the post of officer in the Yayasan Islam (Islamic Foundation) of Trengganu. In the same year, he was elected as the head of PAS Youth (*Dewan Pemuda*) in Trengganu. In 1978, he became the Chairman of the Malaysian Muslim Youth Organization (ABIM) in Trengganu. In that year, he took part in the general elections, contesting both the parliamentary seat at Marang and the State Assembly seat at Manir, but lost both. He contested once again during the elections of 1982 and managed to win the State Assembly seat at Rhu Rendang. In 1982, he was elected to the post of party Vice-President at the same time that Ustaz Yusof Rawa took over as the President of PAS. He became Deputy President of PAS in 1989 when Fadzil Noor took over as the President of the party. In the elections of 1990 and 1995, he managed to retain both his parliamentary and State Assembly seats. During the 1990s, his international profile rose considerably when he was asked to represent PAS on a number of occasions. In 1990, he joined the delegation led by the Turkish leader of the *Refah* party, Necmettin Erbakan, sent to Iraq to help resolve the Gulf conflict that had begun with Saddam Hussein's invasion of Kuwait. In the same year, he was appointed to the Majmak Takrik Mazhab Islam, based in Tehran, Iran. In 1994 he was appointed to the Executive Committee of the International Islamic Movement with headquarters in Istanbul, Turkey. Apart from these posts, he has also been involved in the International Islamic Secretariat for the Defence of *Bait'ul Maqdis* (Jerusalem), based in Jordan, a member of the International Muslim delegation led by German Muslim leaders to settle the disputes between the Mujahideen factions in Afghanistan, and a member of the delegation led by the Turkish Islamist leader Necmettin Erbakan to the capitals of Europe.

References

Ashaari Muhammad. *Perjuangan Teluk: Islam Akan Kembali Gemilang.* Kuala Lumpur: Jabatan Sheikhul Arqam, 1991.

Chandra Muzaffar. "Islamic Resurgence: A Global View". In *Islam and Society in Southeast Asia*, edited by Taufik Abdullah and Sharon Siddique. Singapore: Institute for Southeast Asian Studies (ISEAS), 1986.

————. *Islamic Resurgence in Malaysia.* Petaling Jaya: Fajar Bakti Press, 1987.

Fatimi, S. Q. *Islam Comes to Malaysia.* Singapore: Malaysian Sociological Research Institute (MSRI), 1963.

Jamal Mohd Lokman Sulaiman. *Biografi Tuan Guru Dato' Haji Nik Abdul Aziz: Seorang Ulama serta Ahli Politik Malaysia di Abad ke-20.* Kuala Lumpur: Sulfa Press, 1999.

Jones, Kenneth W. "Socio-Religious Reform Movements in British India". In *The New Cambridge History of India* III, 1. Cambridge: Cambridge University Press, 1989.

Jones, Russell. "Ten Conversion Myths from Indonesia". In *Conversion to Islam*, edited by Nehemia Levtzion. London: Holmes and Meier, 1979.

Hefner, Robert. *Civil Islam: Muslims and Democratization in Indonesia.* Princeton: Princeton University Press, 2000.

Kessler, Clive S. "Archaism and Modernity in Contemporary Malay Political Culture". In *Fragmented Vision: Culture and Politics in Contemporary Malaysia*, edited by Joel S. Kahn and Francis Loh Kok Wah. ASAA Southeast Asia Publication Series. Sydney: Allen and Unwin, 1992.

Muhammad Asad. *The Message of the Quran.* Gibraltar: Dar al-Andalus Press, 1980.

Muhammad Khalid Masud, ed. *Travellers in Faith: Studies of the Tablighi Jama'at as a Transnational Islamic Movement for Faith Renewal.* Leiden: Brill, 2000.

Nik Aziz Nik Mat. "Berceramah: Kesinambungan Tugas Nabi dan Rasul". In *Kelantan: Agenda Baru Untuk Umat Islam*, edited by Tarmizi Mohd Jam. Segambut, Kuala Lumpur: Rangkaian Minda Publishing, 1995.

————. *Islam Boleh.* Ma'ahad ad-Dakwah wal-Imamah, Nilam Puri, Kelantan. 1995.

————. *Kelantan: Universiti Politik Terbuka.* Ma'ahad ad-Dakwah wal-Imamah, Nilam Puri, Kelantan, 1995.

————. *Tafsir Surah Hud.* Ma'ahad ad-Dakwah wal-Imamah, Nilam Puri, Kelantan, 1996.

Nagata, Judith. *The Reflowering of Malaysian Islam.* Vancouver: University of British Columbia Press, 1984.

Rose Ismail, ed. "Hudud in Malaysia: The Issues at Stake". Sisters in Islam (SIS) Forum, Kuala Lumpur, 1995.

S. Hussein Alatas. "On the Need for a Historical Study of Malaysian Islamization". *Journal of Southeast Asian Studies* 4, no. 3 (Singapore, March 1963).

S. Naguib Al-Attas. *Preliminary Statement on a General Theory of the Islamization of the Malay-Indonesian Archipelago*. Kuala Lumpur: Dewan Bahasa dan Pustaka, 1963.

———. *Islam and Secularism*. Kuala Lumpur: Angkatan Belia Islam Malaysia (ABIM), 1978.

Siddique, Sharon. "Conceptualizing Contemporary Islam: Religion or Ideology?" In *Readings on Islam and Society in Southeast Asia*, edited by Ahmad Ibrahim, Yasmin Hussain and Sharon Siddique. Singapore: Institute for Southeast Asian Studies (ISEAS), 1985.

Sidiqqui, Kalim. *Stages of the Islamic Revolution*. London: The Open Press, 1996.

11

THE PAS–BN CONFLICT IN THE 1990s
Islamism and Modernity

AMRITA MALHI

> Expressing fundamental class antagonisms in the countryside, support for the PMIP [today known only as PAS] cannot simply be seen as the product of religious fanaticism nor … can it be seen as an expression of Malay racialism. Rooted in the grievances of a threatened smallholder peasantry, the PMIP, like many populist movements, is a conservative movement of radical discontent. This ambiguity stems from the paradoxical interests and aspirations of its main supporters who, as peasant smallholders, wholly or in part, call for the restoration of the peasant social order … While their social relations remain encased within the traditional mould, the smallholders are the group most vulnerable to the intrusion of outside economic forces.
>
> — Clive Kessler[1]

Introduction
Throughout the 1990s, the approach taken towards Islam by Malaysian Prime Minister Dr Mahathir Mohamad, and his Barisan Nasional

236

(National Front, BN) government, can be characterized as an attempt to co-opt Islamist opposition to his government's "secular" politics and development plans. In an effort to carry this out, Dr Mahathir repeatedly argued that there existed two kinds of Malaysian Muslims — those who advocated a "traditional" and narrow understanding of Islam and its role in society and politics, and those who hold a commitment to a "modernist" and rational interpretation of Islam's teachings. The success of Dr Mahathir's efforts to define the framework within which the relationship of Islam to political competition in Malaysia is understood has been far-reaching. It is apparent that an increasingly wealthy layer of Malay Muslims in Malaysia — or at least those who support Dr Mahathir's interpretations of Islamic teachings — use this dichotomous framework to explain their own relationship to their faith. As anthropologist Patricia Sloane has shown, her Malay Muslim "entrepreneur" interviewees explained to her at length that they were striving towards a "modern" understanding of Islam, in which the active pursuit of wealth was encouraged. Several of Sloane's contacts contrasted this understanding with their real or imagined *kampung* (village) pasts, where to them, Malay Muslims expected to receive a livelihood without much effort, in the politics of "neo-traditionalist", "anti-modern" groups.[2]

That Sloane herself does not question this rhetorical dichotomy between "traditional" and "modern" Muslims is a reflection of another aspect of Dr Mahathir's success in defining a dominant framework for understanding Islam and politics in Malaysia — that is, much of the contemporary academic literature, and the more critical press commentary on this subject takes this traditional–modern divide for granted also. A variety of authors have asserted that the debate over Islam between the two main electoral organizations in Malaysia, both of whom have claimed throughout the 1990s to be "Islamic", demonstrates the existence of these two opposing traditions in Malaysian Islam. It is then usually asserted that the main Islamist opposition party, the Parti Islam SeMalaysia (Pan Malaysian Islamic Party, or PAS), represents the "traditional" grouping, while the BN coalition, led by its dominant party UMNO (United Malays National Organization), hold ideas about Islam which are more suited to managing a modern society and economy. Accordingly, in attempting to offer suggestions on what Malaysia would be like under a PAS-led government, authors

Jomo K. S. and Ahmad Shabery Cheek,[3] and Chandra Muzaffar,[4] have argued that PAS would drive Malaysia towards greater repression and Malay-Muslim chauvinism by implementing a regime characterized by *hudud* laws.[5] Press commentary has focused on the possibility of the oppression of women and non-Muslims, comparing PAS with the Taliban in Afghanistan, as will be discussed further in the section below.[6] Abdullah Ahmad develops this argument to gratuitous lengths, asserting that PAS would have Malaysians whipped, stoned to death, amputated and decapitated, and women prohibited from working, driving, and swimming.[7]

There are serious problems with accepting this conceptual divide between traditional and modern Muslims, primarily with reference to PAS's position within this scheme. Analysis which assumes that PAS is backward-looking and obscurantist reflects a defensiveness about Islam in a multicultural society, particularly in the current international relations climate, and misunderstands PAS's relationship with its supporters. It is in this context that Professor Clive Kessler has made such a useful contribution to understanding Islam and politics in Malaysia. His 1978 work, *Islam and Politics in a Malay State*, quoted above, contrasted with this prevailing view. It showed that PAS, in fact, commands significant grass-roots support, and has historically voiced the aspirations of its supporters — who in turn are rational political agents, not accepting "traditional" villagers — for a more equitable society, regardless of whether or not a PAS government would actually bring this about.

The dichotomy between "traditional" and "modern" societies, and the ideas which correspond to each, has its roots in the sociology of Max Weber. According to this scheme, traditional societies were, or are, characterized by loyalty to kinship networks rather than to a broader class or other social group, birth instead of merit as the basis for holding an office, and a lack of a sophisticated division of labour, where production was largely for subsistence instead of taking place on the scale of modern industrial capitalism. Modern societies are taken to be the opposite of all of the above, organized along the lines of broader, imagined communities such as nation-states, not villages and kinship systems, where public officials are elected in a system of parliamentary democracy, and where education and rationality are upheld as ideals rather than faith. Most importantly, in traditional societies, religion played a role in public life, whereas modern societies are marked by a separation between the state and religious institutions.[8] Throughout much of the discourse on Islam and politics in Malaysia, the BN is assumed to hold a commitment to modernity, whereas PAS is argued to be attempting to push religion "back" into public life.

In contrast to the prevailing view, authors such as Abdul Rahman Haji Abdullah[9] assert that the conceptual dichotomy between "traditional" and "modernist" Islam is not as useful as has been claimed. This development reflects a trend in studies of "Islam" in general, and of Middle Eastern societies, which increasingly argue that the politics articulated by Islamists are not generally a reflection of a desire to return to the past, but a response to or a critique of the nature of the modern world. For example, Zubaida and Sayyid have pointed out that many "Islamists" in fact argue for a move "forward" to an Islamic society, and address their arguments in a language which shows an acceptance of modern political and economic structures.[10] Esposito in turn has noted that Islamist opposition parties such as PAS demonstrate a thoroughgoing commitment to "modern" parliamentary democracy and electoral competition.[11] Furthermore, any idea of a clean split between traditional and modern societies is complicated by the process of industrialization and the integration of capitalist production and distribution on a global scale, with the attendant growth of global financial and communications networks, and mass migration, as well as the possibility for some of study abroad. Societies are not sealed off from each other in neat categories, but contain elements of tradition and modernity within them, and national subjects are connected to ways of thinking which have been brought from beyond their borders.

Based on a selection of the literature addressing Islam and politics produced throughout the 1990s by both the BN and PAS, it is the argument of this chapter that, at least during this time, the debate between government and opposition has in fact been thoroughly "modern", in the sense that both parties are attempting to put forward to the electorate a political vision grounded in modern realities. It has been, however, a central strategy informing the government's rhetoric, aimed at diminishing PAS's electoral support, to describe PAS as backward and traditional, as the following section will attempt to show.

The Indera Kayangan By-election: PAS = Taliban

The Indera Kayangan State Assembly by-election, held in the northern peninsular state of Perlis in January 2002, was won decisively, with an increased majority, by the BN coalition. However, the victory was not without scandal. Apart from the question of bus-loads of possible "phantom voters" arriving on the day of the vote, a controversial television clip was screened on Malaysian national television throughout the campaign. The clip began with a frame depicting a Malay-looking woman, dressed without a scarf or veil, in a contemporary office scene. The male narrator stated in the English-language voice-over, "[they] forbid beautiful women from working, ban entertainment outlets, and consider the assassination of non-Muslim government members by militant terrorists as *sandiwara* [entertainment]". The voice continued, "If this country falls into the hands of extremists and religious militants, it is not impossible that women in this country may face the same fate that befell the Afghan women". The images which follow include the then PAS president, Fadzil Noor, and other party leaders, as well as scenes of veiled Afghan women and children surrounded by the ruins of war. The footage ends with a Quranic verse from the *Surah al-Baqarah* (Chapter of the Cow), "and cast yourself not into perdition with your own hands".[12] The clip also contained an explicitly violent scene showing a kneeling woman, dressed in a *burqa*, being executed by a Taliban gunman, a slow-motion image which was repeated several times.[13]

The clip, ninety seconds long, was aired repeatedly on the government television stations, RTM 1 and 2, and on TV3, a station owned by groups close to the government, during the prime-time nightly news bulletins throughout January 2002.[14] When questioned by the press, the Information Ministry Parliamentary Secretary, Zainuddin Maidin, justified it as reflecting "our [the government's] psychological warfare against the extremists". Furthermore, the Parliamentary Secretary stated that it was a "mere coincidence" that the clip was aired during the Indera Kayangan campaign. Press reports indicate that no distinction appeared to have been made between this clip and the news features among which it was broadcast. It was even described by Deputy Home Minister, Chor Chee Heung, as a "news item for the public".[15]

The screening of this clip during an election campaign in Perlis is significant. In 2002, no PAS candidate was actually standing — keADILan, an opposition party co-operating with PAS within the Barisan Alternatif (Alternative Front), fielded a candidate instead. However, the BN's use of such tactics against the BA stems partly from the large swing to PAS in the preceding national and Perlis state elections, held simultaneously in 1999. Malaysia's largest opposition party, PAS, has created wide grass-roots networks, especially in the northern peninsular states. It won 20 per cent of the aggregate vote in the 1999 state elections, leaving the BN majority in some seats as small as a few hundred votes. For example, in the state constituency of Kayang, the BN won by only 331 votes. In the national constituency of Arau, the BN won with only 1,586 votes. Such a narrow election victory seemed to have come as a shock to the BN, which has since responded with strategies to convince the Malay Muslim electorate to renew its loyalty to BN candidates.

The BN is in this position because, as the 1999 elections demonstrated, PAS poses a serious ideological and electoral threat to the BN's dominance of Malaysian national politics. The BN has responded for more than a decade to the ideological challenge posed by PAS and other Islamist[16] groups with an Islamic rhetoric of its own, as part of a strategy of co-option of the Islamist challenge, and to counter criticism that its own politics are "secular".[17] The government has suppressed extra-parliamentary Islamist groups — the most notable recent example was the 1994 banning of the Darul Arqam group, which had attempted to create an "autonomous" Islamic commune on the outskirts of Kuala Lumpur, alongside a successful business empire. The BN first proscribed Darul Arqam's publications, charging the group with promoting deviant Islam and subsequently arrested its leaders, alleging that they posed a threat to national security.[18] Yet the BN is forced to engage with PAS's politics, even while it has attempted to cast PAS members and leaders as extremists who nurture anti-government sentiment in its schools and organizations, because PAS has held a long-standing commitment to a strategy of *electoral* participation and competition with the BN.[19] In Indera Kayangan in 2002, the BN attempted to associate the electoralist PAS with the Taliban who had seized power without a proven popular mandate, and it was widely argued in the press subsequently that this equation delivered the by-election to the BN.[20]

The equation of PAS with the Taliban, whom the BN government cast in their rhetoric as "retrogressive", was aimed at reducing PAS's appeal for upwardly-mobile Muslims and non-Muslims alike. The clip, aired in English, played on this audience's aspirations for careers in a bilingual (and thus "modern" and "internationally competitive") office culture. It created the image of an extremist, backward-looking threat to these aspirations. For example, under the Taliban, women's opportunities to gain education or work outside the home were virtually abolished. There was also a warning that Malaysia could face the same military and economic consequences as Afghanistan should the Malay Muslim electorate feel too generous towards PAS. The message was delivered in the clip through scenes of ruined homes and of U.S. bombers flying over Afghanistan. As the narrator declared, "You will definitely not want a foreign power to come and bomb this country to liberate women and people repressed by militant groups. Let our people free ourselves from fanatical and retrogressive militant groups to avoid any catastrophes".[21]

The equation was presented to the public in the context of a broader discourse about Islam and extremism, focused at the time on Afghanistan. Within this discourse, popularized by the media worldwide, the Taliban is presented as "backward" by press commentators, working within a system of news-production which has a global audience as its target. The American news network CNN, for example, is accessible to Malaysians through the Astro cable television network twenty-four hours a day. CNN reporters frequently present the view that the "anti-modern" Taliban want to drag their society "back" to the past,[22] regardless of whether or not Taliban-style politics are justified in Islamic teachings. The thrust of the CNN's argument is that the Taliban's interpretation of Islamic doctrine logically leads to this retrograde movement.

Tradition, Modernity, and Modernization

Creating a popular image of PAS as backward-looking and "traditional" is an important part of Dr Mahathir's political strategy. Throughout his long term as Prime Minister, Dr Mahathir has made much of his modernizing credentials. He has made repeated appeals, specifically directed to Malays, to replace their "old values" with ideas of entrepreneurship, an efficient work ethic, and working together under his leadership to create sustained economic growth.[23] Dr Mahathir has consistently presented these ideas as essential if Malaysia is to face up to the challenge of modernization. He has repeatedly asked Malay Muslims to undergo a "mental revolution and cultural transformation", arguing that Malaysia is lagging behind in the global development race, stalled largely by their "traditional" — and therefore unsuitable — ideas. Alongside this rhetoric, as part of his Vision 2020 project, Dr Mahathir has called on all Malaysians to become "psychologically subservient to none", faithful in their religious and spiritual values, and confident of their ability to build a modern economy and society.

Throughout the 1990s, Dr Mahathir's political rhetoric assumed that modernity was a state Malaysia needed to travel towards; it did not already exist. This is most clearly seen in Dr Mahathir's statements on the drive towards industrialization in Malaysia — usually considered a prerequisite for a modern society — which he considers to be a "struggle ... to develop the country".[24] Dr Mahathir believes that Malaysia must go through a process of transformation from undeveloped to a prosperous nation. His view is that, while Malaysia has begun this journey, it "must aim to become a developed country at par with those of Europe and North America. It may not happen tomorrow or next year or even by the end of this [the previous] millennium but we must not be discouraged. Everything must have a beginning".[25] Given the time and the right attitudes, according to Dr Mahathir, Malaysia will reach the level of prosperity enjoyed by many in the West. This is an exact reflection of modernization theory, which holds that the transition from a traditional to a modern society is carried out through a series of stages. In Rostow's 1960 formulation of the theory, this process begins as a result of a "shock", which in non-Western countries usually comes from "some external intrusion by more advanced societies, often, colonialism". This shock brings with it a set of ideas which then filter through that society, "not merely that economic progress is possible, but that economic progress is a necessary condition for some other purpose, judged to be good".[26] This allows for the rise, through initiative or grooming, of a select group of entrepreneurs, willing to take the necessary risks to overcome the resistance posed by traditional ideas. These entrepreneurs build "enclaves of modern activity" so that economic growth becomes the "normal condition" of that society and allows for the triumph of the market, bringing prosperity for all, eventually.[27] It is a formulation that lauds advanced-nation status as the end of history. Modernization then, in Rostow's theory, *is* history, because the history of every less-developed nation is the story of its progress to prosperity and modernity — here, blocked by "traditional elements", there, more advanced because entrepreneurial élites make it possible.

Dr Mahathir's exhortations echo the arguments, renovated a few times, of Western modernization theorists, which shape the development efforts of most developing countries today, with or without external aid. Modernization theory argues that public authority based on religion constitute a "traditional" ideological block to development, so state structures based on Islamic precepts, for example, must do likewise. According to this view, as societies modernize, religion recedes as a feature of public life and increasingly is expressed as a personal faith or system of ethics. The argument is applied with great frequency to Islam. Addressing this specific question, Daniel Pipes, an American consultant on the Middle East and Islam, and a journalist for the *New York Post*,[28] has argued that Muslims are hampered in modernizing by their culture. Pipes claims that modernization theory is discredited, but accepts its premises. He is careful not to attack Muslims for being *Muslim* — his argument is not that Islam holds Muslims back; rather, they cannot modernize because of their shared, pre-modern culture.[29] The character of this culture is not "Islamic", as it is not "inherent in the religion", but "Islamicate", that is, "characteristic of the Muslim experience but not required by the Islamic faith or law". Pipes argues that every Muslim is heavily influenced by the Islamicate world-view, which "derives from the invariant premises of the religion and from fundamental themes established more than a millenium ago",[30] including a disdain for the then inferior Western civilization. Now that the tables are turned and the West is attempting to bring modernity to Muslims, the latter, because of their essential *difference* from Westerners, reject modernization as a Western conspiracy. Pipes goes so far as to assert that Islamicate culture is "the least propitious for modern life".[31] In this way, Muslims are weighed down by a set of religious ideas which need to be marginalized from public life, if the undeveloped countries largely populated by Muslims are ever to develop into prosperous nations.

Pipes' views, unsurprisingly, have gained little popularity among Muslims. However, modernization theory, and the idea that Muslims are trapped in their old ways, have much in common with Dr Mahathir's "progressive" Islam. As a "modernist" Muslim, Dr Mahathir has melded his projected roles of modernizer and Islamist, adapting ideas of economic modernization and applying them so as to make Islam itself the object of "modernization", alongside the society and economy in which it is practised. In this way, he has tried to marginalize PAS's Islamist critique of his modernization plans, while adopting an Islamic vocabulary for his own ends. Dr Mahathir's emphasis on the "work ethic", which he claims is expressed in some verses of the Quran, is an attempt to use Islam as a form of moral and ethical guide, on the individual and institutional level. In this way, Dr Mahathir presents Islam to Malaysians as a religion which is supportive of change and "progress", and entirely appropriate for a "modern" society. This is in contrast with PAS, which uses an Islamic vocabulary to express its critique of Dr Mahathir's development drive, and its consequences. So in a 1995 edition of PAS's paper *Harakah*, a long list of BN scandals involving the mismanagement of public money, together with the banning of several publications and the use of the Internal Security Act, is provided as proof of the BN's immorality, which all serious Muslims should act to prevent.[32]

The premise that the process of "modernization" will lead to a prosperous Malaysia lies at the heart of Dr Mahathir's and the BN's rhetoric about PAS, which is defined as traditional and, moreover, mistaken on Islam. It is because this view is so critical to Dr Mahathir's development plans for Malaysia, as it is for other third-world élites and global superpowers alike, that it has needed to be examined in detail. That societies are divided between "traditional" and "modern" sectors, each with a corresponding set of ideas, is an ideological and rhetorical device used by politicians, planners, international banks, and aid donors in the West and the post-colonial world to support their economic and social prescriptions. Based on this premise, governments like the BN formulate policy for modernizing an undeveloped nation and encouraging economies where production and distribution are carried out subject to the free operation of market principles. Furthermore, once the argument is accepted that nations move through a predetermined series of stages until they reach the "end of history", it becomes much easier for ruling élites to argue that any group in society which questions the process, or highlights the problems it may create, is "blocking" progress, or even looking backwards towards the past. PAS is a target for such accusations because throughout and before the 1990s, they had rejected the methods of the government's New Economic Policy. Moreover, in the context of Dr Mahathir's privatization and deregulation programme for Vision 2020, PAS has actively pointed out that Dr Mahathir's market-oriented modernization plans have left behind pools of poverty, rural and urban, while only a small group of élite Malays have become much better off. PAS has also argued that truly Islamic development would focus more sharply on uplifting the poor and orphans even while it creates Islamic-managed funds.[33]

Islam as a Moral Standard

In pursuing modernization and economic growth, the BN has focused on creating and cultivating a small Malay entrepreneurial class, which possesses modernizing ideas and can lead Malay Muslims away from their "traditional" attitudes. Yet PAS's rhetorical focus on the excesses of this ruling clique has won broad support among those Malays who have found that modernization has not, in fact, propelled them into the ranks of this "New Malay" entrepreneurial class. A recent example of such rhetoric focused on the government's buy-back of Malaysian Airlines shares in 2001 from its controlling shareholder, Tajudin Ramli, at approximately three times the price that each share was worth. The decision to buy out Tajudin was primarily the responsibility of the former Finance Minister, Daim Zainuddin, who has had a long-standing association with Tajudin. Commenting on the ensuing investigation into the buy-back, PAS's then parliamentary leader, Fadzil Noor, is reported to have said:

> Those who are wrong must be punished, including the ministry officials involved. We also hope this mismanagement will not be repeated in other companies in view of the many privatization exercises taking place which may mean many more companies will be bailed out. Will the investigation also include Daim?

This is important because the business community and *rakyat* [people] are aware of Daim's involvement, as some businessmen were his proxies.[34]

This is a statement made in Parliament by a politician aware of the need to position himself against the government's favoured entrepreneurs, while ensuring that he presents himself as close to the *rakyat*. He has made clear links between government ministers, the BN's privatization programme, failed businessman Tajudin, and the mismanagement of public funds.

Such attacks on this network of interests create significant tension for the BN, as they stem from PAS's positioning to present its adherents as true Muslims because they promote clean government, tackle corruption, and defend democracy, and the *rakyat*'s interest. The BN has had to discredit PAS while ensuring that its own followers also appear sufficiently Islamic. The response by the BN has been to present PAS as backward-looking and to show itself as the party of the true progressives. BN's attempts in this area have involved mobilizing selected Islamic teachings, such as those which make allowances for the accumulation of wealth, and presenting them as the "fundamentals of Islam"[35] in order to implement Dr Mahathir's "cultural transformation". At the same time, Dr Mahathir has tried to present his government as an "Islamic" one, and PAS as "deviant", because the government provides for "all the religious needs of Muslims" and attempts to "instill … spiritual values" into the community. In contrast to Dr Mahathir's focus on personal values, PAS, he has argued, uses Islam as part of a "hate campaign" against the government.[36] This kind of exchange between the BN and PAS is evidence of the competition which drives Dr Mahathir's "Islamization" of society and state.

This "Islamization" drive has provided Dr Mahathir with a way to position himself as a defender of Islam and Malay identity, and to embrace calls for more Islam in public life, to counter critiques of the BN government as "secular" and therefore spiritually bankrupt. Arguing for "secularization", as classical modernization theorists would have it, would therefore be unhelpful to Dr Mahathir. Thus, he has argued instead for Malaysia to modernize Islamically, using his favoured, pro-capitalist Islamic teachings and creating an Islamic rationale for the familiar prescriptions for modernization. This is Dr Mahathir's contribution to so-called modernist Islam: using the rhetoric of rational interpretation of Islam's teachings, and with his own political preoccupations in mind, he has adapted classical modernization theory so that it can accommodate Islamic principles, and has elevated those Islamic teachings which can be argued to encourage entrepreneurialism. Dr Mahathir is creating two competing Islams in Malaysia, only one of which is appropriate for those who want to participate in a modern economy and society. Thus, Dr. Mahathir's Islam is a "moral guide", not politics — a set of values and ethics to guide individual or privately-managed action,[37] to motivate Malay Muslims to act in a way which is conducive to national unity and economic growth. For this reason, he has presented the "traditionalists", as exemplified by PAS, as a group of zealots who cannot face up to modernity, with the hope of co-opting those with "modernist" sentiments.

Islam: The Government Version

It is possible to determine exactly how Dr Mahathir has presented his strategy by analysing a selection of his speeches on Islam throughout the 1990s. In these, he has repeatedly stressed the difference between his own and PAS's interpretations of Islam. Dr Mahathir's government has expended large resources to support its arguments about modernization and Islam. One major initiative was a government-funded think-tank, the Malaysian Institute for Islamic Understanding (IKIM). This Institute has been as vocal as Dr Mahathir himself in building an ideological objective on an interpretation of Islam which exhorts Malay Muslims to work harder, accumulate wealth, and rally behind the BN's strong government.[38] Speeches made during the 1990s by leading IKIM figures reproduce Dr Mahathir's arguments and IKIM's website demonstrates its shared agenda with the BN government. The website states that the Institute was launched in 1992 by Dr Mahathir to correct the image of Islam, which it claims is being misrepresented to Malay Muslims. According to IKIM, Islam "has been wrongly portrayed as promoting terrorism, conservatism, fanaticism, backwardness, poverty and degrading stereotypes". In contrast, IKIM claims to present an Islam which "thrives on tolerance and dynamism". Furthermore, IKIM states that its role is to "conceptualize, design and provide the required inputs of Islam" to the development process, which is rooted in the "current reality of the world, [and] the challenges and the prospects that it offers".[39]

Presenting itself as up-to-date and dynamic, IKIM uses rhetoric which interprets Islam as the religion of choice for those who wish to get ahead. This fits neatly with Dr Mahathir's long-term projection of himself and his government as Malaysia's proper modernizers. Despite further statements that IKIM seeks to prove to non-Muslims that Islam is in fact tolerant and progressive, a transcript of its 1992 conference, "Towards the 21st Century: Islam and Vision 2020", shows that IKIM is, in fact, seeking two audiences, the second of which is Malay and Muslim. IKIM's columns appear regularly in Malay-language newspapers, including *Utusan Melayu*, printed in Jawi script, which only Muslims usually learn in schools. IKIM's columns in English-language newspapers are also usually presented as advice to Muslims, indicating that IKIM also seeks to pay sufficient attention to upwardly mobile Muslims fluent in English. For example, a 1993 collection of such columns includes articles from *The Star* and the *New Straits Times*.[40] It would seem that non-Muslims are, in reality, IKIM's secondary target.

IKIM's "Islamic understanding" is focused on assisting Malay Muslims to understand the BN's vision of Islam. Almost all the speeches include oblique references to "groups" in society which refuse to accept Islam's true teachings, although, on occasion, direct references are made to PAS. Yet, it is clear that even where PAS is not explicitly mentioned, the "groups" in question are indeed PAS and its supporters, because both kinds of references lead to the same conclusions. The speeches, largely in standard Bahasa Malaysia, seem aimed at an educated Malay-Muslim audience. There are also one or two in English, directed presumably at a domestic non-Malay audience, and importantly, to international observers. The speeches commonly use allegories from seventh-century Arabian society at the time of Prophet Muhammad to illustrate to the audience that, faced with today's challenges, PAS's "traditionalist" ideas are inadequate. Thus, the early believers of the Prophet's message were broadminded and open to all kinds of learning. This attitude, however, was undermined with the rise of *ulama* in Islam, who began to argue that the pursuit of knowledge which was not specifically Islamic was not necessary. This is precisely what Dr Mahathir's claims is PAS's attitude, as they are alleged not to realize that education and technology are crucial to development.[41]

The intent of these speeches is to underscore the point that, for those who are serious about engaging with modernity, a particular understanding of Islam is required. For example, as part of Dr Mahathir's and IKIM's projection of a modern Islam, they have repeatedly asserted that "real" Islam involves embedding Malaysia into the global "knowledge economy" and building personal and national wealth. As long as some of this wealth is distributed among the poor, its pursuit and possession is argued to be in keeping with the principles of Islam. Thus, IKIM's then Director-General, Dr Ismail bin Haji Ibrahim, argued that the BN's Vision 2020, with its aim of making Malaysia more internationally competitive, partly through scientific and technical innovation, is Islamic, because "Islam is a set of teachings which... aims towards heightened scientific knowledge. In the Quran there are many verses about the importance of science, that is, how human beings have to really use their intellectual capacity to better their lives".[42] Dr Ismail does not name these verses, but Dr Mahathir does elsewhere, for example, from the *Surah al-Ghaasyiyah*, which states, "And the Sky, how is it raised high? And the Mountains, how are they fixed firm? And the Earth, how is it spread out?". This verse is argued to encourage scientific enquiry as humans seek the explanations.[43] For those who feel nervous about the unbridled pursuit of wealth, Dr Ismail adds, "Islam does not forbid its followers from accumulating wealth... because what is emphasized by Islam is that the wealth which is sought should come from sources which are *halal* [permitted]... because those who possess wealth will be able to use that wealth to strive along the path of God".[44]

In both Dr Mahathir's speeches and IKIM's publications, followers of this "real" Islam are frequently contrasted with other groups in society for whom Islamic piety is alleged to mean refusing to engage with knowledge other than Islamic studies. These other groups largely consist of PAS followers. For example, Dr Mahathir has alleged that "some are influenced by PAS that Malay Muslim children should only pursue Islamic studies. Other forms of knowledge are secular and not important. If studied, more time should be given towards supplementary religious activities which are made compulsory by those who are against other forms of knowledge". Furthermore, according to Dr Mahathir, "what is taught during these lectures is not the true teachings of Islam... What is conveyed to the students is anti-government politics".[45] It is on the basis of this allegation that Dr Mahathir accuses PAS of dividing the Muslim community,[46] and refusing to acknowledge that development and economic growth are essential in restoring Islamic countries to their historical prominence. He has characterized the struggle to modernize Malaysia as a religious one, arguing that "This is a *jihad* because when we become an industrialized country... it is not just that we can win, but no one will be able to pressure us".[47]

By contrast, PAS is portrayed as undermining Islamic teachings, clinging to the pre-Islamic past. Dr Mahathir suggested in 1997 that during the time of prosperity experienced by Muslims as Islam first spread through Arabia, there were still figures who "rejected all knowledge which they indicted as un-Islamic, and which did not need to be learned by Muslims".[48] Furthermore, "as time went by, more Muslims and their leaders became involved in power struggles, each claiming that they were fighting for Islam".[49] These allegories about the past, where the force of the Prophet's modernizing Revelation is presented as clashing with traditional Arab society, are always presented as containing a lesson for the challenges of today. The "other groups" of today are also routinely referred to alongside historical references to the pre-Islamic time in Arabia, known in Arabic as the *Jahiliyah*, when Arab tribes rejected or were slow to accept the true and unifying religion of the Prophet. Instead, they preferred to "believe in the religion of their grandparents".[50] These references, commonplace in Mahathir's speeches and forums organized by IKIM, are designed to undermine PAS's Islamic credentials, and discredit their claims as capable managers of a modern economy and society, to be achieved in Malaysia. The word *jahil* has cultural and religious connotations, indicating ignorant people possessing only the most shallow knowledge, and also people who are ignorant of the teachings of Islam. The *jahil* Arab tribes are often presented by Dr Mahathir and IKIM as the uncivilized *opposite* of Islam — they lacked unity and engaged in common feuding; they practised female infanticide; they essentially lived in a condition of moral poverty; and rejected the Prophet's Revelation for a better society. Dr Ismail

makes the point clearly that there are *jahil* people opposing the
government in Malaysia today. He argues:

> God has explained that when Islam was conveyed by the Prophet,
> there were still people with an obstinate attitude, who did not
> want to accept Islam as a way of life... They were too fanatical
> for their old traditions, even though those traditions no longer
> fit with the development of human thinking at that time. In our
> society today we can also see a section of the new generation
> who try to look towards the past; towards old traditions... often
> they have an obstinate and negative attitude.[51]

The strategy is to assert repeatedly that PAS is in fact *jahil*, living
in an ancient past, and therefore incapable of understanding the
demands of the modern world, the world of developed nations. In
combination with devices such as the television clip depicting
the Taliban execution of a woman wearing a *burqa*, Dr Mahathir's
and IKIM's assertions depict PAS as attempting to mastermind the
"return" of Malaysian society to a brutal pre-Islamic past. The
intended message for Muslim listeners or viewers is that PAS is
unable to represent Islamic interests; a party of troublemakers, it is
totally incapable of running a country in the twenty-first century.
This message is not an attempt to improve the public's understanding
of Islam as a religion. It is quite openly a political maneouvre, a
mobilization of *certain* Islamic "fundamentals" which are helpful to
the government.

The BN argues that for Malaysia to modernize, individual Muslims
need "a reformation of thought" so that they can face up to the
present and lead by example those who have reverted to the backward
and ignorant ideas of the Arab tribes before they had even come to
accept Islam. Yet Mahathir's and IKIM's prescriptions for Islam sound
very much like a human resource management manual. One IKIM
publication even has chapter titles such as "The Islamic Conception
of Work", "Management Based on Islam", and "Islam Demands
Brilliance in Commerce and Entrepreneurialism".[52] Dr Mahathir's
modernist Islam appears élite-centric, leaving it wide open to PAS's
criticism that his government is trying to dupe the people with
development[53] as it is oriented only to the needs of the rich, and
upwardly mobile aspirants.

The PAS Challenge

pessanti

While Dr Mahathir urges Muslims to work hard and build the economy, Nik Abdul Aziz, the PAS Chief Minister of Kelantan, and several other leading PAS figures, ask them to be caring and modest, and to live an ethically-guided life, rejecting attachment to status symbols and the temptation to show off.[54] PAS's appeal to its Muslim electorate stems from its ability to critique the BN's development plans from the point of view of an audience it has identified as not materially enriched, and therefore not co-opted by government-led development. This includes the smallholder peasantry mentioned by Kessler in the quote at the beginning of this chapter, but includes many urban dwellers also. In contrast to the government, PAS's rhetoric does not generally involve "berating" the population for failing to carry out their duty as Muslims,[55] but appeals in a much more sophisticated way to their concerns for social justice, which they take seriously precisely because they are Muslims. PAS makes sensitive use of teachings which are just as "fundamental" to Islam as those quoted by the BN, but they do so in such a way as to articulate concerns about the worst ravages of the development and modernization process. Far from attracting devotees of *kejahilan*,[56] or "religious fanaticism", PAS has, since its early successes, attracted a constituency actively considering its political alternatives in responding to *modern* challenges. PAS has in fact been rather careful to address contemporary concerns such as development and poverty — rural and urban. The late PAS parliamentary leader Fadzil Noor, in the statement "PAS shall continue to assess and address the impact of globalization, in so far as it affects the development of a better Malaysia and a better world", has expressed that this is a conscious strategy.[57]

PAS's discussions of "development" certainly demonstrate attention to issues rarely touched upon by the BN or IKIM. It is far beyond the government's frame of discussion to make such statements as "the primary basis of development is the development of humanity".[58] PAS also promises to "prioritize the development of rural people who have been left behind economically".[59] In making statements such as this, PAS is attempting to offer Malay Muslims an Islamic framework within which to raise a critique of uneven development and inequality, and a programme for social change, as expressed in their calls for an

What about the rest?

Islamic state. Broadly, PAS uses the "Islamic State" as a means to contrast its vision of an ethical economy and moral society to the BN's "unIslamic" system, which, for example, allows gambling in Malaysia for the sake of profiting from its tax revenues. This critique is all the more potent, given the weakness of the "secular" opposition in providing an electoral challenge to the BN. PAS's rhetoric is that of a modern, electoral opposition, and throughout its history of activity in post-colonial Malaysia, it has offered consistent, if incomplete, opposition to the market-driven and élite-centred politics of the BN, alongside the showy consumer culture of the rich. Thus, in contrast to the BN members' latest model limousines, Nik Aziz has insisted that Kelantan state government officials should drive ordinary cars.[60] Tarmizi Mohammad Jam, a former writer for *Harakah*, PAS's newspaper, is able to boast that Nik Aziz has also

> cut his salary by as much as forty per cent... he also does not want to receive any of his allowance for Hari Raya [Eid] feasts... Tuan Guru [Nik Aziz] has also warned the people and the organisers of functions which he attends against presenting him with anything in the form of gifts, souvenirs and the like.[61]

Furthermore, PAS can confidently claim that it has taken concrete steps to ease the financial burden on the poor, for example, in the case of road tax. Take the following statement by Nik Aziz as an example of PAS's welfarist rhetoric:

> What's the point of charging road tax when people are already hit with toll. People have to pay the road tax, and pay the toll. Who is all this for? Enough! The people have been bled dry for long enough. We say there is no need for road tax because people need their vehicles now, at least people want to own a motorcycle for travel to and from their workplaces, to the market, and home. Why don't we provide this convenience to the people?[62]

There are several reasons for this kind of rhetoric. In refusing to accept gifts and special allowances, Nik Aziz is able to show in concrete ways that he is not a part of a political culture where favours are traded between the government, "friendly" organizations, and big business. By phrasing his criticisms in moral terms, Nik Aziz is trying to show that he is tackling corruption. His critical attitude towards gratuitous displays of wealth draws on the full potency of Islam as a vocabulary of egalitarianism, not only of commerce. By showing a sensitivity to grass-roots concerns, for instance, by acknowledging that commuters need their vehicles in order to participate fully in the economy, Nik Aziz can help to situate PAS alongside the people it claims to represent. PAS's campaign literature through the 1990s has specifically addressed the problems of poverty for farmers, fishermen, hawkers, and small-time traders,[63] whereas Dr Mahathir's speeches only promise a kind of general "trickle-down" to the poor as the rich grow increasingly wealthy. Furthermore, Haji Hadi Awang, Chief Minister of the PAS-controlled Terengganu state, has pointed out the flaws in the trickle-down argument, pointing to villagers who do not receive piped water and electricity in their homes, "even though they may be living right next to the hydroelectric dam",[64] a typical symbol of development. PAS has placed itself within a critique of the "secular" or "Kemalist"[65] developmentalism, and address its constituency as modern electors, not ungrateful traditionalists. Nik Aziz has explicitly questioned the BN's arguments that Kelantanese Muslims elect PAS because they are poor and "backward", pointing out that many would not be so poor if not for the frequent mishandling of government funds.

PAS is careful also to address its arguments in terms of a desire for a more transparent liberal democracy in Malaysia, a feature of political life which should, in theory, arise with modernization. If PAS were unable to address modern concerns, Nik Aziz would not be able to argue that he trusts the *rakyat* [people] to make capable political decisions at election time, stating: "Thank God the people of Kelantan are more clever than their leaders".[66] Far from looking back in time, PAS is clearly operating, ideologically and practically, within the context of the modern nation-state, and makes frequent use of related concepts, such as "the people" and "democracy". Indeed, Nik Aziz has made clear the idea that Muslims should aspire to more democracy in the political system, because "if Islam is split apart, democracy is also split apart".[67]

A further example of the modern character of the contest between the BN and PAS was their focus on democracy leading up to the

1999 elections, immediately after the jailing of former Deputy Prime Minister Anwar Ibrahim. Fadzil Noor said at the time, "Now, people have started to question what the regime is doing. People are more critical of the issues, such as corruption, cronyism and nepotism... Malaysians, especially Malays, look at PAS in terms of its principles... Our aim is very clear. It is to deny the government the power it has today and to bring back justice".[68] As Bobby Sayyid has pointed out, groups which use such concepts, which assume the existence of nation-states and parliaments, and national citizenries "cannot be described in any meaningful way as being anti-modern".[69] The issue for PAS then is not modernity but the character of the drive towards modernization pursued by the government and its associates. This modernization project has been described as "hegemonic" by John Hilley, reflected by "the long-term promotion of the liberal developmentalist state ... wholesale deregulation and open-market policies".[70] It has been characterized by PAS as involving land-grabbing and false promises of increased wealth for ordinary Malays, who then find that only a small élite can enjoy the luxury facilities built on what was their land. A cartoon in *Harakah* in the period of campaigning for the 1995 federal elections depicted Mahathir as saying to two villagers that in return for their land "everybody would get work". In the next frame, the same villagers are employed on the golf course which Mahathir now enjoys.[71]

It is in relation to this electoral conflict that Professor Clive Kessler's work has been so instructive. As a "conservative movement of radical discontent", PAS channels and gives voice to Malay Muslims' grievances. PAS has historically been a movement of *opposition*, and support for PAS has long been one of the few channels available for Malay dissent in Malaysia. PAS has also, in co-operation with the parties in the now-defunct Barisan Alternatif, formed the backbone of a rare attempt at cross-communal oppositional organization. The ideological challenge provided by PAS has forced the BN a long way from its "secularist" articulation of modernization theory by Dr Mahathir, and forced it to respond with an approach to Islam that makes its politics more palatable to an electorate increasingly receptive to a religious critique. Indeed, before the events of 11 September 2001, this disaffection with the BN had made the PAS critique of BN-style modernization a rallying-point in Malaysian politics.

Yet, as Kessler has also pointed out in his work on Kelantan, PAS is not necessarily able to offer any lasting solution to its constituency's grievances. For PAS, Muslims should work towards moderate capitalism, not drive its excesses, as they would argue the BN's interpretation of Islamic doctrine seeks to do. PAS does not propose any real alternative to the logic of striving for increasing economic growth. Thus, the private-sector, profit-driven ownership of productive resources would be permitted, but some nationalization would be necessary to ensure that the interests of the poor would be protected. PAS refuses to allow *zakat* money collected in Kelantan and Terengganu to earn interest in banks, but at the same time the party speaks the language of efficient capitalist managers, pointing to a focus on the private sector in Terengganu, and the "effective management" of the logging industry to facilitate revenue collection.[72]

Ultimately, PAS proposes a softer version of the same modernization project, offering a new articulation of domination. PAS also exhorts the population to work hard, save money, and avoid complaining about low wages, because, in Nik Aziz's words, "we learn from the *Hadith* that the poor enter heaven hundreds of years before the rich... There's no need to feel lucky if our wage is large, and there's no need to worry if our wage is small".[73] However, if PAS were to come to power in Malaysia, it would find itself managing a complex economy, well integrated with global capitalism, and it would have to reconcile this role with its history of voicing popular opposition to the clear inequalities created by Malaysia's transformation into precisely this kind of economy. PAS would be required to pursue economic growth within a competitive global system and the imperatives of this task, which involve creating profitable conditions for the rich, just as the BN have done, are likely to undermine PAS's ideological credibility as defenders of the people, as they would then be open to similar critiques as the one they have levelled against the BN. This is partly the reason why their notion of an Islamic State is so unclear, because PAS's contradictory character, and often unclear political programme, are a result of its relationship with its grass-roots supporters, and the tension between their expectations and the actual alternative which PAS provides to the BN's politics.

PAS's dilemma is expressed in comments made by Yusuf Rawa, former PAS President, that "to us [PAS] it is not practical to go into

details of what we want to do in an Islamic State. If they want to
see if we operate it well, they must elect us.... All operational
aspects of how and when to do certain things or launch certain
policies, can be taken up later when we do have the Islamic State".[74]
What PAS has found much easier to carry out, however, is the
moralistic proscription of certain behaviour or forms of entertainment
in the states which they control. PAS has found itself in a bind
between, on the one hand, its desire and need to articulate a
convincing vision of a just society, in contrast to what it argues is
a morally bankrupt society ruled by the BN, and on the other, its
ultimate acceptance of the BN's goals, and of the demands of
economic growth and capitalist integration. This ideological dilemma
leads PAS to attempt to implement, and to campaign electorally,
slogans such as *hudud*, siezed upon by the BN as examples of PAS's
fanaticism and inability to rule a multi-ethnic society, yet upheld by
PAS as proof of their unwavering commitment to Islam.

The bitter altercation between PAS and the BN about who are
better Muslims highlights the fact that Islam, as a set of religious
ideas, is not essential and fixed but open to arguments of
interpretation. Islam can be used to rally support for a just economy
and society, and for the mobilization of opposition to the government,
or it can be used as a set of arguments for building a class of
entrepreneurs and shoring up support for unfettered capitalism. This
argument exposes cleavages in Malaysian society based around class,
social mobility, and access to the wealth produced by economic
growth. What PAS offers to Malay Muslims is not only an "idealized
past",[75] as Kessler has put it, but an idealized vision of a just and
equitable future, albeit one which PAS may not be able to provide
when faced with the exigencies of managing a "modernizing"
capitalist economy should the party succeed in coming to power in
the future.

Notes

1. Kessler (1978), p. 167.
2. Sloane (1999), chp. 3.
3. Jomo and Ahmad Shabery Cheek (1992), pp. 79–106.
4. Chandra Muzaffar (1987).

5. For a discussion of *hudud* laws, see M. B. Hooker's contribution in this volume.

6. S. Jayasankaran and Lorien Holland, "The Islamic Party's Malay Dilemma", *Far Eastern Economic Review*, October 2001. <bmalaysia> Archive: http://groups.yahoo.com/groups/bmalaysia. See also note 22 below.

7. Abdullah Ahmad, "Will PAS Reveal Details of its Islamic Polity?" *New Straits Times*, 2 October 2001. <bmalaysia> Archive.

8. See Leys (1996). See also Farrands (1996), pp. 1–21.

9. Abdul Rahman Haji Abdullah (1998), Part 1.

10. Sayyid (1998).

11. Esposito and Voll (1996), chp. 6.

12. Y. S. Tong, "Reel Propagates 'Culture of Fear' via Government Media". *Malaysiakini*, 9 January 2002.

13. <bmalaysia> mailing list, 19 January 2002.

14. Susan Loone, "Justification of RTM Broadcast 'Blatant, Brazen': DAP", *Malaysiakini*, 6 January 2002.

15. See note 12.

16. For an excellent definition of the term "Islamist", refer to Sayyid (1998), p. 17. Here Sayyid states that "an Islamist is someone who places her or his Muslim identity at the centre of her or his political practice. That is, Islamists are people who use the language of Islamic metaphors to think through their political destinies, those who see Islam in their political future". Crucially, "Islamism is a political discourse … that attempts to centre Islam within the political order. Islamism can range from the assertion of a Muslim subjectivity to a full-blooded attempt to reconstruct society on Islamic principles".

17. See, for example, "Kelantan Contoh Membangun Bersama Islam", *Harakah*, 21 April 1995.

18. See Abdul Fauzi Abdul Hamid (2000), pp. 32–65.

19. For a further discussion on Islamism and democracy, see Syed Ahmad Hussein (2002), pp. 74–107.

20. For example, see *Malaysiakini* coverage in January 2002.

21. See note 12.

22. For example, see "Afghanistan: Frozen in Time", *Time*, 29 May 2000, which is available by searching the CNN website. The same website made available a transcript of a CNN news report, dated 22 November 2001, in which Afghanistan is described as not even a "proper country" under Taliban rule. CNN reports have presented the Taliban as backward-looking since they first captured Kabul in 1996, when a report referred

to the Taliban's "fossilised policies". There is no discussion of any previous historical period when such policies were accepted. For a Malaysian version of this argument, see also Mazeni Alwi's "Prophetic Document on the Taliban", a review of Ahmed Rashid's *Taliban: The Story of the Afghan Warlords* in *Malaysiakini*, 24 January 2002. For a discussion of similar arguments applied to Islam before the Taliban existed to be singled out, see Said (1997).

23. Dr Mahathir first expressed this idea in his 1976 book *Cabaran*, and has continued to do so, including in his speech in *Malaysia's Vision 2020: Understanding the Concept, Implications and Challenges*, edited by Ahmad Sarji Abdul Hamid, Appendix 2 (Petaling Jaya: Pelanduk Publications, 1993).

24. See interview with Dr Mahathir, *Utusan Online*, 15 October 2001. http://www.utusan.com.my/utusan/SpecialCoverage/temubual_pm/index.asp?pg=temubual.htm

25. Ibid.

26. Rostow (2000), pp. 100–9.

27. Ibid.

28. Not to be outdone, Pipes too has his own website, complete with a list of recommended readings, and interviews, including one entitled "Islamism is Fascism".

29. Pipes (1983), part 1.

30. Ibid., pp. 90–93.

31. Ibid., p. 188. See also Barber (1996); and Lewis (2002).

32. Abdul Aziz Mustafa, "Undi anda di dunia akan disoal di akhirat", *Harakah*, 28 April 1995, p. 9.

33. Salmah Mat Hussin, "Kelantan laksana 78 perkara berasaskan taqwa", *Harakah*, 28 April 1995, p. 5.

34. Susan Loone, "MAS Passenger Load Down, Revenue Up After Fares Hike", *Malaysiakini*, 13 March 2002.

35. This phrase is repeated throughout Dr Mahathir Mohamad's speech presented at the World Economic Forum in New York in 2002. It is attached to Hardev Kaur's article, "Deviant Muslims' threat of overthrowing moderate Malaysia: PM", *New Straits Times*, 4 February 2002.

36. Ibid.

37. See Hooker (2000), pp. 1–27.

38. See Dr Mahathir's speech, "Facing the 21st Century: *Reformasi* and Challenges for the Regional Muslim Community" at IKIM, Kuala Lumpur, 22 August 1997. Available online at http://www.ikim.gov.my.

"Also to save Muslims, a stable and strong government is necessary". *[Juga untuk menyelamatkan orang Islam, kerajaan yang stabil dan kuat diperlukan].*

39. "Introduction", at http://www.ikim.gov.my/s301-1.htm.

40. *Islam, Budaya Kerja dan Pembangunan Masyarakat: Satu Kefahaman*, edited by Nik Mustapha Haji Nik Hassan and Siti Fatimah Abdul Rahman (Kuala Lumpur: IKIM, 1993).

41. See note 38. *"Orang-orang Islam yang muncul dari Semenanjung Arab pada mulanya adalah pengikut sebenar ajaran-ajaran Islam… mereka berfikiiran luas dan sanggup untuk mempelajari kemahiran-kemahiran, ilmu sains, matematik dan kesenian orang-orang bukan Islam … Mereka membuat kajian mereka sendiri dan menyumbang dengan banyak kepada berbagai cabang ilmu. Akibatnya, mereka menjadi terkehadapan dari segi teknologi. Malangnya, dengan kehadiran ulama-ulama Islam …, kajian-kajian terhadap yang lain selain yang berkaitan dengan agama dan amalan-amalannya dimarahi dan akhirnya dilarang. Dengan ini orang-orang Islam mula mundur"* [The Muslims who appeared on the Arabian peninsula in the beginning were the true followers of Islam's teachings… they were broad-minded and prepared to learn skills, science, mathematics, and the art of non-Muslims … They made their own studies and contributed greatly to many branches of knowledge. As a result, they became technologically advanced. Unfortunately, with the presence of Islamic *ulama*, studies which were not connected to religion and its aspects were disapproved of and finally prohibited. So Muslims began to go backwards].

42. Hon. Dato' Dr Ismail bin Haji Ibrahim, "How Far Does Vision 2020 Fulfil the Requirements of Islam", in *Towards the 21st Century: Islam and Vision 2020*, pp. 29–89. Transcript of IKIM Congress, 3–4 July 1992, Putra World Trade Centre, Kuala Lumpur, Working Paper I, Workshop A, Session I, p. 36. *"Islam adalah merupakan ajaran yang… menuju kepada peningkatan ilmu pengetahuan. Di dalam Al-Qur'an terdapat begitu banyak ayat tentang kepentingan ilmu pengetahuan, iaitu bagaimana seorang manusia itu harus menggunakan daya inteleknya dengan bersungguh-sungguh untuk mempertingkatkan kehidupannya".*

43. Mahathir Mohamad (2001).

44. See note 42, p. 40. *"Islam tidak melarang umatnya mengumpul harta… kerana yang dipentingkan Islam ialah harta yang dicari itu ialah dari sumber yang halal… kerana orang yang mempunyai harta kekayaan akan dapat menggunakan harta kekayaannya itu untuk berjihad pada jalan Allah SWT".*

45. See Mahathir Mohamad (2001), pp. 14–15.

46. See note 38. "This is really against Islam. Kindergartens, pre-schools and religious teachers are responsible for the development of Islamic

knowledge. Instead, they are using this opportunity to provoke feelings of hatred towards the government which is also led by members of the Muslim community". *[Ini sebenarnya bertentangan dengan Islam. Tadika, taska dan guru agama mereka bertanggungjawab mengembangkan pengetahuan Islam. Sebaliknya, mereka menggunakan kesempatan itu untuk membangkitkan perasaan benci kepada kerajaan yang juga dipimpin oleh umat Islam].*

47. See note 24. "This is a jihad because when we become an industrialized country… *bukan saja boleh menang tapi orang tidak akan menekan kita".*

48. See note 38. *"Mereka mula menolak segala ilmu yang mereka dakwa tidak Islam dan tidak perlu dipelajari oleh orang Islam".*

49. See note 38. *"semakin lama, semakin ramai orang Islam dan pemimpin-pemimpin mereka yang terlibat dengan rebutan kuasa, dengan masing-masing mendakwa bahawa mereka berjuang untuk Islam".*

50. See Dr Mahathir's speech, "The Muslim World and Global Cooperation: Preparations for the 21st Century", at Sunway Lagoon Resort Hotel, Petaling Jaya, 25 April 1997, www.ikim.gov.my.
    "Tetapi orang-orang Arab Jahiliah itu lebih suka mempercayai tuhan datuk-nenek mereka".

51. See note 42, p. 57. *"Allah SWT menerangkan bahawa ketika Islam disampaikan oleh Rasulullah SAW maka terdapat orang-orang yang bersikap degil, iaitu yang tidak mahu menerima Islam sebagai satu cara hidup… Jadi mereka merupakan orang yang terlalu fanatik dengan tradisi lama, walaupun tradisi itu telah lapuk dan tidak sesuai lagi dengan perkembangan fikiran manusia ketika itu. Dalam masyarakat kita pada hari ini juga dapat kita saksikan sebahagian dari generasi baru yang cuba melihat ke belakang, kepada adat tradisi lama… maka sering kali mereka menjadi orang yang bersikap degil dan berfikiran negatif".*

52. See note 40.

53. See Nik Abdul Aziz Nik Mat (1995), pp. 206–7.

54. Nik Abdul Aziz Nik Mat (1994).

55. Ibid.

56. Loosely translated as "ignorant", but see also discussion above on *jahil.*

57. Sangwon Suh and Santha Oorjitham, "Battle for Islam", *Asiaweek* 29 no. 3 (16 June 2002), at http://www.asiaweek.com/asiaweek/.

58. Tarmizi Mohd Jam (1991), p. 121.

59. See note 36, p. 121.

60. Tarmizi Mohd Jam (1993), pp. 22–24.

61. See note 58, pp. 38–39. *Nik Aziz "telah memotong gajinya sebanyak 40 peratus… Beliau juga tidak mahu menerima sebarang elaun juadah Hari Raya… Tuan Guru juga telah memberi amaran kepada rakyat dan pihak penganjur*

majlis yang dihadirinya supaya tidak memberikan sebarang bentuk hadiah denderamata dan sebagainya kepada beliau".

62. See note 53, p. 5. *"Apa hendak kenakan road tax kerana sudah kena tol. Ini road tax kena, tol pun kena. Untuk siapa semuanya ini? Sudah! Cukuplah rakyat dihisap darah. Kita kata road tax tidak perlu lagi kerana rakyat memerlukan kenderaan sekarang, sekurang-kurangnya rakyat hendak memiliki sebuah motosikal untuk berulang-alik dari tempat mereka bekerja, ke pasar dan ke rumah. Mengapa tidak diberikan kemudahan ini kepada rakyat?"*

63. See note 60, pp. 122–26.

64. Zakiah Koya, "Hadi on Islamic State and Oil Royalty Controversy", *Malaysiakini*, 4 June 2001.

65. Bobby Sayyid uses the term "Kemalist", after Kemal Ataturk of Turkey, to refer to regimes in Muslim countries which proscribe explicit expressions of religious faith for the sake of "secularism", which in their view is a vital prerequisite for modernization.

66. See note 53, p. 207. *"Alhamdulillah rakyat Kelantan lebih cerdik daripada pemimpin dia"*.

67. Ibid., p. 19. *"Kalau Islam dipecah belah, demokrasi juga dipecah belah"*.

68. See interview with Fadzil Noor by Arjuna Ranawana, "The Issue is Change", *Asiaweek* 25 no. 47 (26 November 1999), at http://www.asiaweek.com/asiaweek/.

69. See Sayyid (1988), p. 88.

70. Hilley (2001), p. 35. For more discussion of the economy under Mahathir, see also Milne and Mauzy (1999), chp. 3.

71. 24 April 1995. For further examples, refer to any edition of *Harakah* in April 1995, all of which are focused on the upcoming federal elections.

72. See Koya, op. cit.

73. See note 53, p. 13.

74. Quoted in Hussin Mutalib (1993), pp. 99–100.

75. See Kessler (1978), p. 167.

References

Abdul Fauzi Abdul Hamid. "Political Dimensions of Religious Conflict in Malaysia: State Response to an Islamic Movement". *Indonesia and the Malay World* 28, no. 80 (2000): 32-65.

Abdul Rahman Haji Abdullah. *Pemikiran Islam di Malaysia: Sejarah dan Aliran*. Kuala Lumpur and Pulau Pinang: Dewan Bahasa & Pustaka, and Pusat Pendidikan Jarak Jauh, Universiti Sains Malaysia, 1998.

Ahmad Sarji Abdul Hamid, ed. *Malaysia's Vision 2020: Understanding the Concept, Implications and Challenges*. Petaling Jaya: Pelanduk Publications, 1993.

Barber, Benjamin R. *Jihad vs McWorld*. New York: Ballantyne Books, 1996.

Chandra Muzaffar. *Islamic Resurgence in Malaysia*. Petaling Jaya: Fajar Bakti, 1987.

Esposito, John L., and John O. Voll. *Islam and Democracy*, chp. 6. New York, Oxford: Oxford University Press, 1996.

Farrands, Chris. "Society, Modernity and Social Change: Approaches to Nationalism and Identity". In *Identities in International Relations*, edited by Jill Krause and Neil Renwick. London: Macmillan, 1996.

Hilley, John. *Malaysia: Mahathirism, Hegemony and the New Opposition*. London, New York: Zed Books, 2001.

Hooker, Virginia Matheson. "Reconfiguring Malay and Islam in Contemporary Malaysia". *Review of Indonesian and Malaysian Affairs* 34, no. 2 (2000): 1–27.

Hussin Mutalib. *Islam in Malaysia: From Revivalism to Islamic State?* Singapore: Singapore University Press, 1993.

Jomo, K. S. and Ahmad Shabery Cheek. "Malaysia's Islamic Movements". In *Fragmented Vision: Culture and Politics in Contemporary Malaysia*, edited by Joel S. Kahn and Francis Loh Kok Wah, pp. 79–106. Honolulu: University of Hawaii Press, 1992.

Kessler, Clive S. *Islam and Politics in a Malay State: Kelantan 1838–1969*. Ithaca, London: Cornell University Press, 1978.

Lewis, Bernard. *What Went Wrong? Western Impact and Middle Eastern Response*. Oxford: Oxford University Press, 2002.

Leys, Colin. *The Rise and Fall of Development Theory*. 5th ed. Indiana: Indiana University Press, 1996.

Mahathir Mohamad. *Malays Forget Easily*. Subang Jaya: Pelanduk Publications, 2001.

Milne, R. S. and Diane K. Mauzy. *Malaysian Politics under Mahathir*. London: Routledge, 1999.

Nik Abdul Aziz Nik Mat. *Kelantan: Universiti Politik Terbuka*. Nilam Puri, Kelantan: Maahad ad-Dakwah Wal-Imanah, 1995.

———. *Tazkirah Jiwa dan Nafsu*. Penang: Dewan Muslimat, 1994.

Pipes, Daniel. *In the Path of God: Islam and Political Power*. New York: Basic Books, 1983.

Rostow, W. W. *The Stages of Economic Growth: A Non-Communist Manifesto*. Reprinted from the 1960 text in *From Modernization to Globalization: Perspectives on Development and Social Change*, edited by T. Roberts and A. Hite, pp. 100–109. Malden, Massachusetts: Blackwell Publishers, 2000.

Said, Edward. *Covering Islam: How the Media and the Experts Determine How We See the Rest of the World*. 2nd edition. New York: Vintage Books, 1997.

Sayyid, Bobby S. *A Fundamental Fear: Eurocentrism and the Emergence of Islamism*. London, New York: Zed Books, 1988.

Sloane, Patricia. *Islam, Modernity and Entrepreneurship among the Malays*. London: Macmillan, 1999.

Syed Ahmad Hussein. "Muslim Politics and the Discourse on Democracy". In *Democracy in Malaysia: Discourses and Practices*, edited by Francis Loh Kok Wah and Khoo Boo Teik, pp. 74–107. Richmond, Surrey: Curzon, 2002.

Tarmizi Mohd Jam. *Kelantan: Harapan, Cabaran dan Visi: Mampukah Ulama Mentadbir?*. Kuala Lumpur: G. G. Edar, 1991.

———. *Kelantan Digugat dan Digigit*. Kuala Lumpur: Pengeluaran Minda Siasah, 1993.

"Towards the 21st Century: Islam and Vision 2020", pp. 29–89. Transcript of IKIM Congress, 3–4 July 1992, Putra World Trade Centre, Kuala Lumpur.

CONCLUSION

12

THE WAY FORWARD
Social Science and Malaysia in the Twenty-first Century

VIRGINIA HOOKER

Clive Kessler was one of the last doctoral students of the late Sir Raymond Firth, who had been one of the first anthropologists to study Kelantan. Firth offered his students insights into the major traditions of European anthropology through his teachers, Malinowski and Sir James Frazer, and through his association with Marcel Mauss. Sir Raymond's lifetime (1901–2002) spanned the entire twentieth century and he witnessed change in all its aspects. These included changes in the theoretical approaches to the study of anthropology, which Kessler has outlined in a tribute he wrote after Sir Raymond's death.[1]

In his tribute, Clive Kessler explains how Sir Raymond's work presented questions which are fundamental to the social sciences, ranging beyond the boundaries of individual disciplines. According to Kessler, Firth's work posed clearly the fundamental questions about the status of *homo economicus*, within analytical frameworks, as a theoretical construct and, within the world of social experience and action, as a social construct; about the relation between the two, especially within those processes of socio-cultural as well as economic transformation known as modernization and development. The central question posed here is whether modernization, or what we more often refer to as "globalization", is necessarily culturally homogenizing — something no anthropologist sensitive to the rich diversity of Firth's "human types" can regard with equanimity — or whether it is possible to achieve "modernity" and to find embodiment for economic and social rationality within a variety of cultural traditions and civilizational forms.[2]

These questions are central not only to the chapters in this book but also to Malaysia's leaders and economic planners. Professor Shamsul's chapter emphasizes the crucial importance of knowledge, particularly of the social sciences, to many aspects of the modern nation-state. He also points out that if both the nation-state and social science are operating effectively, their relationship will be one of tension. While the state has to pursue functional, developmental goals, the social sciences have humanistic and "emancipatory as well as instrumental goals"(see Shamsul in this volume). In his view, to be most useful to the long-term interests of the nation-state, social scientists need to be able to draw from the elements of a vigorous civil society, which is not totally dependent on the state.

The nation-state of Malaysia provides an interesting example of the relationship between the social sciences and a nation's planners because the connection since independence has been close. The economic and cultural development plans, designed to overcome the racial tensions which exploded in 1969, included considerable input from social scientists. Their implementation was, however, the task of government. One Malaysian, trained in medicine and sympathetic to the social sciences, is Malaysia's longest-serving Prime Minister, Dr Mahathir Mohamad. Since his days as a medical student in the late 1940s, he has thought and written about the need for change in Malaysian society.[3] Like students of anthropology, he is aware that change is rooted in cultural transformation. In one of his more recent works, he wrote:

> The NEP (New Economic Policy) was about changing the *bumiputeras* from a farming, petty trading and civil service community to one that was commercial and industrial, comparable in size and wealth to the commercial and industrial

non-*bumiputera* community. Such a change could not be effected unless a cultural transformation, or revolution, took place prior to or during the process (Mahathir 1998, p. 119).

Taking the need for change as his argument, Dr Mahathir develops the issue further to describe how the government had to take upon itself the responsibility of ensuring that the *bumiputera* "went through a cultural revolution of the right kind". He argued that unless this happened, the NEP would fail. In Dr Mahathir's view, the new kind of *bumiputera* culture had to transform itself into one which was "compatible with the running of businesses at all levels", a new understanding of the work ethic, and greater discipline and hard work (Mahathir 1998, p. 120).

Having identified the kind of change necessary, Dr Mahathir describes the process for achieving the revolution: through the example of leaders and seminars, courses and training camps. Dr Mahathir admits that the pace of change has been fast, even too fast, for some. He also admits that effecting cultural change is "a complex, intricate and extensive matter" and that, because so many factors are involved, what will result is "virtually a new people" (Mahathir 1998, p. 121).

Dr Mahathir recognizes that directed cultural change can have serious and damaging consequences if not carefully thought through. "Obviously," he says, "the need in Malaysia has been to retain the spiritual values, while balancing them with a reasonably materialistic creed. This is not easily done. Almost invariably, there will be a pendulum-like swing which may go too far in the other direction, with the total disappearance of any meaningful spiritual values. Therein lies the danger" (Mahathir 1998, p. 128).

It is at this point that Sir Raymond Firth's fundamental questions about modernization (as expressed by Clive Kessler) have direct relevance for the major programmes of the Malaysian nation-state. Sir Raymond's understanding of human diversity led Kessler to ask "whether modernization… is necessarily culturally homogenizing… or whether it is possible to achieve modernity, and to find embodiment for economic and social rationality, within a variety of cultural traditions and civilizational forms" (Kessler 2002). Dr Mahathir may have changed his views since writing *The Way*

Forward, but in 1998 when it was published, he placed his faith in the nobility of the objective and the determination to achieve it. In his own words: "If a determined attempt is made to change the culture to one suitable for the objective in mind, then no matter how foreign or unusual the objective is, it can be achieved. The process is difficult and will take time, but some degree of success can be expected, even with the most backward people. It is not nature that stands in the way" (Mahathir 1998, p. 128).

From the perspective of a national leader, change directed at improved material circumstances for individual citizens may be seen as one of the primary duties of a responsible government. Some social scientists may feel it their duty to respond to government plans for cultural change and suggest amendments, major revisions, or even scrapping the project altogether. It takes courage to make such responses and Professor Shamsul refers to the difficulties which beset both sides, particularly if the social scientists are accused of subverting the nation-state. Even so, the "determined" attempt to which Dr Mahathir refers may not be the only way to work for the objectives he outlines.

The chapters in this book underline the diversity and variety of "cultural and civilizational" forms within the Malaysian state, a richness recognized by Sir Raymond Firth and celebrated by Clive Kessler. In Kessler's view, the diversity of subject should be matched by a richness of methodology.[4] He believes that only an understanding derived from a combined historical, sociological, and anthropological perspective can provide us with an empathetic insight — a *verstehen* — of social reality:

> Human reality can be based neither upon a hard "objectivism" that reduces all cultural phenomena to some underlying material or qualified base, nor upon an idealist insistence on the absolute autonomy of culture, and its total transcendance of the material circumstances which constrain it (and which it must address if it is to serve those who live through it). Both approaches are partial; each, if adopted exclusively, leads to fallacy and absurdity. The material and the ideal, two faces of the one complex social reality, constrain each other, though neither determines or totally overrides the other. Human existence is based upon their dynamic interplay, and an adequate account of any of its particular forms must be similarly grounded. (Kessler 1978, p. 20.)

The authors of the chapters in this volume have not felt constrained by the boundaries of traditional disciplines but have drawn from methodologies which are appropriate to their materials. Each of them, like Clive Kessler, has acknowledged that an understanding of the historical context of contemporary phenomena is an essential component of social scientific analysis.

It is from this historical dimension that the chapters' arguments draw their strength. The examples of change which are described in this book flow from negotiations with, or transformations of, older cultural forms. Dr Mahathir's statements make this point also, although without direct reference to "history".

If we refer again to the concept of paradox, we might say that exhortations for Malays to "change" which have been expressed from the early twentieth century (and through the writings of Abdullah bin Abdul Kadir Munshi[5] even half a century earlier) have possibly had the effect of making them more creative than their leaders had expected. Dr Mahathir lists the Malays' lack of self-confidence in their own abilities as one very negative legacy of colonial rule. Without confidence in successful outcomes, he notes, people are unwilling to experiment with new ideas (Mahathir 1998, p. 122). For this reason, Dr Mahathir introduced the "can do" philosophy, and the slogan "*Malaysia Boleh*" (Malaysia Can!) which was used regularly during the aftermath of the 1997 economic downturn.

As the chapters in this book describe, contemporary Malaysians are showing how they are negotiating change in areas as diverse as gender rights, popular culture, the monarchy, and Islamic modernity. The chapters by Maila Stivens and Joel Kahn, each of which focuses on sections of the middle class, document the complexity of these negotiations. Certainly, individuals need the confidence referred to by Dr Mahathir to face the unknown but they seem to display a much more discerning attitude to the choices available to them than he describes in *The Way Forward*. The women's groups and the younger generation described by Maila Stivens and Joel Kahn display an awareness of their ethnic positions and to some degree their cultural heritage, but they can situate their identity in the broader context of the global culture they have access to through the technology brought to them by Dr Mahathir's development plans. In some areas, such as the monarchy (as described in Anthony Milner's chapter), new meaning is being invested in older forms. The survival of those forms depends on creative adaptations and an active desire by Malaysians to play a role in their contemporary lives.

Popular culture, the monarchy, and gender rights are areas in which individual input to the form of change is to a large degree possible. Changes to Islam are a different matter because humans are face-to-face with God's revelation and His omnipotence. Change to revealed scripture is not possible but, as several chapters describe, the administration of religion is changing and the *hudud* code of Kelantan, although not enacted, is a challenge to the balance of federal and state legal jurisdictions. Again in Kelantan, Nik Aziz, in his role of a gifted religious teacher, is changing the way Kelantanese understand the Quran by presenting it in terms of their own daily lives. Its immediacy is at odds with the distance they feel from the federal capital and the politics of the urban élite whom they envisage residing there. Yet all, Nik Aziz assures them, are subject to the Will of God, which will be visited on them ultimately in His everlasting universe. Beyond Kelantan, nation-state, region, and even the global universe, Nik Aziz conveys to his audiences that God's Kingdom is immutable and eternal. The transformation from the relentless changes and challenges of the ephemeral world to the eternal and unchanging state of the next world are concepts which lie outside both social science and national development programmes but are subjects about which Nik Aziz and other religious teachers know a great deal.

On a more mundane level, what areas of Malaysian life might the social sciences contribute to in the near future? Some of the possibilities could include:

1. The phenomenon of generational change — in politics, religious leadership, communal leaders, intellectuals, artists and activists (no area will be immune to this change).
2. New expressions of class difference — where class might be defined by different markers and not confined to ethnicity or occupation.
3. Different symbols to represent power and authority — greater variety of options, perhaps including more non-Malay elements.

4. Greater interest in non-Malay indigenous cultures, especially those of the Orang Asli (Original Peoples) and established communities of Chinese and Indians.
5. Sustained and serious study of non-government, grass-roots organizations as influential elements in the nation-state.
6. Increased recognition of the existence of multiple identities and their effect on individual choice and behaviour.
7. Alternatives to the nexus between Islam and Malay — an examination of the possibilities for understanding Islam in Malaysia other than through its almost total identification with one ethnic group.
8. A more fluid approach to what constitutes the "history" of Malaysia — the confidence to explore the past with imagination and without the constraints of the so-called "national interest", using sources which have so far not been considered as "historical".
9. Law is crucial to Islam, which itself is a theology in legal form. Careful legal drafting is thus a major area for further attention.

The agenda for the social sciences is long and challenging.

Sir Raymond Firth, a scholar during the colonial interlude in Malaysia's history, was influenced by what he learned from his studies in Malaya. One of his gifts to succeeding generations is the concept of variety and diversity as a legitimate and scientific framework for analysing change. Certainly, it was an inspiration for Clive Kessler, whose first work in Malaya was accomplished with a sensitivity and intelligence which have rarely been equalled. This book is dedicated to Clive Kessler and to the contributions he has made to greater rational and informed understanding of social science in and about Malaysia.

Notes

1. Clive S. Kessler (2002).
2. Ibid.
3. See further Khoo Boo Teik (1995).
4. I wish to thank Norani Othman for the following points and the selection of the quotation from Clive Kessler's work.

5. In the 1830s and 1840s, Abdullah bin Abdul Kadir, clerk, translator and
    teacher to Europeans in Singapore and Penang, urged Malays to respond
    positively to change and to participate actively in the advances of the
    modern world.

References

Kessler, Clive S. *Islam and Politics in a Malay State: Kelantan 1838–1969*.
    Ithaca and London: Cornell University Press, 1978.
———— . "Raymond W. Firth 1901–2002". *Australian Journal of Anthropology*,
    13, no. 2 (2002): 219–24.
Khoo Boo Teik. *Paradoxes of Mahathirism: An Intellectual Biography of Mahathir
    Mohamad*. Kuala Lumpur and New York: Oxford University Press, 1995.
Mahathir bin Mohamad. *The Way Forward*. London: Weidenfeld & Nicolson,
    1998.

INDEX